ENVIRONMENTAL CRIME AND CRIMINALITY

CURRENT ISSUES IN CRIMINAL JUSTICE
VOLUME 15
GARLAND REFERENCE LIBRARY OF SOCIAL SCIENCE
VOLUME 984

Current Issues in Criminal Justice

Frank P. Williams III and Marilyn D. McShane

General Editors

STRANGER VIOLENCE
A Theoretical Inquiry
by Marc Riedel

CRIMES OF STYLE
*Urban Grafitti and the
Politics of Criminality*
by Jeff Ferrell

UNDERSTANDING CORPORATE
CRIMINALITY
edited by Michael B. Blankenship

POLITICAL CRIME IN
CONTEMPORARY AMERICA
A Critical Approach
edited by Kenneth D. Tunnell

THE MANAGEMENT OF
CORRECTIONAL INSTITUTIONS
by Marilyn D. McShane
and Frank P. Williams III

INNOVATIVE TRENDS
AND SPECIALIZED STRATEGIES
IN COMMUNITY-BASED CORRECTIONS
edited by Charles B. Fields

THE WINDS OF INJUSTICE
*American Indians
and the U.S. Government*
by Laurence French

ALTERED STATES OF MIND
Critical Observations of the Drug War
edited by Peter Kraska

CONTROLLING STATE CRIME
An Introduction
edited by Jeffrey Ian Ross

MEDIA, PROCESS, AND THE SOCIAL
CONSTRUCTION OF CRIME
Studies in Newsmaking Criminology
edited by Gregg Barak

ACADEMIC PROFESSIONALISM
IN LAW ENFORCEMENT
by Bernadette Jones Palombo

AFRICAN-AMERICAN ORGANIZED CRIME
A Social History
by Rufus Schatzberg and Robert J. Kelly

AFRICAN AMERICANS AND THE
CRIMINAL JUSTICE SYSTEM
by Marvin D. Free, Jr.

ENVIRONMENTAL CRIME
AND CRIMINALITY
Theoretical and Practical Issues
edited by Sally M. Edwards,
Terry D. Edwards, and Charles B. Fields

POLICING CHANGE, CHANGING POLICE
International Perspectives
edited by Otwin Marenin

Environmental Crime and Criminality
Theoretical and Practical Issues

Edited by
Sally M. Edwards
Terry D. Edwards
Charles B. Fields

Garland Publishing, Inc.
New York and London
1996

Library of Congress Cataloging-in-Publication Data

Environmental crime and criminality : theoretical and practical issues /
    edited by Sally M. Edwards, Terry D. Edwards, Charles B. Fields.
            p.   cm. — (Garland reference library of social science ; vol.
984)   (Current issues in criminal justice ; v. 15)
    Includes bibliographical references and index.
    ISBN 0-8153-1756-5 (alk. paper)
        1. Offenses against the environment—United States.   2. Environmental
law—United States—Criminal provisions.   I. Edwards, Sally Mitchell,
1953–   . II. Edwards, Terry D.   III. Fields, Charles B.   IV. Series.
V. Series: Garland reference library of the humanities. Current issues in
criminal justice ; vol. 15.
HV6403.E59   1996
364.1'4—dc20   95-31266
                                                                     CIP

Cover illustration by Gordon Jones.

Printed on acid-free, 250-year-life paper
Manufactured in the United States of America

Contents

Series Foreword

One of the primary goals of this series has been to explore new areas of criminology and criminal justice, topics that constitute the frontiers of the field. This work, edited by Sally Edwards, Terry Edwards and Charles Fields exemplifies that purpose in its coverage of environmental crime. While corporate and political crime developed slowly into mainstream criminology over the last half century, environmental crime, as an area of emphasis is still in its infancy. It is unusual to have many varied and informative perspectives early in a subject's development. This volume, however, demonstrates that many people are already examining environmental crime perhaps as an extension of both the greater environmental movement and the broadening of the popular parameters of crime.

The varied selections here constitute both an overview and introduction to the topic and a thoughtful treatment of the issues. As is usual in preliminary works, many questions are raised as well as answered. We believe that readers will find the collective essays in this work to be readable, insightful and thought provoking.

Marilyn D. McShane
Frank P. Williams, III

Acknowledgments

We wish to acknowledge several individuals whose encouragement and support were instrumental in getting this book to press. Our colleagues at Appalachian State University, the University of Louisville, and California State University at San Bernardino, encouraged the project from the beginning. A special note of thanks goes to Richter Moore, friend and mentor, who continues to inspire us all.

The series editors of Current Issues in Criminal Justice and cherished friends, Frank Williams and Marilyn McShane, should be applauded for their vision and foresight in the production of this series.

Finally, we wish to thank the chapter authors, whose innovative work in the area of environmental crime and criminality will continue to challenge us.

Introduction

The 1970s witnessed a virtual "explosion" of environmental laws, many including criminal as well as civil provisions. But barring exceptional and highly sensational cases, such as the Distler case in Kentucky or the Kepone case in Virginia, the utilization of criminal penalties in the enforcement of the environmental laws has been haphazard, if not totally nonexistent. Criminal prosecution of environmental violations at the state or local level was unheard of prior to the 1980s. At the federal level, it wasn't until 1982 when the U.S. Environmental Protection Agency (EPA) established the Office of Criminal Enforcement that federal efforts kicked into "high gear," pursuing environmental violators criminally rather than civilly.

Throughout the 1980s and into the 1990s, the criminal prosecution of environmental violators steadily increased. Corporate America simply viewed civil penalties as merely another cost of doing business. It was cheaper to pay the civil fine and pass these "expenses" on to customers than to incur the significantly higher costs incurred in preventing the violation(s). Furthermore, civil penalties do not carry the social stigma or negative publicity of criminal penalties. However, there was a growing belief among the public that some environmental violations were time bombs, the equivalent of holding a gun to someone's head for 20 years or more.

Despite the increased activity of utilizing criminal statutes for prosecuting environmental violations, there has been little academic research concerning this form of sanctioning. Our initial research focused on what the states were doing, since they have primacy of regulatory enforcement over many of the national environmental laws.

We quickly discovered that what little research there was focused on federal issues. Existing research was also very diffuse among issues concerning criminal environmental violations.

Often the research focused on the sensational or extraordinary cases rather than routine. There has been little inquiry into the necessity of calling environmental violations "crimes" or specifically defining an "environmental crime." Furthermore, there is a dichotomy concerning the research regarding environmental crimes; we have questions concerning theory and philosophy as well as questions relating to practical questions. Philosophical questions concern human relationship with nature. Theoretical questions delve into what constitutes an environmental crime and why it is committed. The practical questions concern the difficulties investigators and prosecutors encounter when engaged in the investigation or prosecution of environmental crimes. Despite our academic inattention to criminal environmental enforcement, it is a growing concern for the practitioners in the field: regulators, police, and attorneys. The International Association Chiefs of Police (IACP) formed an Environmental Crimes Committee in 1992, and the American Bar Association has had an Environmental Crimes Committee for several years. The committees have come into existence due to activity among practitioners. Environmental issues frequently arise for state and local police as well as state and local attorneys.

The idea for this book was conceived as a result of the fragmented research we encountered and in response to the growing activity in the field. We had difficulty finding theoretical or philosophical guideposts for our research on state activity concerning the investigation and prosecution of environmental crimes. Few scholars have investigated the issue from the perspective of white-collar crime, court decisions, and practical aspects of the investigation and prosecution of environmental crimes. What is lacking is a coherent focus, an open discussion of what exactly is known and where researchers and practitioners need to go from here. It is the assimilation of existing knowledge on which future research can be based that is the grounding for this book. We have accumulated the leading research on environmental crimes, and this text is a single source of the cutting edge of research on environmental crime. The book is not divided into specific categories, for, as with environmental crime, topics and subject matter tend to overlap, but roughly the "sections" concern theoretical, practical, philosophical and future issues concerning environmental crimes.

Chapter one, Gerhard O. W. Mueller's "An Essay on Environmental Criminality," contains a broad historical overview of environmental crimes. Written from a criminological, and, specifically, a white-collar crime perspective, Mueller provides us with a review of the ten basic problems or "problem clusters which made it difficult to deal with the environmental questions by invocation of criminal laws." These problem clusters, he suggests, need further research and inquiry. The problem clusters include problems concerning qualification and quantification, strict liability, vicarious liability, corporate liability, proof, abuse of power, inadequate enforcement, changing priorities, countervailing trends towards decriminalization, and countervailing penalization policies.

Freda Adler's chapter "Offender-Specific vs. Offense-Specific Approaches to the Study of Environmental Crime," is a long overdue discussion of the theories of criminality (offender-specific approaches and explanations) and the theories of crime (offense-specific approaches and explanations). She demonstrates "the difference between how theories of criminality and theories of crime are used to formulate research and ultimately policy on environmental crime." Adler gives us much food for thought when considering the nature of environmental crimes and how we can develop mitigative policies.

In chapter three, moving from the theoretical to more explicit practical issues of environmental crimes, Debra Ross's "A Review of EPA Criminal, Civil, and Administrative Enforcement Data: Are the Efforts Measurable Deterrents to Environmental Criminals?" involves a thorough analysis of the effectiveness of the U.S. EPA's Office of Criminal Investigation in preventing violations of key environmental laws. She highlights the difficulty facing the agency since it is only one member of the prosecutorial team. Much of the decision making for prosecutions lies in the hands of the Department of Justice. This chapter is an excellent example of the practical and operational interagency problems faced when trying to investigate and prosecute environmental crimes.

In chapter four, the emphasis is on the individual. Donald Rebovich's "Prosecutorial Decision Making and the Environmental Prosecutor: Reaching a Crossroads for Public Protection" assesses a survey of local prosecutors concerning the factors that influenced them the most in deciding whether or not to prosecute a particular criminal environmental violation. The results of his research are very insightful concerning both the motivations of local prosecutors and the difficulties they encounter. Rebovich's article underscores the research needed to thoroughly understand the phenomena of environmental crimes.

Valerie Cass in "Toxic Tragedy: Illegal Hazardous Waste Dumping in Mexico" provides us with an excellent case study into a specific environmental crimes problem. This chapter also underscores the international component of environmental crimes and the necessity of not only intergovernmental cooperation but also international cooperation to fight this growing activity. Dumping our toxic wastes, both legally and illegally, carries with it ethical considerations as well as practical investigative and prosecutive difficulties. Cass's case study sheds much-needed light on this troubling environmental crime development and the difficulties that arise when trying to combat this problem.

Moving from the theoretical and practical considerations of environmental crimes to a more philosophical discussion of environmental crime requires some explanation. The philosophical discussions offer a framework for research into this topic as well as a blueprint for how to approach the environmental dilemma. As with any issue, the philosophical musings will not be monolithic in their reasoning and meaning. In chapters six and seven we offer two widely divergent but useful viewpoints to put environmental crimes into contextual focus.

In chapter six, Mark Seis's "A Native American Criminology of Environmental Crime" provides us with an insightful assessment of environmental crime from the perspective of the Seneca Indians during a specific time in their history. According to Seis, the relationship of the Seneca Indians with the environment was grounded in "a proactive rather than reactive criminology." Thus, the Senecas worked at preventing environmental degradation rather than using stopgap measures after the damage as been done. We agree with Seis there is much to learn from this culture, even though, as Seis readily admits, we cannot go back to that lifestyle.

Nanci Koser Wilson, in chapter seven, tackles the philosophical issues concerning environmental crime from a very different perspective. "An Ecofeminist Critique of Environmental Criminal Law" provides us with the ecofeminist perspective of environmental crime. She critiques current environmental criminal laws from a position that successfully integrates a social and environmental analysis. As with Seis's discussion of the environment, Wilson's ecofeminist perspective allows one to think of the problem in a different light. This additional perspective leads us not only to new research questions but also to different solutions to the problem that traditional analysis does not allow us to contemplate. The wider range of perspectives of philosophies we can utilize when assessing environmental problems, the better armed we will be and the more effectively we can deal with those problems.

Chapters eight and nine bring us to another host of problems concerning environmental crime. One concerns the definitions of environmental crime. From most of the chapters in this reader, one may conclude environmental crimes concern violations of criminal laws carrying criminal liability and/or penalties. However, this may represent a very narrow definition of the problem. For example, would a terrorist poisoning a municipal water supply be committing an environmental crime or merely an act of terrorism? Was Saddam Hussein's release of oil into the Persian Gulf an environmental crime or an act of war? The answers to such questions need to be addressed in future research efforts. However, in chapters eight and nine an oft-overlooked and nontraditional aspect of environmental crimes is considered: monkeywrenching and/or the ecoterrorist.

Scott Hays, Michael Esler, and Carol Hays in "Radical Environmentalism and Crime" offer a very insightful overview of the activities and rationale underlying monkeywrenching. Monkeywrenching, or ecoterrorism, refers to activities by radical environmentalists to combat environmental degradation and pollution. These activities include tree spiking, the removal of survey stakes, disabling bulldozers, and the felling of billboards, to name just a few. The radical environmentalists who engage in these activities believe traditional methods of working through the political system such as lobbying, campaigning, and reliance on the courts are doomed to failure because the political system is too wedded to the social and economic forces that lead to environmental degradation. Are their activities, indeed, environmental crimes? We can provide no dispositive answer to that question; however, the article by Hays et al. (as well as the following chapter by Shevory) offers some answers concerning these issues.

We included two chapters on monkeywrenching because it does bring to bear a whole host of questions as to what specifically constitutes an environmental crime. Furthermore, Tom Shevory, in "Monkeywrenching: Practice in Search of a Theory," addresses the issue from a different perspective. Shevory, in chapter nine, explores the historical, philosophical and theoretical underpinnings of the monkeywrenching phenomena. He traces the roots of radical environmentalism in the broader historical context of civil disobedience and dissent. His efforts, too, will enable us to tackle the question of definitions.

The last two chapters in this book take a different tack from the previous contributions, more appropriately dealing with what do we need to know and where do we go from here. In chapter ten, Sally Edwards's "Environmental Criminal Enforcement: Efforts by the States" assesses empirical data gathering to ascertain state activity in investigating and prosecuting environmental crimes. A majority of the current research into environmental issues concerns federal activity. However, states have primacy enforcement responsibilities for many federal environmental laws. This chapter contains the results of surveys administered to all state police organizations and state attorneys general to ascertain the level of activity and commitment by the states to environmental crimes. The research generates more questions than answers and provides a multitude of avenues of further research before we can be able to understand the nature of environmental criminal investigations and prosecutions in our federal system of government.

Finally, William D. Hyatt and Tracy L. Trexler in "Environmental Crime and Organized Crime: What Will the Future Hold?" offer us much to think about as to the future. Hyatt and Trexler outline where we need to go from here concerning research into environmental crimes and highlight two specific issues: organized crime and the internationalization of environmental crime. Their chapter underscores the real problems environmental crime portends for us if we do not rise to the occasion and implement proper corrective measures.

Environmental Crime and Criminality

CHAPTER ONE

An Essay on Environmental Criminality

Gerhard O. W. Mueller

> "Hurt not the earth,
> Neither the sea, Nor
> the trees. . ."
>
> Revelation 7: 3

Waste management and environmental protection are essential for survival. Instinctively, felines bury their body waste. Paleolithic man took drinking water upstream, bathed midstream, and disposed of waste downstream. The medieval city located the tanners' quarter at the edge of the walled city where the stream that traversed it exited. Instinct? Consensus? Regulation? Penal proscription?

Roman private law had a highly developed set of rules concerned with environmental protection. The many petty annoyances which might cause injury or disease were highly regulated by imposition of civil liability, such as the property owner's liability for objects thrown out of or falling from a building (*Institutes*, 4.5 Section 1). Indeed, from that time on, the concept of police was primarily associated with regulating the environment of the city and its citizens rather than with the prevention of common crime. Yet it seems environmental protection remained, at best, a matter of the social welfare policing function of the cities; perhaps because environmental destruction of potentially catastrophic consequences was generally unknown. Yet, already the *Law of the Twelve Tables* (451 B.C.) addressed itself to environmental crimes with potential catastrophic impact: the destruction of the crop apparently was made a capital offense; "Whoever enchants away crops . . ." (*Law of the Twelve Tables VIII*: 8a).

The common law of crimes did not deal with environmental problems resolutely. Pollution was regarded as a misdemeanor of the nuisance variety. In America especially, land, water, and air resources were vast, seemingly immune to any human depredation. Even the Industrial Revolution regarded natural resources as nondepletable or, in any event, viewed industry's effluent as an affordable price of progress. Belching smokestacks were the gauges of prosperity. Developing countries still largely ascribe to this philosophy. Matters could not begin to change until a worldwide awareness would emerge that natural resources are depletable indeed and that environmental pollution does not respect international boundaries.

The event most responsible for the creation of a worldwide environmental consciousness and conscience undoubtedly was the United Nations' World Congress on the Environment, held in Stockholm in 1972. The danger to human survival inherent in unbridled environmental exploitation and pollution was keenly recognized and measures for environmental protection assiduously debated. Persistent calls for the heavy guns of criminal law permeated the assembly, as they are always heard when humankind perceives a new danger which it does not know how to deal with in a civil manner. Yet it was the era of decriminalization, and Sweden had been in the forefront of the decriminalization movement. The International Association of Penal Law, one of the United Nations' principal resources in crime prevention and criminal justice, warned against rushing into criminal legislation. We first had to know the facts; we then would have to research the potential effects of various possible measures before we could recommend or endorse one or another of a multitude of possible (including penal) measures to deal with the perceived danger of environmental endangerment.

It is now two decades later. World consciousness about the danger to the environment has indeed been created and maintained. The number of organizations concerned with environmental protection proliferates. The literature has become so vast that even specialists have difficulties keeping up with it. The number of periodicals keeps growing.

In most countries of the world, legislation dealing with the environment is in a constant state of growth and flux. International conventions are being drafted and ratified. The United Nations' Environmental Program, a direct outgrowth of the Stockholm conference, has become one of the world's busiest bureaucracies, and its periodic congresses contribute significantly to environmental protection worldwide. Unhappily, despite the warnings of 1972, legislatures have resorted to criminal sanctions without the cause and effect studies which were then advocated. Indeed, what is most astounding is that the two turbulent decades since Stockholm have produced very little in the nature of criminological research with respect to environmental control.

In the United States, at the federal level, the first environmental legislation, The Rivers and Harbors Act (now 33 U.S.C. Section 407) dates from 1899. Yet it was not until the 1960s that this act was interpreted as prohibiting the discharge of pollutants into navigable waters (See, *United States v. Standard Oil*, 384 U.S. 224 [1966]). Only in the 1970s did Congress enact pollution-specific civil and criminal legislation. These statutes can be conveniently grouped into three categories: hazardous waste, water pollution, and air pollution. Among the most important acts is the federal Resource Conservation and Recovery Act (RCRA) (42 U.S.C. Sections 6901-6992k), which, inter alia, imposed upon the states certain minimal requirements regarding criminal violations with respect to treatment and disposal of hazardous substances. This statute thus endeavored to achieve a certain degree of uniformity of state criminal legislation. Federal enforcement of federal environmental criminal provisions began in earnest with the passage of this act. Both the federal Environmental Protection Agency and the Department of Justice established prosecution guidelines and, in 1978, a Hazardous Waste Task Force. "Knowing" violations, anywhere from the source to the polluter, were targeted for prosecution.

Water pollution was attacked by the federal Water Pollution Control Act of 1972, amended by the Clean Water Act of 1977 (33 U.S.C. Sections 1251-1376) as well as the *RCRA*. These laws contain provisions for specific violations under a regulatory scheme that seeks to regulate discharges from point sources, such as industrial plants or municipal sewage treatment facilities, by imposing quality standards. The penalties for "knowing endangerment" are substantial—up to 15 years of imprisonment and/or a fine up to $250,000.00. Corporate offenders may be fined up to $1 million. The statutes also require minimum sanctions for state legislation.

In the sphere of air pollution, the ineffective Air Quality Act of 1967 (Pub. L. No. 90-148, 81 Stat. 485 [1967]) was substantially amended by the Clean Air Act Amendments of 1970 and 1977 (42 United States Code, Sections 7401-7671q). Under these laws the administrator of the Environmental Protection Agency is required to set national standards of air quality. It is up to the states to enforce these standards by state legislation and control. In addition, the legislation contains penal sanctions for "knowing" violations (113 (c)), with, inter alia, misdemeanor penalties up to 1 year of incarceration and of up to $25,000.00 in fines.

At the state level, the last two decades have seen a spectacular growth of regulatory and penal legislation. The federal aim of relative uniformity of state legislation has been accomplished only modestly. Many states merely enacted laws which comply with federal minimum standards, others have adopted more stringent requirements, and many fall in between, by threatening fines of up to $25,000.00 and incarceration up to one year for "knowing" (or, in some states, reckless) transportation, storage and disposal of hazardous waste in violation of standards. The situation is similar with respect to waste pollution, whereas in the case of air pollution only a few states have embodied the statutory language and enforcement provisions, including penalties, of section 113(c) of the Clean Air Act (deCicco & Bonano, 1988).

It appears, then, that in the United States there is a legal framework for combatting environmental pollution by means of criminal sanctions and that the framework has federal and state components which are not necessarily in harmony between and amongst themselves. This lack of coherence itself is the source of many problems, yet far more problems are inherent in the objective itself of dealing with environmental problems by means of the criminal sanction. To recognize such problems does not mean to yield to them. Rather, recognition is simply the first step toward designing solutions that are criminologically sound.

A decade ago, in an analysis of offenses against the environment and efforts at their prevention, from an international perspective, the problem clusters which made it difficult to deal with environmental questions and concern by invocation of criminal laws were isolated (Mueller, 1979: 56):

These were:

- The problems of qualification and quantification;
- The problem of strict liability;
- The problem of vicarious liability;
- The problem of corporate liability;
- The problem of proof;
- The problem of the abuse of power;
- The problem of inadequate enforcement;
- The problem of changing priorities;
- The problem of the countervailing trend towards decriminalization; and
- The problem arising from countervailing penalization policies.

In the following sections, these ten problems are reviewed in light of legislative and judicial developments and, particularly, on the basis of such empirical studies as have been conducted during the past decade (Chappell & Moore, 1989; Meinberg et al., 1988). Not surprisingly, criminological research in the area of environmental pollution is as new to criminologists as penal sanctions for environmental crimes were to criminal lawyers. Entering the sphere of environmental criminality, we are indeed entering unfamiliar territory, in which the police officers in blue or green uniforms, with silver badges on their chests, are conspicuous through their absence and where standard-setting and enforcement rests with anonymous bureaucrats, for the most part.

The Problem of Qualification

Traditional crimes are recognized, characterized, and grouped by the harm they create: harm against life, against property, etc. To the public these harms are clear and immediate. With crimes against ecology, the harm seems to lie somewhere between Greek mythology and the distant future. Individual contributions to harm creation seem microscopic and apparently incapable of endangering the cosmos. Disapprobation of pollution activities has been low. Even after the passage of the federal antipollution acts, many judges have viewed pollution as "merely" an economic crime, often committed involuntarily and thus not deserving of criminal disapprobation. Such offenses have been likened to the "public welfare offenses" which, traditionally, were only *mala prohibita*, not *mala in se*, thus not morally delinquent acts (Kuruz, 1985: 93).

Unlike perpetrators of treason, murder and robbery, pollution offenders frequently have been rewarded by the state for "productivity and ingenuity," rather than being prosecuted (Goldsmith & Bunyard, 1984: 138). In the Netherlands the media have even been criticized for rooting for the pollution defendant UNISER, in a case in which defendants received prison sentences up to 25 years (Brants & de Roos, 1984). We may wish to regard such cavalier attitudes toward ecological criminality as out of step with the growing public awareness of the danger which pollution poses to the environment. Over the last two decades, civic and political organizations concerned about the environment have made enormous strides in creating public awareness about the threatened environment. A variety of surveys found that the populace at large regards pollution offenses as serious criminality. Thus, a national survey by Marvin Wolfgang and his associates found that "knowing" factory water pollution which causes a single death, or twenty persons to become ill, is rated in severity between rape causing physical injury and smuggling heroin into the country (Wolfgang et al., 1985; Klaus & Kalish, 1984; Schrager & Short, 1980; Cullen et al., 1982; Cullen et al., 1983; and Dodd et al., 1977).

Even in the 1970s, a multi-country study conducted by the United Nations Social Defence Research Institute (now United Nations Interregional Crime and Justice Research Institute, UNICRI) had found that sample populations in the United States, India, Indonesia, Iran, Italy, and Yugoslavia regarded factory pollution as equally serious as some of the most severe street crimes (Newman, 1978). The crisis of non-recognition of the serious nature of environmental criminality appears to near its end. Policy makers and the populace begin to agree on the harm which ecological mismanagement entails. Indeed, a new ecology-conscious life-style is beginning to emerge, a life-style which is said to be necessary to avoid an environmental catastrophe (Estrin & Swaigen, 1978).

Alas, there is as yet a considerable amount of scientific uncertainty about the consequences of pollution. Environmental damage which at first appears catastrophic and permanent may turn out to be temporary and reversible. Scientific predictions often are tentative and conjectural but may be received with the greatest alarm by environment-conscious advocacy groups and politicians. The global warming issue, for example, which still divides scientists, has become the rallying ground for environmentalists who see doom around the corner. The long-range climatological consequences of the "greenhouse" effect are subject to many non-quantifiable factors that may counteract global warming trends. Yet, scientists who predict climate changes as severe as those for the last ice age, which resulted in the extinction of many species and the redistribution of land and sea masses, may well be right. Equally difficult is the measurement of the impact of countermeasures, such as reduction of carbon monoxides (Wright, 1991), and particularly the contribution to greenhouse avoidance which each person can make by using less aerosol spray. That is the root of the problem of harm recognition.

Obviously, not all spheres of environmental harm are as complicated as those of the greenhouse effect. Thus, the effect on the quality of life of a given neighborhood by industrial waste dumping is more easily recognizable than the greenhouse effect. River pollution is far better understood, and counteractable, than ocean pollution.

Turning from the recognition of environmental harm, in general, to the qualification of environmental harms in the various pieces of legislation, we encounter further problems. When is a harm to the environment serious enough to constitute a penal offense? Past Canadian legislation restricted itself to "serious [and intentional] acts of pollution," a standard which provided little guidance and led to few prosecutions. More recent legislation extends to "serious and dramatic breaches," a term which indicates that the legislator has all but given up on qualifying the criminal harm of pollution (Duncan, 1986). The essence of the Canadian crime of pollution, that of "substantial harm to the environment without any overriding social justification," has been criticized as so vague as to stifle prosecution (Commentary, 1986). In the United States, the lack of standards and of clarity of standards encourages frustrating appeals. In one case, it lead to two reviews by the United States Supreme Court and three by the Court of Appeals where a conviction of polluting a stream was ultimately upheld and the individual defendants were sentenced to 30 days incarceration and the company was fined $50,000.00 (DiMento, 1986). The problem with respect to environmental offenses is that of meaningful segmentalization and quantification of environmental harm, after it has been qualified.

The Problem of Quantification

Water pollution (sewage) criminality may provide us an example for the quantification of environmental harm, adequate for recognition and capable of proof. The United States, United Kingdom, Germany, and France all have made studies in quantifying unacceptable pollution levels at the source. Thus, the United States Clean Water Act has quantitatively (and qualitatively) clarified oil and hazardous substance discharges (La Force, 1980). Exceeding the level of "permissible" pollution results in a "sin tax" that may simply amount to part of the cost of doing business while failing to convey the message that pollution is harmful. Such pollution taxes were found to be imperfectly enforceable. Research has demonstrated that a polluter's actual level of waste is independent of proportional changes in the expected penalty for pollution tax evasion and that the marginal cost of actual waste reduction equals the unit tax on reported waste (Harford, 1978).

In the United Kingdom, a major study has been completed on the effect of regional enforcement by the regional water authorities of source pollution by effluent exceeding consent limits. In effect, such consent limits determine the harm level justifying prosecution. Yet, many factors other than merely exceeding the consent levels determine whether a prosecution will be instituted (Richardson, Ogus & Burrows, 1983; and Richardson, 1982/83). Above all, moral judgment on the part of controllers and the community was found to be "all-pervasive in pollution control" (Hawkins, 1984). Germany has a similar system of "effluent charges." The effluent charge law (*Abwasserabgabengesetz*) of 1976 provides that parties discharging waste pay for the abatement costs directly or indirectly imposed on society. The act provides in great detail for the nature and quantity of effluent and the cost of their emission. This cost was found to be modest and as not impairing the economic situation of industries and municipalities (Brown & Johnson, 1984). A similar system of effluent discharge fees exists in France, where standards are arrived at contractually between polluters and control agencies (*Contrats de branche*). Lack of data makes it difficult to assess the impact of this scheme.

There are areas with unsatisfactory conditions, leading to the speculation that fees are too low, prompting polluters to prefer violations over more costly controls (Harrison & Sewell, 1980). Canada has moved in the same direction, though it has led to the criticism that it encourages the perception of pollution as socially acceptable (Ison, 1985). Nevertheless, the process of "negotiated rule-making" has succeeded in quantifying pollution harm. If based on research, the emission of pollutants may well be kept at a level which allows abatement through the pollution taxes imposed on excess effluent, or by preventing such excesses in the first place, thus securing a healthy environment.

The scheme is here to stay, and in the United States it is being adopted by more and more regulatory agencies (Susskind & van Dam, 1986). Moreover, the idea of fixed rate taxes on all products and services which require environmental renewal or clean-up is now being seriously considered by the United States Congress. Thus, if it costs $100.00 a ton for the safe disposal of hazardous waste, a "green tax" of $100.00 per ton ought to be added to the purchase price of all materials which produce $100 worth per ton of toxic waste. The World Watch Institute has calculated an elaborate cost scheme, with a total dollar figure of $130 billion per year for the preservation of the environment in this time of depletion of resources. These taxes would correct the failure of the market in balancing the ecology. What holds up the implementation of the scheme is simply the feared adverse impact on the economy. Thus, a gradual imposition of "green" taxes is likely to be considered (Shabecoff, 1991), even though some researchers argue that such taxes are impossible to calculate or would be economically unfeasible (Braithwaite, 1981/82).

The Problem of Strict Liability

While it may be premature to celebrate the victory of the *mens rea* principle (*Schuldprinzip*) over strict criminal liability, as a persistent critic of strict criminal liability, this author welcomes the fact the recent American federal and state criminal legislation requires *mens rea*, usually in the form of *scienter*, for criminal liability. (Under the Clean Water Act, the violation may be "willful or negligent") (Riesel, 1979;

Riesel, 1985; and Harris, Cavenaugh & Zisk, 1988). Indeed, if deterrence is the prime motivation for the penal provisions of environmental statutes, how could legislation possibly extend to criminal liability for innocent and guilty violators alike (Bledsoe, 1980)? It seems, however, that industry itself played a major role in eliminating strict criminal liability for health and safety offenses from the proposed federal criminal code, in effect trading a system of civil penalties for strict liability (Frank, 1984). While American criminal legislation on environmental offenses now extends the *mens rea* principle to all offenses, it appears that Canada's fifty-odd environmental penal statutes still operate with strict criminal liability, prompting one commentator to suggest this is yet another indication legislators do not view pollution as a particularly disgraceful or even serious crime (Dumont, 1977). As yet, there is no empirical research on either United States or the Canadian approach.

The Problem of Vicarious Liability

Vicarious liability is the imposition of liability for the act of another. In criminal law it is a variant of strict criminal liability. Even though strict criminal liability has been removed from American environmental criminal law, vicarious liability persists to some extent. This "quasi-strict" liability applies to corporate officials for the act of their corporations, and vice-versa. Any "responsible corporate officer," including even the company lawyer, may incur criminal liability under any of the federal environmental acts, and that despite the "scienter" requirement of these laws. The problems arise particularly as to superiors in the corporate hierarchy with the power to authorize or to stop a given activity, as well as with sub-alterns, whose knowledge of wrongdoing may be inferred from the responsibilities and activities with which they were entrusted (See, *United States v. Johnson and Towers, Inc.*, 741 F. 2d 662 (3rd Cir. [1984]), *cert. denied*, 53 U.S.L.W. 3597). Perhaps the rationale for this form of vicarious liability may rest on the assumption that the laws and their standards have been around long enough to have become familiar in the regulated community. Yet, such as assumption is hard to maintain in the case of a lowly foreman and his worker, who were told that their corporate employer did not have the appropriate license for the dumping in question. Such an impartation would appear to be inconsistent with the legislation's scienter requirement, and thus counterproductive to deterrence.

Corporate Criminal Liability

Since most major polluting activities are carried on by private corporate entities if not by municipalities and other governmental agencies, the complex questions of corporate criminal liability require consideration in any scheme intended to control pollution (Mueller, 1957). Among all the criminological aspects of pollution control, the topic of corporate crime was the first one to have received criminological attention (half a century ago) (Sutherland, 1940; Sutherland, 1946), and it has received the most intense research and policy attention since the awakening of the ecological conscience (Adler, Mueller & Laufer, 1991). Nevertheless, as recently as 1988, the late Donald R. Cressey, justifiedly spoke of a "poverty of theory in corporate crime research" (Cressey, 1989: 31).

Much of the recent research is concerned with corporate behavior with regard to cost-beneficial decision-making as to pollution activities (Ermann & Lundman, 1982; and Hochstedler, 1984). Some research has investigated the question of the lawlessness of corporations. One study finds that 11 percent of major corporations have been involved in at least one major delinquency in the decade of the 1970s (Ross, 1980). Clinard and Yeager (1980) found that, during 1975/76, 60 percent of corporations subject to the jurisdiction of 25 federal regulatory agencies had violated the law and that 13 percent accounted for over half of all these violations. Increasingly, it is being demonstrated that corporate immunity from prosecution and their obliviousness to deterrence are a myth (Cullen & Dubeck, 1985). This reflects, no doubt, the increasingly punitive thinking toward corporations on the part of the public (Braithwaite, 1985; Downing & Kimball, 1982/83).

Some research explored the question why corporations do or do not commit crimes, especially in the environmental category. "Bottom-line" thinking, in other words the profit motive, is a powerful incentive (Barnett, 1981), but so is the corporate image amongst the public (Albanese, 1984). Apparently the public views with disfavor the power of corporations to "bargain" the level of compliance with environmental standards (Braithwaite, 1985; Downing & Kimball, 1982/83). Moreover, there is more than a suspicion that corporations favor certain types of regulation because these protect them against potential competitors entering the market (Downing & Kimball, 1982/83).

There is growing evidence that the imposition of corporate criminal liability can be effective in regulating and controlling corporate conduct with respect to environmental pollution. In a study of the oil-tanker industry, Epple and Visscher (1984) determined that the incentives, including potential fines, "facing oil transporters affect the frequency and size of oil spills. . . Vessel size, the price of oil, the enforcement of pollution control regulations, and the risk associated with variance in spill size affect the oil transporter's decisions concerning expenditures on measures for spill prevention" (p. 29). Corporate deterrence works by prompting corporations to alter their activities for the purpose of compliance. Yet there is evidence to the contrary. Using economic efficiency as a gauge to analyze the effectiveness of imposing criminal sanctions to deter socially undesirable conduct, Byam (1982) concluded that "criminal sanctions increase the costs of imposing legal rules without producing a concomitant benefit to society" (p. 582). At best, the price of a product or service is passed on to the consumer. Since "the total cost to society of corporate offenses is the sum of the cost of violations, the cost of detection agents and the cost of administering fines," he comes out in favor of a system of private sector enforcement whenever the chance of detection is close to unity and public sector enforcement whenever that chance is less than unity.

While the evidence on the effectiveness of corporate criminal liability for environmental offenses remains ambiguous, there is growing certainty among scholars about the effectiveness of criminal sanctions for corporate officers responsible for the making of decisions for the economic ("acquisitive") benefit of the corporation. Dershowitz (1961/2) provided the following formula, which probably still holds true: "The rate of acquisitive corporate crime . . . will (a) vary directly with the expectation of net gain . . . and will (b) vary inversely with the certainty and severity of the impact with which the criminal sanction personally falls upon those who formulate corporate policy" (p. 280). Indeed, modern policy regarding the subject favors criminal liability for corporate officials who formulate and control policy with respect to law-violative pollution and the prosecution of the corporate entity itself

(Iseman, 1972; and Schneider, 1987), and such is the law in the United States (See, *United States v. Park*, 421 U.S. 685 [1975]). Controversy exists simply as to whether imprisonment or a fine is the most effective sanction (Schneider, 1987; Nielson, 1978; Groveman & Segal, 1985; Comment, 1984; and Posner, 1980).

Due to the *scienter* requirement in American pollution laws, there remains the problem of determining which officer in the corporate hierarchy had the decision-making power and abused it for the creation of a violation of environmental criminal law. There is evidence to support that blame for white collar crime is passed downwards in the hierarchy (Braithwaite, 1985; and Meinberg et al., 1988), yet there are highly varied ways in which large organizations hold individuals and subunits responsible for corporate wrongdoing (Braithwaite & Fisse, 1985).

The Problem of Proof

Problems of proof permeate the sphere of environmental criminality. There is the difficulty in establishing the quantum of proof of ecological damage which may justify legislative penal intervention. Similarly, quantum of proof problems as to whether the requisite harm is constituted mark criminal litigation. The legal characterization of the quantum of proof may vary from the vaguest (as in Canadian law) to the most exacting scientific measure, as under the United States Water Quality Improvement Act of 1970 and subsequent amendatory legislation (Epple & Visscher, 1984). By the very nature of pollution, some acts, especially those of catastrophic proportion, are easily detectable and tend to be reflected in crime statistics, while most are so insignificant as to escape notice, detection, and prosecution. These are the bulk, numerically (Meinberg, 1986). The number of prosecutions remains low because of lack of knowledge of the true risk and long-term effects on the environment and on persons of exposure to hazardous chemicals covered by legislation. Moreover, proof may be difficult to obtain owing to a shortage of investigators; after all, guessing the resources requisite for effective environmental law enforcement in itself is a hazardous job (Albanese, 1984; and Russell, Harrington & Vaughan, 1986). DiMento (1986) identified four evidentiary problems in environmental criminal prosecutions: (1) the difficulty of securing adequate evidence to prove the case beyond the requisite legal standard of proof of guilt beyond a reasonable doubt; (2) the establishment of the causal connection between the act and the harm; (3) the identification of the proper individual defendants (Fisse, 1984); and (4) proof of their *mens rea* (DiMento, 1986).

Access to corporate information, for purposes of identifying decision-makers responsible for the act in question, has been a problem (Barnett, 1981) but can be overcome by the state's subpoena power, since the self-incrimination privilege does not protect legal entities (see, *Bellis v. United States*, 417 U.S. 85 [1974]). Indeed, it might be argued that since it is easier to obtain evidence against corporations than against individuals, corporate criminal liability for environmental crimes should be preferred over individual criminal liability. Yet, while this may be true from the perspective of proof, it does not hold equally true from the perspective of deterrence, as indicated earlier. The fact is the problems of proof in criminal prosecutions have been largely overcome since first complained about over 30 years ago.

The Problem of the Abuse of Power

The theme "abuse of power" refers to the age-old problem of the *pacta leonis*: when the lion makes a contract with the lamb, it is the lion who dictates the terms. Corporations, especially when they combine to represent an entire industry, are indeed in a leonine position in dealing with governments seeking to regulate them. The relationship between the regulated and the regulators is indeed a semi-contractual one, in that legislation results from a process in which the views of both sides are considered and in that specific standards are frequently subject to negotiation (Meinberg et al., 1988). Some maintain the thesis of a capture by ruling class interests in the environmental arena (Braithwaite, 1985). More powerful businesses, so it has been demonstrated, are favored by regulators and prosecutors over less powerful businesses (Yeager, 1987); "little thieves are hanged but great ones escape" (Meinberg et al., 1988: 65). Frequently a symbiosis develops between regulators/enforcers and the regulated which, for the sake of smooth working relationships, sacrifices the common good (Adler, Mueller &

Laufer, 1991). Nowhere is this more evident than in developing countries where polluting industries wishing to locate there often "have the power to influence governments and officials, surreptitiously and officially, into passing pollution legislation favorable to the industry. The desire to industrialize outweighs the desire to preserve the environment" (Adler, Mueller & Laufer, 1991: 297). Yet, research in Britain suggests that nefarious symbiosis need not result even where processes of negotiation are part of the enforcement routine, especially when there is public accountability and scrutiny (Weait, 1989; Richardson, 1982/83).

The Problem of Inadequate Enforcement

Over a decade ago, many scholars expressed a concern over the unwillingness to enforce legislation enacted for the purpose of protecting the ecology. Indeed, in the 1970s, the U.S. Environmental Protection Agency "had referred only 130 cases to the U.S. Department of Justice for criminal prosecution. Only six of the cases involved major corporate offenders. The government actually charged only one of these corporations, Allied Chemical, which admitted responsibility for 940 misdemeanor counts of discharging toxic chemicals into the Charles River in Virginia, thereby causing 80 people to become ill" (Adler et al., 1991: 297; see also Clinard & Yeager, 1980). Since then the situation has improved significantly, thanks largely to public and congressional pressure.

The Problem of Changing Priorities

Government may set aside vast tracts of land for purposes of recreation and to serve as a lung for the ecological renewal cycle. Environment-endangering activities are prohibited. Yet when there is a fuel crisis, government is under pressure to allow environment-endangering oil drilling on this land. The prime example of changing priorities was provided by Japan's "Pollution Diet," which unanimously repealed a provision of the Basic Law for Environment Pollution

Control that had posited a balance between the conservation of life environment and the needs of economic development (Upham, 1979/80). Thus, developers and individuals are not required to take environmental factors into account in their planning programs. This policy resulted in massive pollution problems, producing the widespread Minamata and Itai-Itai diseases, leading to the so-called Big Four environmental cases. In consequence, Japan's attitude changed once again, this time in favor of stricter controls (Peterson & Wade, 1985).

The former German Democratic Republic is another case in point. Its 1968 penal code did not mention crimes against the environment and actually exculpated those who created environmental damage "in pursuit of important economic benefit." Near catastrophic consequences of this policy led to stringent anti-pollution legislation in 1968 and 1970. Such legislation was viewed with envy by Western commentators (Sand, 1973). Alas, either the legislation came too late, or it posed the problem of government prosecuting itself (as owner-polluter) or both. In any event, when Germany became united in 1991, the West acquired a well-nigh dead Eastern environment. And the situation is not much different in the other new Eastern European democracies, where the environment had been subjugated to economic exploitation.

The situation is particularly disheartening in developing countries, where belching smokestacks are viewed as a sign of economic progress and environmental concerns are postponed for later solution. Yet, the ecology is a global unity and pollution recognizes no international frontiers. It is therefore in the interest of industry-exporting developed countries to respect the ecology of the developing countries. An economically feasible solution is by no means in sight, although the actions of some developing countries, notably Brazil with respect to the Amazon basin, give cause for hope.

The Problem of the Countervailing Trend Towards Decriminalization

This, and the following section, refer to the inherent clash of principles—first noted at the Stockholm Environment Congress (1972)—between the aim of decriminalization, on the one hand, and that of subjecting important, severely dangerous activities, like pollution, to prohibition by penal law (Kaiser, 1985; Ross, 1984; and Finkle, 1983).[1] What has emerged, however, is a somewhat pragmatic, if not research and experience-based, distribution of functions. Penal law has its role to play, as has been noted throughout, and as shall be discussed closely in the next section. But so has the civil law, as the range of options developed over the last decade demonstrates. Most advocates for civil alternatives to either prosecution or imprisonment note the various and previously noted difficulties inhering in the penal approach, or they refer to the cost-beneficial nature of more civil approaches.

Among the civil choices ranks foremost the one favored by "routine activities" proponents, namely removal of incentives for violation. Thus, ships and boats are prohibited from discharging liquid waste, especially waste oil, into navigable waters. Yet they are forced to do so owing to a dearth of pump-out stations. If these were created in adequate number, with cost efficient charges for their use, vessels would not be forced to pollute the waters (Rea, 1982).

Some argue the state's regulatory power could be used to force industry into establishing self-regulatory systems or intra-company self-policing schemes (Braithwaite, 1984). Additionally, the previously discussed environmental tax for pollution activities may well prove its worth in providing the wherewithal for clean-up activities (Trezise, 1975). A similar function can be performed by the creation of superfunds from industry sources, out of which environmental clean-up costs can be covered (Starr, 1986). New ways can be found for assuring victims of spills and other pollutants a remedy (Estrin, 1986). In drastic pollution cases remedies such as divestiture, license revocation (though not without its market problems), and probation could be used and further developed (Wilson, 1986). Indeed, probation upon conviction of a criminal offense opens up a whole range of appropriate sanctions short of imprisonment, including community restitution (Merritt, 1984), community service (DiMento, 1986), or even a mandated advertisement in *The Wall Street Journal* advertising and apologizing for patterns of pollution (Goldsmith & Bunyard, 1984). Probation permits sentences to remain essentially civil, yet, within given frameworks, to be customized so as to maximize the goal of environmental protection.

The Problem Arising from Countervailing Penalization Policies

If there is one overriding factor which prompts most environmentalists to opt for the criminal sanction, it is the concern that nothing short of punishment can demonstrate the seriousness of the ecological situation. These punitive demands occur at a time when the decriminalization policy is on the decline, at a time of general conservatism and of more retributive attitudes toward crime and punishment. Having earlier been charged with laxity, the U.S. Environmental Protection Agency stepped up its enforcement policy. Between October 1983 and March 1986, close to 180 indictments were found and 130 convictions or pleas of guilty obtained, mostly from management defendants (Starr, 1986). For the period October 1, 1982 to July 1, 1986, 205 criminal charges were filed, nearly all against individuals.

Under the Clean Water Act, criminal enforcement began in earnest in 1986. While only 123 violators had been indicted during the four-year period 1982-1985, 123 indictments were obtained during the first nine months of 1986 alone. Ninety percent of individuals indicted were convicted, although only one in five received a prison sentence. The most severe sentence was a two-and-a-half year prison term for a chief business executive convicted of dumping toxic chemicals. Judges have at their disposition increased penalty schemes (Long, 1984) and appear more willing than ever to press for harsher sentences, and more and more judges are willing to impose punitive sentences (Goldsmith & Bunyard, 1984). At least one study has determined that penal enforcement has a significant deterrent effect (Epple & Visscher, 1984). Indeed, even traditionally non-punitive Swedes call for penal liability for environmental offenses as needed for the purpose of deterrence (Erikson, 1988). However, far more empirical research on this complicated issue is needed before we can come to an acceptable conclusion on appropriate punishments for given environmental crimes.

Conclusion: Criminological Classification of Environmental Criminality

The foregoing concentrated on environmental or ecological crime as it is understood by most criminologists: a serious though nevertheless regulatory crime of *accretion*, i.e., by which individual offenders threaten an overall harm by individual contributions. This accretion of individual pollutants results in overall harmful consequences. This form of criminality has produced some research of its own, and certain principles may well be emerging. Inasmuch as accretion pollution is largely a white-collar, organizational form of criminality, the large body of research on white-collar and organizational crime is available for its study. Yet environmental criminality extends to three other criminological realms, each with its own body of research. These shall be briefly alluded to.

There is above all the growing involvement of organized crime in the disposal of waste, especially hazardous waste. While environmental crime by accretion is committed by legitimate enterprises which, for the most part, act more or less lawfully on the margin of ill-defined permissibles, organized crime acts conspiratorially in an effort to violate laws deliberately for vast financial gain. The role of organized crime in hazardous waste disposal is only now being recognized (Block & Scarpiti, 1985; Rebovich, 1986; and Szasz, 1986). The larger body of research on organized crime in general would seem to be equally applicable to environmental organized crime.

There is next the criminological phenomenon of environmental criminal disaster. Instances are the Bhopal, India, toxic chemical emission, the Chernobyl, USSR nuclear contamination, and the *Exxon Valdez* oil spill in Alaskan waters, (Adler et al., 1991). Accretion is not the issue in ecological disasters. The event itself brings about immediate harm, death, and destruction of life and the environment. The principles for the criminological study of such environmental disasters differ from those suitable to environmental accretion offenses. Rather, such principles are to be found in the body of knowledge of disaster criminology. Human behavior preceding, immediately before, during the onset of, during the enveloping event, immediately after, and during the recovery phase of a disaster has been identified and studied. Each of the phases is marked by its own form of criminality. First there is negligent malfeasance and intentional misfeasance (e.g., embezzlement, bribery, corruption) which creates the condition leading to a disaster (which, thus, is man-made). From the point of view of prevention, this phase deserves the greatest criminological attention. During the disaster itself criminality is usually minimal and sometimes excusable (due to panic), while the post-disaster phase knows its own form of criminality, including but not necessarily looting and other offenses against property as well as offenses against the person, with fraud being the most prevalent. For the post-disaster criminality, the general theories of criminology are suitable for crime prevention efforts.

Finally, there is an entirely new form of environmental criminality. It was vividly envisaged by the novelist Frederick Forsythe who, in his 1979 novel *The Devil's Alternative*, conjured up a terrorist plot which resulted in a vast oil slick in the North Sea (Forsythe, 1979). There have indeed been a number of terrorist (and sometimes state-terrorist) acts which resulted in near-catastrophic environmental pollution (Mueller & Adler, 1985), culminating in January 1991 in the vast oil spill in the Persian Gulf, apparently resulting from the intentional dumping of crude oil out of Iraqi-occupied Kuwaiti oil terminals. This spill threatens the entire ecology of the Persian Gulf, including the drinking water supply of all riparian countries. As to all environmental terrorism, the accumulated wisdom on pollution criminality offers little insight, but terrorism criminology has much to offer.

All environmental criminality is marked by the fact that it does not respect international boundaries. It is actually or potentially a form of international crime, thus calling for the invocation of principles of international comparative criminology for its study and principles of international criminal law for its control.

At this point, Donald Cressey's (1989) lament about the poverty of crime research comes to mind. The lack of theory is equally glaring in environment-specific crime research. While this chapter may point toward the applicability of extant theories to the four criminological types of environmental criminality, there is a long way to travel before theories of criminality and theories of crime can be usefully deployed for research on and prevention of environmental crime.

NOTES

1. The People's Republic of China has developed a triple strategy to ensure environmental protection, ranging from the law enforcement (penal) approach to the civil approaches of market exchange and exhortational campaigns.

CASES CITED

Bellis v. United States, 417 U.S. 85 (1974).

United States v. Johnson and Towers, Inc., 741 F. 2d 662 (3rd Cir. 1984), *cert. denied*, 469 U.S. 1208 (1984).

United States v. Park, 421 U.S. 685 (1975).

United States v. Standard Oil, 384 U.S. 224 (1966).

STATUTES CITED

Air Quality Act of 1967 (Pub. L. No. 90-148, 81 Stat. 485, 1967)

Clean Air Act (42 United States Code Sections 7401-7671q)

Clean Water Act of 1977 (33 U.S.C. Sections 1251-1376)

Resource Conservation and Recovery Act (RCRA) (42 United States Code Sections 6901-6992k)

The Rivers and Harbors Act (now 33 U.S.C. Section 407)

REFERENCES

Adler, Freda, Gerhard O. W. Mueller & W. S. Laufer (1991). *Criminology.* New York: McGraw-Hill.

Albanese, Jay S. (1984). "Love Canal Six Years Later: The Legal Legacy." *Federal Probation* 48: 533-538.

Barnett, Harold C. (1981). "Corporate Capitalism, Corporate Crime." *Crime and Delinquency* 27: 4-23.

Bledsoe, L. (1980). "Criminal Liability for Public Welfare Offenses: Gambler's Choice." *Memphis State University Law Review* 10: 612-632.

Block, A. A., & F. R. Scarpiti (1985). *Poisoning for Profit.* New York: William Morrow.

Braithwaite, John (1981/82). "The Limits of Economism in Controlling Harmful Corporate Conduct." *Law and Society Review* 16: 481-504.

_____ (1984). *Corporate Crime in the Pharmaceutical Industry.* London: Routledge and Kegan Paul.

_____ (1985). "White Collar Crime." *Annual Review of Sociology* 11: 1-25.

Braithwaite, John & Brent Fisse (1985). "Varieties of Responsibility and Organizational Crime." *Law and Policy* 7: 315-343.

Brants, Chrisje, & Theo de Roos (1984). "Pollution, Press and the Penal Process: The Case of UNISER in the Netherlands." *Crime and Social Justice* 21/22: 128-145.

Brown, Gardner M., Jr., & Ralph W. Johnson (1984). "Pollution Control by Effluent Charges: It Works in the Federal Republic of Germany, Why Not in the U.S.?" *Natural Resources Journal* 24: 929-966.

Byam, John T. (1982). "Comments: Economic Inefficiency of Corporate Criminal Liability." *Journal of Criminal Law and Criminology* 73: 582-603.

Chappell, D., & R. D. Moore (1989). *The Use of Criminal Penalties for Pollution of the Environment: A Selective and Annotated Bibliography of the Literature.* Ottawa: Minister of Supply and Service, Canada.

Charles, M. T., & J. C. K. Kim (eds.) (1988). *Crisis Management.* Springfield, IL: Charles C. Thomas.

Clinard, Marshall B., & Peter C. Yeager (1980). *Corporate Crime.* New York: Free Press.

Comment (1984). "L.A. Jails Company Officer for Breaking Pollution Laws." *Business Insurance* (April 2): 2.

Commentary (1986). "Canadian Proposal for Crimes Against the Environment." *Environment* 28 (June): 2-5.

Cressey, D. R. (1989). "The Poverty of Theory in Corporate Crime Research." In F. Adler & W. S. Laufer (eds.), *Advances in Criminological Theory.* New Brunswick, NJ: Translation.

Cullen, Francis, B. Link, & C. Polanzi (1982). "The Seriousness of Crime Revisited." *Criminology* 20: 83-102.

Cullen, Francis, R. Mathers, G. Clark, & J. Cullen (1983). "Public Support for Punishing White Collar Crime: Blaming the Victim Revisited." *Journal of Criminal Justice* 11: 481-491.

Cullen, F. T., & P. J. Dubeck (1985). "The Myth of Corporate Immunity to Deterrence and the Creation of the Invincible Criminal." *Federal Probation* 49: 3-9.

deCicco, John, & Edward Bonano (1988). "A Comparative Analysis of the Criminal Environmental Laws of the Fifty States: The Need for Statutory Uniformity as a Catalyst for Effective Enforcement of Existing and Proposed Laws." *Criminal Justice Quarterly* 9 (4): 216-294.

Dershowitz, A. M. (1961/2). "Comment—Increasing Community Control Over Corporate Crime: A Problem in the Law of Sanctions." *Yale Law Journal* 71: 280-306.

DiMento, Joesph F. (1986). *Environmental Law and American Business: Dilemmas of Compliance*. New York: Plenum Press.

Dodd, David, Richard Sparks, H. Genn, & D. Dodd (1977). *Surveying Victims*. New York: Wiley.

Downing, Paul B., & James N. Kimball (1982/83). "Enforcing Pollution Control Laws in the U.S." *Policy Studies Journal* 11: 56-65.

Dumont, H. (1977). "Canadian Criminal Law and the Protection of the Environment." *McGill Law Journal* 23: 189-206.

Duncan, L. F. (1986). "Pollution *is* Crime." *Environmental Law Centre Newsletter* 4: 1-2.

"EPA Pushes Criminal Sanctions" (1986). *Chemical Week* 139: 16-18.

Epple, D., & M. Visscher (1984). "Environmental Pollution: Modeling Occurrence, Detection, and Deterrence." *Journal of Law and Economics* 27: 29-60.

Erikson, I. (ed.) (1988). *Miljobrott och straff*. Stockholm: National Crime Prevention Council.

Ermann, M. David & Richard J. Lundman (1982). *Corporate and Government Deviance: Problems of Organizational Behavior in Contemporary Society* (2nd ed.). New York: Oxford University Press.

Estrin, D. (1986). *Handle with Caution: Liability in the Production, Transportation and Disposal of Dangerous Substances.* Toronto: Carswell.

Estrin, D., & J. Swaigen (1978). *Environment on Trial: A Handbook of Ontario's Environmental Law* (rev. ed.) Toronto: Canadian Environmental Law Research Foundation.

"Exxon's Liability in Oil Spill Is Restricted by a U. S. Judge" (1991). *The New York Times* (February 10): L 24.

"Feds Crack Down on Corporate Polluters" (1986). *Inc.* 8 (September): 20-21.

Finkle, P. Z. R. (1983). "Canadian Environmental Law in the Eighties: Problems and Perspectives." *Dalhousie Law Journal* 7: 257-276.

Fisse, Brent (1984). "The Duality of Corporate and Individual Criminal Liability." In E. Hochstedler (ed.), *Corporations as Criminals.* Beverly Hills, CA: Sage.

Forsythe, F. (1979). *The Devil's Alternative.* New York: Ahiara International Co., S.A.

Frank, Nancy F. (1984). "Choosing Between Criminal and Civil Sanction for Corporate Wrongs." In E. Hochstedler (ed.), *Corporations as Criminals* (pp. 85-102). Beverly Hills, CA: Sage.

Goldsmith, E., & P. Bunyard (1984). "Industrial Pollution: Getting Away with the Crime." Editorial. *Ecologist* 14: 138-140.

Groveman, Barry C., & John L. Segal (1985). "Pollution Police Pursue Chemical Criminals." *Business and Society Review* 55: 39-42.

Harford, J. D. (1978). "Firm Behavior Under Imperfectly Enforceable Pollution Standards and Taxes." *Journal of Environmental Economics and Management* 5: 26-44.

Harris, C., P. O. Cavenaugh, & R. L. Zisk (1988). "Criminal Liability for Violations of Federal Hazardous Waste Law: 'Knowledge' of Corporations and Their Executives." *Wake Forest Law Review* 23: 203-236.

Harrison, Peter, & W. R. Derrick Sewell (1980). "Water Pollution Control by Agreement: The French System of Contracts." *Natural Resources Journal* 20: 765-786.

Hawkins, Keith (1984). *Environment and Enforcement: Regulation and the Social Definition of Pollution.* Oxford: Clarendon Press.

Hochstedler, E. (ed.) (1984). *Corporations as Criminals.* Beverly Hills, CA: Sage.

Ilgen, Thomas L. (1985) "Between Europe and America, Ottawa and the Provinces: Regulating Toxic Substances in Canada." *Canadian Public Policy* 11: 578-590.

Institutes of Justinian.

Iseman, R. H. (1972). "The Criminal Responsibility of Corporate Officials for Pollution of the Environment." *Albany Law Review* 37: 61-96.

Ison, T. G. (1985). "Book Review—*A Contract Model for Pollution Control.*" B. J. Barton, R. T. Franson, and A. R. Thompson. *Canadian Bar Review.*

Kaiser, G. (1985). *Kriminologie* (7th edition). Heidelberg: C. F. Muller Juristischer Verlag.

Klaus, Patsy, & Carol Kalish (1984). *The Severity of Crime.* Bureau of Justice Statistics Bulletin (NCJ-92326). Washington, DC: U.S. Government Printing Office.

Kuruz, Michelle (1985). "Putting Polluters in Jail: The Imposition of Criminal Sanctions on Corporate Defendants Under Environmental Statutes." *Land and Water Review* 20: 93-109.

La Force, N. (1980). "Environmental Crimes." *American Criminal Law Review* 18: 345-370.

Law of the Twelve Tables.

Long, C. (1984). "Criminal Prosecution of Environmental Laws: Semi-White Collar Crime." *Federal Bar News and Journal* 31: 266-272.

Meinberg, Volker (1986). "Probleme der Verfolgung von Umwelt— Straftaten aus Kriminologischer Sicht." *Schriftenreihe der Polizei-Fuhrungsakademie* 4: 270.

Meinberg, Volker, Donnen, H. Hoch, & W. Link (1988). "Environmental Crime—Economic and Everyone's Delinquency, Empirical Studies of the Implementation of Environmental Criminal Law in the Federal Republic of Germany." In Gunther Kaiser and Isolde Geissler (eds.). *Criminal Justice: Criminological Research in the 2nd Decade at the Max Planck Institute Freiburg.* Freiburg, Germany: Max Planck Institute {R 48533}.

Merritt, F. S. (1984). "Corrections Law Developments—Community Restitution—An Alternative Disposition for Corporate Offenders." *Criminal Law Bulletin* 20: 355-360.

Mueller, Gerhard O. W. (1957). "Mens Rea and the Corporation: A Study of the Model Penal Code Position on Corporate Criminal Liability." *University of Pittsburgh Law Review* 19: 21-50.

_____ (1979). "Offenses Against the Environment and Their Prevention: An International Appraisal." *The Annals* 444: 56-66.

_____ forthcoming. *Disasters and Catastrophes— American Law Governing Human Behavior Before, During and After the Events.*

Mueller, Gerhard O. W., & Freda Adler (1985). *Outlaws of the Ocean--The Complete Book of Contemporary Crime on the High Seas.* New York: Hearst Marine Books-William Morrow.

Newman, Greeme R. (1978). "Perceptions of Deviance." Reports No. 1, India; No. 2, Indonesia; No. 3, Iran; No. 4, Italy (Sardinia); No. 5, Yugoslavia; No. 6, U.S.A. United Nations Social Defence Research Institute.

Nielson, R. P. (1978). "Should Executives be Jailed for Organization Behavior That Causes Consumer and Worker Injuries and Death?" *Labor Law Journal* 29: 582-585.

Peterson, Michael R., & Larry L. Wade (1985). "Environmental Pollution Policy in Japan: A Public Choice Hypothesis." In Alexander J. Groth and Larry L. Wade (eds.), *Public Policy Across Nations: Social Welfare in Industrial Settings.* Greenwich, CN: JAI Press, Inc.

Posner, R. A. (1980). "Optimal Sentences for While-Collar Criminals." *American Criminal Law Review* 17: 409-418.

Quarantelli, E. L., & Jane Gray (1986). "Research Findings on Community and Organizational Preparations for and Responses to Acute Chemical Emergencies." *Public Management* (March): 11-14.

Rea, R. A. (1982). "Hazardous Waste Pollution: The Need for a Different Statutory Approach." *Environmental Law* 12: 442-467.

Rebovich, D. J. (1986). "Criminal Opportunity and the Hazardous Waste Offender: Confronting the Syndicate Control Mystique." *National Environmental Enforcement Journal* 3 (December): 3-7.

Richardson, Genevra (1982/83). "Policing Pollution: The Enforcement Process." *Policy Studies Journal* 11: 153-164.

Richardson, Genevra, A. I. Ogus, & Paul Burrows (1983). *Policing Pollution: A Study of Regulation and Enforcement*. Oxford: Clarendon Press.

Riesel, Daniel (1979). "Air and Water Act Enforcement Problems—A Case Study." *Business Lawyer* 34: 665-723.

_____ (1985). "Criminal Prosecution and Defense of Environmental Wrongs." *Environmental Law Reporter* 15: 10065-10081.

Ross, Irwin. (1980). "How Lawless Are Big Companies? A Look at the Record Since 1970 Shows That a Surprising Number of Them Have Been Involved in Blatant Illegalities." *Fortune* 102 (December): 56-62.

Ross, Lester (1984). "The Implementation of Environmental Policy in China: A Comparative Perspective." *Administration and Society* 15: 489-516.

Russell, Clifford S., Winston Harrington, & William J. Vaughan (1986). *Enforcing Pollution Control Laws*. Washington, DC: Resources for the Future.

Sand, P. H. (1973). "The Socialist Response: Environmental Protection in the German Democratic Republic." *Ecology Law Quarterly* 3: 451-505.

Schneider, Mark W. (1987). "Criminal Enforcement of Federal Water Pollution Laws in an Era of Deregulation." *Journal of Criminal Law and Criminology* 73: 642-674.

Schrager, Laura Shill, & James F. Short, Jr. (1980). "How Serious a Crime? Perception of Organizational and Common Crimes." In Gilbert Geis and Ezra Stotland (eds.) *White Collar Crime: Theory and Research*. Beverly Hills, CA: Sage.

Shabecoff, Philip (1991). "Environmental Tax Urged for Some Products." *The New York Times,* commenting on World Watch Institute, *State of the World Report* I (25) (February 10): 1.

Siman, B. (1977). *Crime During Disaster.* Unpublished doctoral dissertation, University of Pennsylvania, Philadelphia, PA.

Starr, J. W. (1986). "Countering Environmental Crimes." *Boston College Environmental Affairs Law Review* 13 (3): 379-395.

Susskind, L., & L. van Dam (1986). "Squaring off at the Table, Not in the Courts: All Too Often Government Regulations End Up as the Subject of Lawsuits." *Technology Review* 89: 36-44.

Sutherland, Edwin H. (1940). "White Collar Criminality." *American Sociological Review* 5: 1-12.

_____ (1946). *White Collar Crime.* New York: Dryden.

Szasz, Andrew (1986). "Organizations, Organized Crime and the Disposal of Hazardous Waste: An Examination of the Making of a Criminogenic Regulatory Structure." *Criminology* 24 (1): 1-27.

Trezise, D. (1975). "Alternative Approaches to Legal Control of Environmental Quality in Canada." *McGill Law Journal* 21: 404-427.

"UN/WCED Proposals for International Environmental Law Development, Toward the Year 2000" (1986). *Environmental Policy and Law* 16: 90-96.

Upham, F. (1979/80). "After Miramata: Current Prospects in Japanese Environmental Litigation." *Ecology Law Journal* 8: 213-268.

Weait, Matthew (1989). "The Letter of the Law? An Enquiry into Reasoning and Formal Enforcement in the Industrial Air Pollution Inspectorate." *British Journal of Criminology* 29 (1): 57-70.

Wilson, J. D. (1986). "Re-thinking Penalties for Corporate Environmental Offenders: A View of the Law Reform Commission of Canada's Sentencing in Environmental Cases." *McGill Law Journal* 31: 313-332.

Wolfgang M., R. M. Figlio, P. E. Tracy, & S. I. Singer (1985). *The National Survey of Crime Severity*. Washington, DC: U.S. Department of Justice, Bureau of Justice Statistics.

Wright, Karen (1991). "Heating the Global Warming Debate." *The New York Times Magazine* (L) (February 3): 1.

Yeager, P. C. (1987). "Structural Bias in Regulatory Law Enforcement: The Case of the U.S. Environmental Protection Agency." *Social Problems* 34: 330-344.

CHAPTER TWO

Offender-Specific vs. Offense-Specific Approaches to the Study of Environmental Crime

Freda Adler

Criminological research in environmental crime is little more than a decade old.[1] Many obstacles have hindered studies of this topic. To begin with, there are those who argue that by and large these offenses fall outside the purview of criminological theory and research because many are not criminal but rather regulatory. Moreover, researchers investigating environmental crime are faced with the same complex of problems encountered in the study of other types of white-collar and corporate crime, including the need for massive funding, industries' reluctance to release voluntarily information about their own illegal acts, access to corporate records, the low level of visibility of day-to-day corporate activities, lack of official national statistics, and non-comparable recording systems of regulatory agencies. Add to this the fact that offending corporations may operate in many different jurisdictions, some of which regard a given activity as illegal, others not. The possibility for research in countries outside the United States is often even worse, especially in the developing countries, where corporations are subject to little control thereby making it easy to keep secret various slip-shod practices.

Despite these drawbacks, scholars have managed to conduct research in a number of areas including air pollution estimation. One study indicates 9 percent of all deaths in the U.S. may be attributed to it (Mendelsohn & Orcutt, 1979). Other studies include the dumping of radioactive wastes in Canada (Howard, 1980), water pollution (Epple & Visscher, 1984), sulphur dioxide air pollution control in the European Economic Community (EEC) countries and Switzerland (Hill, 1982/83), estimation of the actual amount of environmental crime in Germany (Wittkamper & Wulff, 1987), the discharge of trade effluent into sewers in England and Wales (Richardson, 1982/83), behavioral theories of corporate regulation (Ullman, 1982/83), and the causes of individual disasters (Albanese, 1984). With the increasing number and diversity of crimes against the environment, including primarily catastrophic events which have shocked the conscience, such as Chernobyl, the *Exxon Valdez* oil tanker spill, Bhopal, and the pollution of the Persian Gulf, there is likely to be much more attention paid by criminologists to theory building and research in this area.

Theoretical Perspective

Criminological research and, ultimately, policy decisions can be guided by two different theoretical approaches to the crime problem. To start with the familiar, the first approach involves theories of criminality. These are the traditional well-established sociological theories that seek to explain criminal behavior in terms of the social environment. They explain why some groups of people are more likely to engage in criminal behavior than others. Typical explanations focus on frustrations of people deprived of legitimate means to reach their goals, the learning of criminal values and norms, and the breakdown of social control wielded by formal (law enforcement) and informal (family, religion, profession) institutions. These mainstream theories have been used by most of us to formulate research and policy for over half a century. The second perspective, rapidly gaining acceptance, is based on theories of crime. It has appeared in the criminological literature during the past decade. According to Michael Gottfredson and Travis Hirschi (1989) there is a fundamental difference between theories of criminality and theories of crime. Summarizing their argument, theories of criminality are offender-specific. They look at why people commit crime. In other words, what are the factors that explain criminal behavior? Theories of crime, on the other hand, are offense-specific. They identify the conditions under which those persons who are prone to commit crimes will in fact do so. Crimes are viewed as events. These events have characteristics. They take place at given times and places, require expertise or skills on the part of the perpetrator, and involve various situational factors that influence their commission.

With this brief summary of the distinction between two approaches used to study crime in general, we shall turn to the major objective of this chapter: to demonstrate the difference between how theories of criminality and theories of crime are used to formulate research and ultimately policy on environmental crime.

Explanations of Crimes Against the Environment: Traditional Theories of Criminality

The theory of criminality used most frequently by criminologists, thus far, to explain why corporations commit crimes is strain theory. Put succinctly, strain theory argues when there are limitations on legitimate opportunities to attain one's goals, people may turn to illegitimate means instead. When applied to corporate crime it suggests that officers of corporations are sometimes willing to abandon morality for the rewarding objectives of security, money, power, prestige and, more importantly for survival of the company. In the area of environmental crime, take, as an example, the generators of hazardous waste. The cost of hazardous waste disposal has increased steadily since the 1940s and has become a major factor in the economics of some industries. Pharmaceutical companies for example, spend about $125 per 55 gallon drum for legal waste disposal (Rebovich, 1986). Other industries pay as much as $550 a drum. These exorbitant costs can, indeed, cut into profit margins and may even cut companies out of the competitive race. Cheaper, albeit illegal, means of disposal then, may make the difference in a corporation staying in business. A case study from the petroleum industry (The Mahler operations) demonstrates the point (Block & Bernard, 1988):

Russel W. Mahler's enterprises specialized in receiving waste oils and re-refining these into lubricants. His business reputation was so outstanding that his refueling contacts ultimately included the Strategic Air Command bomber fleet, U.S. Naval Vessels, and Air Force One. Let us examine his practices:

(1) In 1978, the U.S. Coast Guard detected an oil spill in Newtown Creek which runs into New York's East River across Waterside Plaza, near the United Nations. The spill was traced to an overflowing catch basin of Mahler's Newtown Oil Refining Company, which subsequently was sold to another company by Mahler.

(2) Starting in 1979, large amounts of waste oil and other toxic materials were fouling the waters at a pumping station on Lake Onondaga. Sanitation Department investigators found that the Northeast Oil Service tank farm had dumped 40,000 gallons of waste oil into the Syracuse sewer system. Northeast Oil Service was owned by Mahler.

(3) Later on, Hudson Oil dumped truckloads of waste oil into a borehole in Pittston, Pennyslvania, into an abandoned mine shaft. From there, it seeped into the Susquehanna River, ultimately fouling the waters of the Chesapeake Bay. Hudson Oil was controlled by Mahler.

(4) In 1981, a new company owned by Mahler called Quanta (in which he consolidated most of his operations which had been shut down elsewhere) transported about 150,000 gallons of waste oil from an illegal dump on Staten Island, New York. The oil reappeared as fuel oil in New York apartment buildings. When burned, it emitted extremely high levels of PCBs and bromoform.

According to Block and Bernard (1988) the Mahler case is by no means unique.

> The lubrication re-refining industry was a major part of the American petroleum industry in 1960, with over 150 companies producing about 18% of the nation's total lubricant consumption. . . .By 1982, however, 90% of these companies were out of business, and the remaining companies produced less than 5% of the nation's lubricant consumption. There were many reasons for this dramatic decline in the re-refining industry. Lubricant oils were increasingly complex, with sophisticated additives to meet the needs of high performance engines. These additives account for as much as 25% of the total volume of the oil, and increase the cost and difficulty of re-refining. . . The quality of re-refined oils declined in response to this increasing complexity. This resulted in a decline in their use, including a ban on their use by the military and a drop in the price they would bring. . . Additional costs were also imposed on the industry by new toxic waste disposal regulations that increased the cost of disposing of the acid sludge that remained after re-refining. . . As a result, refined lube

oil prices declined while costs were increasing and most re-refineries went bankrupt (p. 120).

The new toxic waste disposal regulations were contained in the Resources Conservation and Recovery Act of 1976 (RCRA), by which the toxic waste disposal industry was subjected to stringent standards, making toxic waste disposal far more expensive. Industrial bankruptcies were not the only result. Unethical entrepreneurs developed illegal opportunities to generate profit. "Midnight dumpers" (companies ready to dispose of hazardous and toxic waste at below market price anywhere including waterways and abandoned mine shafts) made their appearance throughout the country. Some producers of hazardous wastes began "hiding" them in used oil. This used oil, now contaminated with PCBs (polychlorinated biphenyl compounds) and other toxins, was then used by unscrupulous re-refiners to produce (contaminated) heating oil. Unethical consumers of heating oil (landlords) bought this cheaper and less flammable product, which, when burned, produced even more toxic substances and simply spewed the poisons in the air through their smokestacks:

> Thus, a new illegal means for making money was presented to waste oil dealers (and toxic producers) at the same time that their traditional legal means for making money suddenly disappeared (Block & Bernard, 1988: 120).

Explanations of crimes against the environment need not be limited to strain theory. Sutherland, for example, posited that white collar criminality, like common forms of criminal behavior, is learned[2]. The learning includes (a) techniques of committing the crime, which are sometimes very complicated and (b) the specific direction of motives, drives, rationalizations, and attitudes (Sutherland, 1939). Applying this principle to the chemical, petroleum, electronics and pharmaceutical industries, it may well be that corporate officers accept some illegal activities as unavoidable in the exercise of their normal functions. For example, it may be a common business practice to turn over hazardous waste to any hauling firm presenting a license with the state's seal of approval. They may, in fact, do so for competitive reasons, in spite of the fact that they are not always ignorant of the fact that their wastes may be dumped down the city's sewers or even burned with fuel oil. Well aware of the shortage of disposal sites and, in many instances, suspicious of those with whom they are dealing, industrial managers typically fail to conduct any follow up on where or how their wastes are actually disposed of. Moreover, industry does not normally alert officials when they suspect illegal dumping. According to the United States Environmental Protection Agency, the main reason why management fails to do so is because they are reluctant to report their low-bid haulers to the authorities. Nor are they obligated to do so legally. Managers learn how to "look the other way" and competition may require that they do so (Szasz, 1986).

While governments struggle to develop regulatory legislation, it appears that some industries have informally created their own rationalization for avoiding it. This is suggestive of the one proposed by Charles Dickens: "Do other men for they would do you. That's the true business precept." Such attitudes took root over 2000 years ago. They echo the ethos of ancient Carthage, as stated by Polybius, "at Carthage, nothing which results in profit is regarded as disgraceful." In our modern corporate society big business often sets the moral level of the market place and this is bound to remain low as long as the executives involved believe, and teach their successors, that there is a difference between ordinary morals and business morals.

Social control theory provides yet a third way criminologists might explain criminality against the environment. The thrust of the argument is: as social control of institutions such as the criminal justice system and regulatory agencies break down, individuals are free to deviate. There is little doubt that in the past governments have frequently been unable to prosecute major industries because of poor enforcement techniques, on the one hand, and the collective political power (sometimes coupled with bribery and corruption) of industry, on the other. We shall return to this discussion in the next section.

Explanations of Crimes Against the Environment: Theories of Crime

To reiterate, theories of crime attempt to identify conditions under which persons who are prone to commit crime will in fact do so. In the commission of a crime the presence of an offender is only one of the necessary components. Crimes also require conditions that are independent of the offender. The crime of illegal dumping of toxic waste, for example, requires not only a generator who needs to dispose of such waste but also a place in which to dump it and a dearth of law enforcers.

Experts have made the argument that in order to prevent crime and to formulate crime control policy, the study of criminal behavior has to be closely tied to the criminal acts themselves, including the characteristics of the crime which have an impact on an offender's decision and which help to determine why an offender chooses to commit one act rather than another. Two theories of crime that make these assumptions are rational choice and routine activities. The rational choice perspective, formulated by Derek Cornish and Ronald Clarke (1986), takes into account the whole criminal event which encompasses the motivation of the offender *and* the situational factors surrounding the crime. "Rational" refers to the fact that criminals weigh the probability of success under certain conditions and consider alternatives. "Choice" refers to the fact they make decisions. Crimes are committed, then, after a rational decision has been made to do so, and this decision includes calculating risks and benefits and selecting a particular offense according to various criteria (Cornish & Clarke, 1987). Violators of environmental law, for example, make decisions based on the chance of apprehension, the availability of employees who are willing to commit the offenses, the cost differential between legal and illegal operation and, frequently, technological expertise. Characteristics of offenses then become key to understanding the commission of the crime. These characteristics include where, when, how, and by what types of persons offenses are committed.

To demonstrate the application of rational choice theory to environmental crime, consider, once again, the illegal dumping of hazardous waste. In an analysis of case documentation for all such cases disposed of between 1977 and 1984 in four U.S. states having a high concentration of such crimes (72 firm defendants and 121 individual defendants), Rebovich (1986) found that there are two types of crimes— those committed by the hazardous waste generators and those by treatment/storage/and disposal (TSD) firms. Large generating firms were more apt to dispose of their hazardous wastes on-site without involving agreements with haulers or treaters. Thus, they were relatively protected from discovery. These large industries were insulated further by law enforcers' lack of understanding of their manufacturing procedures

(Rebovich, 1986). Most illegal dumping, however, was conducted by a small number of persons who were knowledgeable in disposal and who "satisfied" licensing standards. The offenses were committed by systematically defrauding the waste generators. They guaranteed a service never actually provided. In some instances they would stockpile the waste in drums and declare bankruptcy before disposal. The illegal *modus operandi* of disposal includes dumping in isolated areas, storage in drums that dissolve over time, filling of unlined landfills, and burning. Offenders also report that they made use of boreholes leading to abandoned mines. Some dumped the waste into convenient sewers or nearby bodies of water and took advantage of the technological inadequacies and carelessness of inspectors. With the increasing amount of hazardous waste, the number of legal sites for disposal decreases and the cost of legitimate disposal steadily rises. Correspondingly, the amount of illegal dumping rises.

Turning from two characteristics of the offense—*how* it is carried out and *where*—to another characteristic, namely, who the persons tending to commit it are, an interesting point arises. Is hazardous waste crime synonymous with syndicated (organized) crime? Findings from the Rebovich (1987) study of industries in the northeast United States suggested it is not:

> In the sample, hazardous waste offenses committed as acts of a formal, criminal monolith were rare. The generator offenses were criminally organized only on the most fundamental level. Organization usually took the form of simple criminal conspiracies. These criminal arrangements often were ongoing but were primarily designed for illegal profit without the typical hallmarks of traditional syndicate racketeering (e.g., threats of violence or corruption of officials). . .

> The usual form of organized hazardous waste criminal behavior in the sample was a loosely knit, independent criminal unit based on the triadic nature of the legitimate hazardous waste disposal processing cycle (i.e., generator, hauler, and treater). Early criminal offenses grew from simple, individualized offenses (e.g., midnight dumping) that were eventually prone to failure due to enforcement advancements and rose to a point where small detection avoidance enterprises were formed.

> Overall, these criminal units were without the size and centralization of traditional syndicate crime but did manage to improvise a degree of criminal sophistication through the workplace structure. The units sometimes sprouted into networks of TSD facility personnel and "outsiders" like unethical disposal/treatment brokers and private laboratory chemists whose help could build an aura of legitimacy around criminal activities (p. 4).

While organized crime accounts for a small portion of illegal dumping in the U.S., it is nevertheless involved "in those parts of the nation where garbage hauling and landfilling was historically controlled by organized crime" (Szasz, 1986: 8) before the new hazardous waste market had come into existence. The infrastructure was in place. Organized crime needed only to switch from hauling garbage to hauling hazardous waste—a much more profitable cargo. According to Szasz (1986):

> Landfill owners not directly associated with organized crime could be bribed to sign manifests for shipments never received or to accept hazardous waste that was manifested elsewhere. . . In addition, known organized crime figures started or seized control of a network of phony disposal and "treatment" facilities. . . Licensed by the state, these outfits could legally receive hazardous waste and sign off on the manifest. They would then either stockpile it on site (where it would stay until it exploded, burned, or otherwise came to the attention of the authorities) or dump it along roadways, down municipal sewers, into the ocean, or elsewhere (p. 9).

Routine activity theory is closely linked to the rational choice perspective. It also explains criminal events in terms of characteristics of the crime rather than of those of the offender. According to Lawrence Cohen and Marcus Felson (1979) each criminal act requires the congruence of three elements: motivated offenders, suitable targets, and the absence of capable guardians to prevent the would-be offender from committing the offense (Cohen & Felson, 1979). To demonstrate the applicability of routine activity theory to environmental crime, specifically toxic waste disposal, we shall now separate the component parts.

Motivated Offenders

In terms of environmental crime, the number of potential offenders grows with the increasing need to dispose of waste generated by industries that produce steel, paper products, plastics, petrol, chemicals, pharmaceuticals, armaments, and munitions (including nuclear) as well as by power-producing enterprises and municipalities (sewage and household waste).

Suitable Targets

Suitable targets are necessary for a criminal event to take place. Crimes against the environment have many such targets—air space, especially surrounding factories (and some residential and office buildings), rivers, oceans, isolated dumping grounds, sewers, landfills and abandoned mine shafts. Estimates of the amount of waste discharged into these "targets" are difficult to make. We do, however, have a few statistics. For example, a survey by the United States Environmental Protection Agency found 150 metric tons of hazardous waste were generated in the United States by 14,000 regulated manufacturers, almost three-quarters of it produced by the chemical industry (Rebovich, 1986: 5). It estimated that 90 percent of it was illegally dumped (Krajick, 1981). Estimates of the number of hazardous waste dumping sites are also rare. One survey sets the figure at 378,000, of which 10,000 are said to require immediate attention (Szasz, 1986).

Absence of Capable Guardians

Motivated offenders and suitable targets have to converge (according to routine activities theory) with an absence of capable guardians to prevent the would-be offender from committing the crime. Guardians of the environment include law enforcement officers and even ordinary citizens who alert authorities to visible activities of waste transporters, to chemical odors, or to strange nocturnal noises of "midnight dumpers" (where the only thing needed is". . .a truck and a lack of regard for public safety") (Wolf, 1983: 440).

Guardianship involves the enforcement of statutory and regulatory law—a task that, to date, has been done poorly. Protecting the "suitable targets" against the discharge of waste involves many different types of problems, including untrained enforcers, difficulty of identifying violators, co-optation of the regulators by those being regulated, financial benefits of paying a fine over complying with standards, ineffective licensing (of ships' captains, for example), the imaginative methods of illegal disposal with which enforcement has not caught up, bribery, corruption, weak penalties for violations and too few sanctions. Moreover, there is often tension between regulatory agencies which use cooperative techniques to gain compliance and criminal enforcement agencies, which use more punitive forms of pressure. Criminal enforcement agencies distrust cooperative regulation which, they claim, overlooks some technical violations, makes too few inspections, and accepts excuses for noncompliance (Rebovich, 1987). Another "guardianship" problem arises from the fact that legislators place too much faith in the manifest system. The manifest is a document that states the amount, content and disposition of hazardous waste shipments. This document is turned over to state agencies once the shipment reaches its final destination. In theory, it appeared good. In practice, it does not work. This testimony from a U.S. House of Representatives Subcommittee Hearing (1980) sums up the problem:

> Gore: "What enforcement efforts are you making to prevent the abuse of the manifest system?"
>
> Edwin Stier (New Jersey Division of Criminal Justice): "The only way the manifest system is going to be properly, effectively enforced is through the proper analysis of the information that comes from the manifest. . . Anyone who assumes that a manifest system which looks good on paper can control the flow and disposition of toxic waste without the kind of support both technical and manpower support that is necessary to make it effective, I think, is deluding himself. [However]. . . we aren't looking specifically for manifest case violations. We aren't pulling every manifest that is filed with the department of environmental protection and looking for falsification of manifests specifically because we don't have the time, the resources, or the specific lead information to do that" (p. 140).

There is yet another problem with guardianship of the environment against offenses. The criticism is made that the industries which generate hazardous waste had a great deal to say in the shaping of the federal legislation which concerns their own operation. What they wanted, and were somewhat successful in attaining, was regulation that would necessitate few changes in their operations. They insisted that government should not interfere with industrial decisions and that industries should not be responsible for disposal of their wastes. The responsibility should be that of the hauler. They wanted, and got, limitations to their liability (Szasz, 1986).

In sum, routine activity theory argues that three components must converge in order that a criminal act take place—motivated offenders, suitable targets, and absence of guardians. If all three components are in place and one of them is strengthened, crime is likely to increase. If, for example, the proportion of offenders and suitable targets stays the same, a decrease in the amount of regulation (guardians) will alone increase the crime rate by multiplying the opportunities for crime.

Theory to Practice: Situational Crime Prevention

Both the rational choice and the routine activity perspectives are particularly important for the development of crime-control policy and of situational crime prevention, which consists of changing the conditions and circumstances that influence the commission of specific crimes. While mainstream criminological theories formulate prevention policy in terms of manipulating the factors in the social milieu that are associated with criminal behavior (models which include education, poverty reduction, etc.), situational crime prevention seeks to eradicate the opportunities for crime to be committed (Clarke, 1980). According to experts social crime prevention programs that attempt to change offenders have had minimal impact—a fact which has led to a search for solutions that are offense rather than offender-specific (Brantingham & Brantingham, 1990). Situational crime prevention looks at the "intersection of potential offenders with the opportunity to commit offenses and at offenders' decisions to commit particular offenses at particular times and places" (Brantingham & Brantingham, 1990: 25). The approach is based on the idea that the specific characteristics of specific offenses should be factored into prevention models (Clarke & Mayhew, 1980). To demonstrate, consider the following two examples in which steps were taken to make it more difficult for offenders to carry out specific crimes:

1. [S]ignificant changes were made to the design of a church that was built in a "difficult" part of town near pubs and bars. Another church and other buildings in the neighborhood suffered break-in and vandalism, and had graffiti problems. In particular, the windows of an existing church were frequently broken. The design for the new church was changed to put its large windows at an angle to the street. The windows were made from plexiglass. To break windows or vandalize the church, an offender would have to make a major effort—walk across some open ground and attack plexiglass. Drinking problems and related property crime problems continued in the area, though no problems occurred at the new church.

2. There is a international example of something that has happened in video stores. To eliminate shoplifting, video stores are switching how they display the videos they have for rental. Early on they tended to place the actual VHS or Beta rental cassettes out on the shelves. People selected a cassette and carried it to a central desk for rental. This is similar to the situation found in many smaller lending libraries. It has the virtue of reducing staff time spent on telling customers whether particular videos are still available for rental: if they are on the shelves they are available.

   The situation has now largely changed: most stores display the small empty boxes that the videos originally came in, or they display small plastic display cards with advertising material. The customer must go to a central desk to determine whether a particular video is available, and if so, rent it before actually taking possession of the cassette. This is similar to the controlled stacks situation found in major research libraries: it occupies more staff time, but cuts casual user pilferage (Brantingham & Brantingham, 1990: 30).

Transferring situational crime prevention techniques to crimes against the environment involves the same principles—i.e., reduce the commission of crime by designing models that eliminate the crime opportunities. As Rebovich (1986) demonstrates:

> The key to successful enforcement is to redesign enforcement strategies to cut off industry-specific criminal opportunities. Without timely attention to the critical opportunity points, architects of hazardous waste crime will be permitted to build their criminal subcultures in the workplace and to see that such subcultures become firmly entrenched.
>
> For enforcement interests, the closing of these opportunities for hazardous waste crime will be quite feasible in some cases and formidable in others. A chief explanation for past enforcement lapses is that, in the beginning, crime enforcement could not catch up technically with legislatures' desires to eradicate hazardous waste crime through newly fashioned criminal laws. Problems of effort duplication and inexperience with confronting improper disposal as a criminal activity could not realistically be avoided. As time has gone by, enforcement effectiveness has improved and should continue to do so with the emerging knowledge of the offender's characteristics and with the increase of technical training.
>
> The task of countering criminal assistance networks is more of a problem. This entails more than simply identifying "outsider" operatives. The task also includes deciding the appropriate course of action to pursue against those committing what may be unethical, but non-criminal, acts in non-regulated enterprises (e.g., treatment brokering). Crushing these assistance networks will be integral to reducing opportunities for the successful commission of hazardous waste crimes.
>
> In the future, two areas that should be watched very closely are, on the generator end, the new breed of emerging hazardous waste generator offenders and, on the treatment/disposal end, the citing of new TSD facilities. . . A host of heretofore unregulated industry procedures related to hazardous waste generation/treatment are now regulated. . . [These regulations] are meant to crack down harder on hazardous waste violators but may unintentionally play a part in widening the population of hazardous waste criminals. [In effect, they lower] the cut-off volume level of those previously exempt because of low levels of waste generation. . . [T]he new cost of compliance may be seen as prohibitive to some small

generators and may serve to heighten the incentive to seek opportunities for illegal disposal as an alternative.

The future also offers some new challenges for enforcement in the disposal/treatment industry. TSD facility siting has turned into a protracted struggle in [some] states seriously limiting the available outlets for legal disposal and increasing the chances that more waste generators/handlers will opt for illegal disposal. But, for those new facilities that are sited, enforcement will be expected to meet the challenge of short-circuiting criminal subcultural development within them. The operation of these facilities and the resultant quality of public health, will be only as good as the attention given to them by both regulatory and criminal enforcement and the effectiveness of the implementation of enforcement methods.

The key term, then, for hazardous waste crime enforcement is *opportunity anticipation*. Enforcement personnel must be willing and able to anticipate how regulatory/criminal law changes and market developments might rearrange future crime opportunities or compel more to search for such opportunities. Without this forethought, enforcement is in danger of being one step behind those who choose to profit from the illegal disposal of hazardous waste (p. 6).

Strengthening the guardianship of the environment also depends on the relationship of regulator/regulatee. Industry's information about regulators influences compliance with environmental law. There appears to be an association between the status of the communicator, his or her professionalism, and the degree of compliance. Legislative acts carry more weight than judicial orders, and administrative agency directives carry the least (DiMento, 1989). Regulators who appear knowledgeable, efficient and fair engender the most respect (Bardach & Kagan, 1982). Agencies have more impact if their procedures and rules are articulated clearly and consistently and are backed up with explanations that give them legitimacy. Moreover, there is more compliance when government focuses on specific rules rather than on a general debate on government vs. business in the regulatory function (DiMento, 1989).

In sum, environmental crime has, indeed emerged as a major social problem—and one that is likely to increase as new products and processes are being developed, especially in the chemical industry. Hazardous waste disposal, for example, is currently a $3 billion to $4 billion business (Feder, 1991). With new regulations expanding the spectrum of materials classified as hazardous wastes, and the decrease in the number of legal disposal sites, there will probably be an increasing amount of motivated potential offenders. Situational crime prevention appears to offer solutions that more traditional methods have not yet been able to effect. Many new questions are being asked: Where are the vulnerable spots in the corporate structure? Where are the most suitable targets? Which techniques of discovery afford the greatest promise; among them, long-range photography, aerial surveillance, regular inspections, e'ectronic and mechanical monitoring? In October 1994, the first satellite capable of detecting oceanic oil spills was launched, an advance that will assist greatly in curbing water pollution. How much waste (the potential polluter) is generated? Which regulations foster compliance? Prevention planning also needs to take into account new developments in industry, economic trends affecting vulnerable industries, and the existence of financial problems in specific corporations. Situational crime prevention does not necessarily involve more enforcers, but it does involve a more creative strategy.

NOTES

1. Environmental crime is different from environmental criminology. Environmental criminology is a term used to encompass the study of spatial patterns in crime; environmental crime refers specifically to theory, research, and policy in the area of crimes against the environment.

2. This concept was quickly adopted by scholars in other countries: "Crime en col blance" in France, "Criminalita in Colletti bianchi" in Italy and "Weisse-Kragen-Kriminalitat" in Germany. See G. Geis and C. H. Goff, "Introduction," in E. H. Sutherland (1983), *White Collar Crime: The Uncut Version*, New Haven: Yale University Press, pp. XI-XII.

REFERENCES

Albanese, Jay S. (1984). "Love Canal Six Years Later: The Legal Legacy." *Federal Probation* 48: 533-538.

Bardach, Eugene, and Robert Kagan (1982). *Going by the Book: The Problem of Regulatory Unreasonableness.* Philadelphia, PA: Temple University Press.

Block, Alan A., and Thomas J. Bernard (1988). "Crime in the Waste Oil Industry." *Deviant Behavior* 9: 113-129.

Brantingham, Patricia L., and Paul J. Brantingham (1990). "Situational Crime Prevention in Practice." *Canadian Journal of Criminology/ Revue Canadienne de Criminologie* 32 (January): 17-40.

Clarke, Ronald V. (1980). "Situational Crime Prevention: Theory and Practice." *British Journal of Criminology* 20: 136-147.

Clarke, Ronald V., and Tim Hope (1984). *Coping with Burglary: Research Perspectives on Policy.* Boston: Klewer-Nyhoff.

Clarke, Ronald, V., and Pat Mayhew (1980). *Designing Out Crime.* London: HMSO.

Cohen, Lawrence E., and Marcus Felson (1979). "Social Changes and Crime Rate Trends: A Routine Activity Approach." *American Sociological Review* 44: 588-608.

Cornish, Derek B., and Ronald V. Clarke (eds.) (1986). *The Reasoning Criminal.* New York: Springer-Verlag.

_____ (1987). "Understanding Crime Displacement: An Application of Rational Choice Theory." *Criminology* 25: 933-947.

DiMento, Joseph F. (1989). "Can Social Science Explain Organizational Noncompliance with Environmental Law?" *Journal of Social Issues* 45: 109-132.

Epple, D., and M. Visscher (1984). "Environmental Pollution: Modeling Occurrence, Detection, and Deterrence." *Journal of Law and Economics* 27: 29-60.

Feder, Barnaby, J. (1991). "A Disappointing Deal for Browning." *The New York Times* (February 22): D1.

Geis, Gilbert, and Colin H. Goff (1983). "Introduction." In Edwin Hardin Sutherland (ed.), *White Collar Crime: The Uncut Version.* New Haven: Yale University Press.

Gottfredson, Michael, and Travis Hirschi (1989). "A Propensity-Event Theory of Crime." In William S. Laufer and Freda Adler (eds.), *Advances in Criminological Theory* (pp. 57-67). New Brunswick, NJ: Transition.

Hill, Michael (1982/83). "The Role of the British Alkali and Clean Air Inspectorate in Air Pollution Control." *Policy Studies Journal* 11: 165-174.

Howards, R. (1980). *Poisons in Public: Case Studies of Environmental Pollution in Canada.* Toronto: James Lorimer.

Krajick, K. (1981). "When Will Police Discover the Toxic Time Bomb? and Toxic Waste Is Big Business for the Mob." *Police Magazine* (May): 6-20.

Mendelsohn, R., and G. Orcutt (1979). "An Empirical Analysis of Air Pollution Dose Response Curves." *Journal of Environmental Economics and Management* (June 6): 85-106.

Rebovich, Donald (1986). *Understanding Hazardous Waste Crime: A Multistate Examination of Offense and Offender Characteristics in the Northeast.* New Jersey Department of Law and Public Safety, Division of Criminal Justice (June).

_____ (1987). "Policing Hazardous Waste Crime: The Importance of Regulatory Law Enforcement. Strategies and Cooperation in Offender Identification and Prosecution." *Criminal Justice Quarterly* 9: 173-184.

Richardson, Genevra (1982/83). "Policing Pollution: The Enforcement Process." *Policy Studies Journal* 11: 153-164.

Sutherland, Edwin H. (1939). *Principles of Criminology* (3rd ed). Philadelphia, PA: Lippincott.

Szasz, Andrew (1986). "Corporations, Organized Crime, and the Disposal of Hazardous Waste: An Examination of the Making of a Criminogenic Regulatory Structure." *Criminology* 24 (1): 1-27.

Ullman, Ariel A. (1982/83). "The Implementation of Air Pollution in German Industry." *Policy Studies Journal* 11: 141-152.

U. S. House of Representatives Subcommittee Hearing (December 16, 1980). *Organized Crime and Hazardous Waste Disposal.* Subcommittee on Interstate and Foreign Commerce.

Wittkamper, G. W., and M. Wulff (1987). "Nienhusen, Umweltkriminalitat—Heute und Morgen." *BKA-Forschungsreihe* 20, Weisbaden.

Wolf, Sidney M. (1983). "Hazardous Waste Trials and Tribulations." *Environmental Law* 13: 367-491.

CHAPTER THREE

A Review of EPA Criminal, Civil, and Administrative Enforcement Data: Are the Efforts Measurable Deterrents to Environmental Criminals?

Debra Ross

White collar crime presents unique challenges to those who study it. Compared with other criminological inquiry, this field is of recent origins, beginning with Sutherland's (1940) examination and analysis of white-collar crime. Frequently problems are encountered with definitions, data availability, and interpretation. Furthermore, there is a dearth of reliable information on the impact or costs of white collar crime and even fewer studies on effective forms of deterrence or punishment of white collar crime. This article represents one such effort to measure or assess the deterrent effects of various remedies on one particular type of white-collar crime: environmental crime.

The U.S. Environmental Protection Agency (EPA), generally, has broad discretion to pursue whatever action it deems necessary in order to ensure compliance with federal environmental laws. Over the past decade, in the wake of rising numbers of environmental violations, the EPA has adopted a three-prong approach to insure environmental violators are properly detected, deterred, and punished: criminal prosecutions, civil judicial actions, and administrative sanctions (Coleman, 1989; U.S. EPA, 1990a; U.S. EPA 1990b; and U.S. EPA 1991a). This chapter examines the degree to which the deterrent effect of these enforcement options can be measured or assessed, given current data and information on the programs. Specifically, it examines the characteristics of and data from the programs implemented by the U.S. EPA's Office of Enforcement and evaluates the role and effectiveness of these programs in preventing and combatting environmental crimes.

The underlying premise for this research is that wrongful or deviant behavior is generally deterred more by criminal prosecution than by civil or administrative action. Therefore, the criminal prosecution of environmental violations ought to be more effective in the deterrence of environmental crime when compared to civil and administrative actions. This hypothesis is examined by analyzing various EPA data sets and assessing the "measurable" deterrent effects of each of the actions.

Considering current fiscal "belt-tightening," and given the "downsizing" in most federal agencies, an evaluation of current enforcement efforts and an assessment of the effectiveness of the various enforcement "tools" appear in the best interest of those combatting environmental crime. In order to contain white collar crime, government and private sector planning and decisions require a firmer base of knowledge than now exists. Who are the perpetrators and who are the victims? What harm is done to our environment and to our individual health and well being? As we plan for future public action in this area, decisions must be made on how government should best respond: with criminal, civil, or regulatory remedies, or with some mix of these. These, and other, problems will be addressed within this article.

Methods

This research involved the examination of various data obtained from the EPA relating to the three options available in cases of environmental violations: administrative, civil, and criminal. In order to study the "effectiveness" of the EPA's enforcement efforts, various data sets were examined, then compared and contrasted.

For civil actions, two data sets were reviewed. The first, a Civil Enforcement Docket ("Docket"), is maintained by the EPA, contains information on all environmental civil judicial cases filed by the U.S. Department of Justice (DOJ) and is updated quarterly. For the period FY 71 to FY 91, this docket contained 3189 cases. For each of the 3189 available civil cases, the following data were obtained: the date the case was filed with the DOJ, the date of its conclusion, the EPA region in which the violation occurred, the statute(s) violated, the verdict, the penalty assessed[1], and the cost recovery awarded[2]. The second data set for civil actions was taken from the EPA's *Enforcement Accomplishments Report* for various fiscal years.

In analyzing the criminal case data, two data sets were again employed. The first, the *Summary of Criminal Prosecutions Resulting from Environmental Investigations* ("Summary") (U.S. EPA, 1991b) was obtained from the EPA's National Enforcement Investigations Center (NEIC) in Denver. This document contains a summary of the federal environmental criminal cases, arranged in chronological order, filed during the federal fiscal year. It is organized by the date of the first indictment/information filed in federal district court for that case. This report represents the best information available but still does not include every environmental case brought to federal court. Data from October 1, 1983 to May 31, 1991 formed one set of figures examined in this research.

In order to evaluate this document, a data base was created, the information entered, then the data were converted to a file for statistical analysis. Once the data from the *Summary* was coded and entered, frequencies were obtained on the number of cases and defendants charged and convicted as well as the number and nature of the statute(s) violated. The evaluations were made collectively, as well as by each of the ten EPA regions. The number of cases that were successfully prosecuted were counted in two different ways, by the number of cases per company and also by each court issued case number. There were some discrepancies between the two different methods of tallying the number of cases. Quite clearly, the number of cases by court number would be a much more accurate picture of the total number of cases that are successfully prosecuted by the EPA, given that within a particular company there may be more than one court case filed and prosecuted, each with its own court case number. Similar to the data for the civil actions, the second source of data for criminal actions was also the EPA's *Enforcement Accomplishments Report* for various fiscal years.

Original data and information regarding the administrative cases processed by the EPA were, unfortunately, not available. As a rule, each environmental statute is "enforced," administratively, by a particular federal agency (e.g. OSHA, OSM, etc.). The responsible agency then becomes primarily responsible for addressing violations and collecting data on the actions and penalties meted out. Obtaining original data from each of the responsible federal agencies was beyond the scope of this research. Therefore, to analyze administrative actions, secondary data, published by the Office of Enforcement in the *Enforcement Accomplishments Report*, by fiscal year, was evaluated.

The analysis of these various data sets offers insight as to which, if any, of the options are effective and to what degree in combatting and preventing the occurrence of environmental crimes. One measure of effectiveness is the number of violations detected, prosecuted, and convicted, given the number of businesses and individuals who are regulated by the EPA. This research compares the number of violators who have been "successfully" dealt with within each enforcement action as compared to the number of generators of hazardous waste that are under the EPA Office of Enforcement's jurisdiction.

Assessing the Available Data

EPA Reported Data

Criminal: According to the EPA's *Enforcement Accomplishments Report* for FY91, the Office of Enforcement operated at or near record levels by pursuing the prosecution of more cases than each preceding year. The EPA referred a record combined total of 474 civil and criminal cases to the Justice Department in FY91, surpassing FY90's record total of 440. Out of these 474 cases, a record 48 EPA criminal cases were successfully prosecuted, resulting in a conviction and sentencing. There is no information on how many of the civil referrals were successfully prosecuted or how many are still pending. A record 104 defendants, individuals and corporations, were charged in EPA criminal cases in FY91. A total of 72 defendants, individuals and corporations, were convicted and sentenced for environmental crimes as a result of EPA investigations in FY91, tying the record set in FY89 (See Table 1). Penalties were obtained in 85 percent of the cases concluded in FY91. The courts sentenced defendants to pay a record $14.1 million in fines (before suspension) for environmental crimes investigated by EPA, up from the previous record of $11.6 million in FY89 (U.S. EPA, 1992a).

Table 1: Defendants Charged and Convicted for Violating
Environmental Laws by Fiscal Year
(EPA Reported Data—Criminal)

Fiscal Year	Number Charged	Number Convicted	% Convicted
FY82	14	11	78.57
FY83	34	28	82.35
FY84	36	26	72.22
FY85	40	40	100.00
FY86	98	66	67.35
FY87	66	58	87.88
FY88	97	50	51.55
FY89	95	72	75.79
FY90	100	55	55.00
FY91	104	72	69.23
Totals	**684**	**478**	**69.88%**

The largest penalty assessed in FY91 was $6,184,220, obtained in a Clean Water Act judicial case. The second largest penalty was assessed in a Resource Conservation and Recovery Act (RCRA) judicial case which settled for $5,405,000. Both penalties were higher than the second highest penalty assessed in FY90 in the Texas Eastern Pipeline Case which was $3,750,000 (U.S. EPA, 1992a). EPA's criminal enforcement program produced an increase in jail time served in FY91. After suspension of sentence was accounted for, there was a record of 610 months of imprisonment in FY91 compared to the 222 months of imprisonment after suspension in FY90. Courts also ordered a record of 1,713 months of probation in FY91, an increase from the 1,176 months in FY90 (U.S. EPA, 1992a).

Civil: According to the EPA's *Enforcement Accomplishments Report* for FY91, the EPA obtained almost $320 million in cash civil penalties from FY74 through FY91 in some 12,530 civil judicial and administrative cases. With $73.1 million in civil penalties assessed in FY91 (a 21 percent increase over FY90), the EPA civil enforcement effort resulted in the assessment of the largest amount of civil fines in EPA's history. In FY91 alone, 23 percent of all civil penalty dollars in EPA's history were assessed. The Office of Enforcement referred a total of 393 civil cases to the DOJ in fiscal year 1991, up from 375 referrals in fiscal year 1990 (U.S. EPA 1992a). When the data are examined as to the different environmental laws being violated, the most statutes violated were: Clean Air Act, Clean Water Act (CWA), Comprehensive Environmental Response, Compensation, and Liability Act (CERCLA), Resource Conservation and Recovery Act (RCRA), and Toxic Substance Control Act (TSCA).

Administrative: According to the recent EPA's *Enforcement Accomplishments Report* for FY91, about $41.2 million, or 56 percent, of all EPA federal penalty dollars in FY91 came from civil and criminal judicial cases. The remaining $31.9 million, 44 percent, came from administrative cases. There were more administrative cases than judicial cases. Some 89 percent (1,250) of all cases with penalties were administrative enforcement actions, compared to 11 percent (152 cases) that were judicial actions (U.S. EPA, 1992a). Considered on an agency-wide basis, the number of dollars, and cases from the judicial and administrative cases in FY91 are similar to the ones in the past five fiscal years. In FY91 there were 3,925 total administrative actions initiated by the EPA. The type of environmental laws violated in the majority of administrative actions from FY72 to FY91 were the Clean Water Act (CWA) and Safe Drinking Water Act (SDWA), with the Federal Insecticide, Fungicide, and Rodenticide Act (FIFRA) not far behind. In FY91 alone, the Clean Water Act and Safe Drinking Water Act had 2,177 (55 percent) of these initiatives (U.S. EPA, 1992a).

Original Data

Criminal: There were a total of 311 cases successfully prosecuted, resulting in charges being filed against 611 defendants, of whom 570 were convicted (Table 2). For FY83 through FY90, and for the first half of FY 1991, there were 268 defendants who violated only one environmental law, 184 violated two, 99 violated three, 11 violated four, 4 violated five and only one defendant violated six environmental laws. The majority of the cases (79.7%) that were prosecuted involved defendants violating one or two laws. The environmental laws that were violated most often were the Clean Water Act (CWA), with 189 violations; followed by the Solid Waste Disposal Act (SWDA) and RCRA, each with 181 violations.

Table 2: Defendants Charged and Convicted for Violating
Environmental Laws by Fiscal Year
(EPA Original Data—Criminal)

Fiscal Year	Number Charged	Number Convicted	% Convicted
FY82	N/A*	N/A*	N/A*
FY83	36	30	83.33
FY84	37	29	78.38
FY85	35	27	77.14
FY86	95	94	98.95
FY87	69	68	98.55
FY88	97	86	88.66
FY89	78	76	97.44
FY90	65	64	98.46
FY91	99	96	96.96
Totals	**611**	**570**	**93.29%**

When the number of defendants charged and convicted was identified by EPA region, some interesting results occurred. Region 4 (Atlanta) had a much higher occurrence of environmental crimes (charges and convictions) than did the other regions (Table 3): 102 defendants charged and 92 convictions, a 90.2 percent conviction rate. These figures pose interesting questions in that Region 4 does not have the highest number of hazardous waste generators when small-[3] and large-quantity generators[4] are examined (Table 4). Regions 2, 5, and 9 each have more hazardous waste generators than does Region 4 but fewer environmental violators than Region 4. Region 4 does have the highest number of small quantity generators than the others, in fact, it has almost twice as many.

Table 3: Defendants Charged/Convicted by Region: FY82-FY91
(EPA Original Data)

Region (#)	Charged	Convicted	% Convicted
Boston (1)	71	63	88.73
New York (2)	48	48	100.00
Philadelphia (3)	55	53	96.36
Atlanta (4)	102	92	90.20
Chicago (5)	66	63	95.45
Dallas (6)	61	55	90.16
Kansas City (7)	38	36	94.74
Denver (8)	43	40	93.02
San Francisco (9)	47	47	100.00
Seattle (10)	80	73	91.25
Totals	**611**	**570**	**93.29**

Table 4: Number of Generators of Hazardous Wastes by EPA Region

Region(#)	Large Quantity Generators	Small Quantity Generators	Total
Boston (1)	2,281	11,395	13,676
New York (2)	27,532	15,930	43,462
Philadelphia (3)	7,412	18,149	25,561
Atlanta (4)	6,759	27,472	34,231
Chicago (5)	13,492	45,382	58,874
Dallas (6)	6,979	13,545	20,524
Kansas City (7)	2,306	10,026	12,332
Denver (8)	1,218	4,441	5,659
San Francisco (9)	18,896	18,900	37,796
Seattle (10)	1,959	4,777	6,736
Totals	**88,834**	**170,017**	**258,851**

Besides Region 4 (Atlanta), the other nine regions seem to have comparative numbers of defendants being charged and convicted for violating environmental laws. The number of crimes that are charged seem to be approximately the same as the number of convictions. It is of interest to note from year to year the regions vary in the number of violators being charged and convicted. When each individual region is examined there is more diversity from one year to the next, which is not seen collectively. For example, Atlanta has very few defendants charged in FY85, but the highest number is for FY90 and FY91. An analysis of the enforcement programs by region may be able to identify a program more effective than that in another region.

From a review of this data, it appears the EPA criminal enforcement effort is in need of expanding if it is to operate effectively to prevent, deter, catch, and prosecute environmental criminals. Given the current ability of the EPA, considering its budget and personnel constraints, one could say the criminal enforcement program is effective. However, it follows that the number of investigators be increased if environmental crimes are going to be eradicated or substantially decreased. Given a staff of less than 150 criminal investigators for the entire United States, the number of successful prosecutions obtained each year may not be that low, especially when the amount of time needed to investigate, prepare, and prosecute a case in criminal court is taken into consideration.

Criminal sanctions are the least widely used because of the amount of time needed to investigate a case from detection to conviction. If more personnel were allocated and relied upon more heavily, the existing environmental crime problem may be effectively reduced. An increased amount of personnel would be able to detect and prosecute more of the violators in the regulated community. More investigators should increase the number of successful prosecutions thus increasing overall effectiveness. Besides criminal actions, the EPA has the power and authority to use other forms of actions. Civil and administrative actions are used more frequently than criminal sanctions and they will be discussed next.

Civil: As discussed above, the data file of all civil enforcement cases filed and concluded by the EPA's Office of Enforcement was obtained, although there were some problems evaluating this data. One of the major problems was that these data were hard to manipulate in preparation of statistical analysis. The relationship between the date each original case was filed, as opposed to the date it was concluded, was one that would have been extremely helpful in the analysis of the civil enforcement effort, but was unavailable for this study. Even though there were many problems, some interesting patterns of the civil enforcement program were identified.

The civil data file contained information for all the cases filed from FY71 through the beginning of FY92. Altogether, 3,189 cases were filed and 2,602 cases concluded; there were 587 cases not concluded, for reasons unknown. Unlike the criminal data, only the number of cases, not the number of defendants is known. As would be expected, the civil numbers are much greater than the criminal ones, but if the number of defendants were examined, instead of cases, the numbers would most likely be even larger. This should be kept in mind when the civil data are compared to the criminal and administrative data. Similar to the data for criminal cases, the number of civil cases filed and completed does not vary much year by year. The use of civil actions began slowly and continued that way from FY71 through FY74; then from FY75 to the present, the number of civil actions increased dramatically from the beginning four years, but during the mentioned time frame has leveled off from year to year. The total number of civil cases may be much higher than criminal cases because civil cases are easier to track and not as time consuming (U.S. EPA, 1992a). There are a variety of possible outcomes in a civil action case. The most common outcome is a consent decree with a penalty (1600 cases, 62 percent of all cases). From there, the type of result drops to 12 percent (297 cases) ending with a consent decree and no penalty, 8 percent (196 cases) consent decree and cost recovery. Unfortunately, 584 cases have no written result since these cases have not yet been concluded for unknown reasons.

The number of environmental laws being violated in civil cases is similar to those in criminal cases. Most cases involved defendants who had violated either one or two environmental laws. There were 1,584 cases of businesses that were charged with violating only one environmental law and 1,099 cases that violated two laws representing 84 percent of all cases. Only 11 percent of the cases violated three laws, 3.2 percent four laws, and 1.1 percent violated five or more laws. The EPA civil data file only collects data for up to five violations, so it is not possible to know if any more than five laws have been violated in any one case. Similar to the criminal violations, the laws violated the most, civilly, are the Clean Water Act and Clean Air Act, followed closely by CERCLA and RCRA.

When the data were examined by EPA region (Table 5), the region with the most civil violations was Region 5 (Chicago), with 669 violations. Region 2 (New York) was not far behind with 493 violations. Most of the other regions were in the 150 to 250 violation ranges. This result is contrary to the criminal results, given that Chicago and New York have the highest number of generators of hazardous waste (See Table 4). On the whole, the number of civil cases that have been filed is much larger than the number of criminal cases filed. Even though this is true, the effectiveness of the civil enforcement program is still debatable since only 10 percent of the regulated population was prosecuted civilly. Granted, this is a higher percentage than for criminal prosecutions, but it is still quite low to be a deterrent. Since civil cases are filed much more regularly than criminal cases, the researcher expected a much larger number of cases that would have been filed. Over a twenty year period, there have only been 3,189 civil cases filed. On average, that is only 150 cases each year. When the number of generators of hazardous waste is examined, it becomes difficult to imagine how the EPA could believe its enforcement program is effective in the fight against environmental crime.

Table 5: Civil Violations and Criminal Convictions by Region:
FY82-FY91 (EPA Original Data)

Region (#)	Civil Violations	Criminal Convictions
Boston (1)	190	63
New York (2)	493	48
Philadelphia (3)	242	53
Atlanta (4)	312	92
Chicago (5)	669	63
Dallas (6)	342	55
Kansas City (7)	159	36
Denver (8)	152	40
San Francisco (9)	213	47
Seattle (10)	211	73

Comparing and Contrasting the Data Sets

Criminal: Upon review of the various data sets, it becomes quite apparent that a variety of discrepancies exist in the number of cases reported as successfully prosecuted by the Office of Enforcement. There could be several reasons for this inconsistency. When the number of court case numbers were counted, there was a larger difference between the EPA's original data and the EPA's reported data. For example, in FY83, there were 20 different successful court cases identified, but the EPA reports only 12. In FY86 there is a very large deviation between the number of successful prosecutions, 53 for the original data and 26 reported by the EPA. In other years the differences range from 3 to 10 cases.

The *Summary* lists each case by company name, by fiscal year. In some instances a company may have anywhere from one to five different court case numbers. This may account for some of the discrepancies identified in this analysis. When the number of companies is examined, there still are some inconsistencies but not as large as when case numbers were used. For example, using information from the *Summary*, in FY86 the number of cases, by company, was 37, while the EPA *Enforcement Accomplishments Report* for the same period indicates only 26 cases successfully prosecuted. These discrepancies are especially important in light of the claim the EPA's Office of Enforcement is doing a "record-breaking" job each year. Because of these contradictions, both this analysis of the raw EPA data and the EPA's published results should be viewed with care until the study is replicated.

Not only are there discrepancies within the number of cases successfully prosecuted but also in the number of defendants charged; these differences range from 2 to 36 defendants. FY86 and FY88 show a very large difference between numbers found and those reported by the EPA. For FY86, a review of the *Summary* found 94 defendants were prosecuted, but the EPA *Enforcement Accomplishments Report* for the same period indicated only 66 defendants. In FY88, the difference was 36 defendants (86 compared to 50). Again, questions explaining these differences have not been answered. One explanation may be that the EPA *Enforcement Accomplishments Report* does not include defendants who may have their decisions reversed or set aside on appeal. The appeals information was not contained in the *Summary* and could not be accounted for through this analysis. If a result was reversed at a later time, the case would have been removed from the total successful cases, which may be reflected in the EPA published data but not in the data obtained from the EPA.

Another difference between the original and reported data was the ten different regions were not examined individually by the EPA. The EPA's enforcement efforts are certainly enhanced by breaking down the number of defendants and cases by the ten different regions. Besides the various discrepancies found between the original and reported data, the current evaluation of effectiveness, by any measure, has low validity and reliability since it is not exactly clear why these discrepancies in the basic data are occurring.

Civil: The original data evaluated in this research apparently included much more information than the EPA publishes. Unfortunately, the raw data were hard to manipulate in their original form and advanced statistical analysis was difficult. Within the raw data there was a date that each case was filed and concluded. Out of the 3,189 cases included, only 2,602 have been concluded, a 81.59 percent conclusion rate. It was difficult to validate which cases were completed, which were not completed, and why. There was a variable for the result of the case, but this too was blank in many instances within the data. The existing criminal, civil, and administrative data sets are not compatible and at present cannot be linked. Therefore, comparative analysis is difficult, if not impossible. Table 6 does show the number of total administrative, civil, and criminal actions brought against violators of environmental laws since the criminal enforcement office was created in 1983, but any direct comparisons should be taken "with a grain of salt."

Table 6: EPA Reported Data: Administrative, Civil and Criminal
Actions (FY 82-FY 91)

Fiscal Year	Administrative	Civil	Criminal
FY82	864	112	20
FY83	1848	166	26
FY84	3124	251	31
FY85	2609	276	40
FY86	2626	342	41
FY87	3194	304	41
FY88	3085	372	59
FY89	4136	364	60
FY90	3804	375	65
FY91	3925	393	81
Totals	**29,215**	**2,955**	**464**

Discussion

A major problem in measuring the effectiveness of these three
options is that the number of violators who are caught and criminally
prosecuted pales in comparison to the total number of generators of
hazardous waste that operate in this country. As of 1992, there were
258,860 known generators of hazardous waste in the United States (U.S.
EPA, 1992b). While in FY92 there were only 81 criminal cases
resulting in 48 successful prosecutions of 82 defendants by the DOJ on
behalf of the EPA. That means only .0317 percent of the regulated
population were criminally convicted for violating environmental laws
in 1992. Even if most of the 258,860 generators are in compliance with
the law, having such a small number of the total regulated population
convicted for violations seems to be an ineffective deterrent against
violations by others. If the business community knows that there is such
a small chance of detection then they may decide to violate the laws
and take the risk of being caught. The deterrence picture is not much
better when one examines administrative and civil actions, even though
these options are take by the DOJ and EPA much more often than
criminal actions.

According to the data evaluated, the number of successful prosecutions has increased (U.S. EPA, 1991b; U.S. EPA, 1992a). But does this mean that the problem is being solved or that there are just more violators each year? The EPA has tried very hard to create an office committed to the vigorous enforcement of environmental law, but its effort is not great enough to even put a dent into the problem of environmental crime. How can it be possible to have an effective enforcement effort when there are less than 150 criminal investigators responsible for 258,860 generators of hazardous waste? If allocated proportionally, each investigator would be responsible for regulating approximately 1400 generators each year.

For each environmental law, there is an office that concentrates on the problems with violators of that law. These offices must work together within the Office of Enforcement in order to develop, investigate and refer criminal environmental cases to the DOJ. In this highly structured organization, there are many problems that can affect the number of criminal cases actually prosecuted. It is because of the time involved in developing a criminal case and the coordinating efforts required by the numerous EPA and DOJ offices involved, that the use of administrative and civil judicial actions are more common than criminal actions (U.S. EPA, 1992b). The environmental crime problem will continue to exist until all of the offices become more cohesive and willing to use criminal actions instead of administrative and civil judicial actions. Unfortunately, the administrative, civil, and criminal databases are not linked and it is impossible to analyze their comparative effectiveness. It was the hope that these databases could be utilized for an in-depth analysis of the effectiveness of the EPA's Office of Enforcement. When an integrated data system for enforcement is created, a replication of the current study should be done. Unfortunately, at present time, only a descriptive analysis of the individual criminal, civil and administrative programs can be performed.

Table 5 depicts the number of total administrative, civil, and criminal actions brought against violators of environmental laws since the criminal enforcement office was created in 1983. As seen the number of administrative actions is much higher than the civil and criminal actions.

According to the information in the EPA's *Enforcement Accomplishments Report*, published yearly, the Office of Enforcement is doing an effective job in prosecuting environmental crimes. But according to this research the EPA's potential is far from being reached. The EPA's published report does not include information on the number of generators of hazardous waste. The EPA publishes the number of successful cases without giving a benchmark to compare them to. By just looking at the numbers of successful cases one may conclude that the EPA is effective; however, these numbers can be misleading, especially when the number of generators in the regulated population is compared to the number of prosecutions.

At face value, the number of cases and companies that are being prosecuted civilly, criminally and administratively is increasing, but only by a relatively small margin. When the number of hazardous waste generators in the United States is considered, the picture of effectiveness is blurred. There are 258,851 small- and large-quantity generators of hazardous waste in 1992, and this number is increasing each year (U.S. EPA, 1992b). When the number of administrative, civil, and criminal actions are added for the FY91 the total is 4,366 (3,925 administrative actions, 393 civil actions, and 48 criminal cases). If 4,366 is divided into the total number of generators (258,851), only 1.69 percent of the regulated population is currently facing the possibility of being prosecuted for violating any of the possible environmental laws.

With such a low rate of apprehension, it is no wonder why many businesses may choose to violate the laws instead of being in compliance with them as previously mentioned studies have shown. It is much more economically feasible to run the risk of being caught and paying a fine of $100,000 (on average--using EPA figures) than to spend the money to be in compliance or dispose of hazardous waste properly. If this country is really serious about preventing and prosecuting environmental crimes, it needs to establish federal and state programs that are provided with the budget and personnel to do the job correctly. The EPA should re-evaluate its enforcement program and develop new, more effective ways of having the business community voluntarily comply, since it is impossible to have the amount of personnel needed to regulate all of the businesses that are capable of violating our environmental laws.

Suggestions For Responding To Environmental Crime

Environmental crime knows no jurisdictional boundaries. Getting caught violating the environmental laws may be nothing more than "part of doing business." The way the penalty system works at the present time, businesses do not have anything to lose by violating the laws. It is because of the lack of cohesiveness between the EPA's various enforcement offices and lack of personnel and budget that the data available to analyze the effectiveness of the EPA is extremely limited. The EPA needs to create a greater chance of detection within the regulated community if businesses are to be deterred from violating environmental laws. It is impossible for a handful of criminal investigators and civil and administrative investigators to regulate the entire community.

In 1990 the "Pollution Prosecution Act" was mandated but the funds were never allocated (Matulewich, 1991). Fortunately, this was rectified in 1992 when Congress did manage to fund some of the programs, most notably funding the portion requiring the EPA to employ at least 200 criminal investigators by the end of FY94. If the EPA's enforcement effort is to be effective, the number of investigators must meet the standards set in this Act and the budget must be increased. Again, the hypothesis is that environmental crime is really no different from other "traditional" crime and that criminal prosecutions would be more effective in the fight against environmental violators. If this is the case, then the EPA should devote more time, money, and effort into developing a productive criminal investigative team. If need be, maybe the personnel from the administrative and civil offices should be put to use in the criminal enforcement office.

Possibly, the Administrative, Civil, and Criminal Offices could be combined and work together jointly; then the number of successful prosecutions should rise and the amount of time wasted would decrease. Another suggestion would be to analyze the individual EPA region's programs. It seems these enforcement programs vary significantly from region to region, which may be adversely affecting the number of successful prosecutions obtained. These enforcement programs should be consistent from region to region. This would offer uniform deterrence and prevent "forum shopping" by business.

Conclusion

An analysis of the three options available to the EPA should also test the hypothesis that criminal prosecutions are a more effective deterrent and preventive method in combatting future environmental crimes than are either administrative or civil actions. Unfortunately, the preliminary findings of this research quickly revealed the data from these three actions are not readily compatible. Therefore comparable effectiveness, although elusive from a clearly statistical and objective standpoint, was possible in descriptive terms. What this chapter then offers is a description of the types of enforcement actions available and how often they are utilized in the prevention and prosecution of environmental crimes. The hypothesis that criminal actions are more effective as a deterrent was measured, but further research is required to develop accurate and compatible data across the different enforcement actions. The EPA needs accurate, readily accessible data for the analysis of their enforcement programs.

The disposal of hazardous wastes in the United States is not a new problem. What is relatively new, however, is the public's heightened awareness of this environmental problem. In the last decade, well-planned, aggressive team approaches to environmental law enforcement have been the key to successful prosecutions for the illegal disposal of hazardous waste. Through experience and proper training, law enforcement officers can detect and investigate environmental crimes successfully. This, in turn, may ultimately serve as a deterrent to those who attempt to shortcut the system at the expense of the public's health.

Respect for the law will inevitably erode if the most severe sanctions are not brought against the most deliberate, serious violators. The message has gotten out that the U.S. Environmental Protection Agency and U.S. Department of Justice are serious about criminal enforcement and these efforts are increasing every day. Everyone in society, businesses and individuals, needs to do their part to make this world environmentally safe for present and future generations. Unfortunately, as reflected by this research, there are many problems with the EPA's enforcement effort. The biggest problem lies in the fact that the EPA's budget and personnel are constantly being reduced, while the public wants the enforcement effort increased. Because of the low numbers of enforcement personnel at both the state and federal levels, it is virtually impossible to regulate every business to be in compliance with these standards.

This chapter examines the different enforcement actions available to the U.S. Environmental Protection Agency. Enforcement data were analyzed to understand how the EPA's Office of Enforcement operates and whether or not it is effective in the fight against environmental crimes. Theses preliminary findings suggest the EPA is trying its best, but its best is not good enough. More effective programs and actions need to be developed and implemented in a timely fashion. Additionally, the EPA needs to have an integrated data system created and in working order as soon as possible. With an integrated computer system the administrative, civil, and criminal actions can be linked and analyzed in order to understand which are more effective. These preliminary findings also suggest the EPA create programs addressing prevention and deterrence, not just rely on programs and efforts that deal with environmental crime once it has occurred.

Environmental crimes are far-reaching, dangerous, and complex crimes affecting our society and world. They are crimes that may directly affect our health today as well as in future generations. Efforts to detect and deter these crimes should be effective and culminate in prosecution to the fullest extent permitted. Without meaningful, measurable data, records, and information, the true deterrent effects of enforcement efforts may continue to be just an elusive target.

NOTES

1.   "Assessed Penalty" is defined as: 1) the dollar penalty owed to the United States, as agreed to in a consent decree, or 2) the final amount of a civil penalty imposed by a judge or an administrative law judge.

2.   The "cost recovery awarded" is defined as the total dollar amount owed the United States awarded under CERCLA authority and Superfund.

3.   Small-Quantity Generators: Handlers which generate 100-1000 KG of hazardous waste during any calendar month, or generate less than 1 KG of acutely hazardous waste, or generate less than 100 KG of any residue or contaminated soil, waste, or other debris resulting from the cleanup of a spill into or on any land or water, of acutely hazardous waste, or accumulate 100-1000 KG of hazardous waste or less than 1 KG of acutely hazardous waste.

4.   Large-Quantity Generators: Handlers which generate greater than 1000 KG of hazardous waste during any calendar month or generate 1 KG or more of acutely hazardous waste or generate more than 100 KG of any residue or contaminated soil, waste or other debris resulting from the cleanup of a spill into or on any land or water, of acutely hazardous waste, or accumulate greater than 1000 KG or more of acutely hazardous waste.

REFERENCES

Coleman, James William (1989). *The Criminal Elite: The Sociology of White Collar Crime.* New York: St. Martin's Press.

Matulewich, Vincent A. (1991). "Environmental Crime Prosecution: A Law Enforcement Partnership." *FBI Law Enforcement Bulletin* 60: 20-25.

Sutherland, Edwin (1940). "The White Collar Criminal." *American Sociological Review* 5: 1-15.

United States Environmental Protection Agency (1990a). *Environmental Criminal Enforcement: A Law Enforcement Officer's Guide.* Washington, DC: U.S. Government Printing Office.

United States Environmental Protection Agency (1990b). *Meeting The Environmental Challenge: EPA's Review of Progress and New Directions in Environmental Protection.* Washington, DC: U.S. Government Printing Office.

United States Environmental Protection Agency (1991a). *Enforcement Accomplishments Report, Fiscal Year 1990.* Washington, DC: U.S. Government Printing Office.

United States Environmental Protection Agency (1991b). *Summary of Criminal Prosecutions Resulting from Environmental Investigations.* Denver: National Enforcement Investigations Center.

United States Environmental Protection Agency (1992a). *Enforcement Accomplishments Report Fiscal Year 1991.* Washington, DC: U.S. Government Printing Office.

United States Environmental Protection Agency (1992b). *EPA RCRIS National Oversight Database.* Washington, DC: Office of Communications, Analysis and Budget Division.

Appendix A

United States EPA Regional Offices: Jurisdictions

Region 1 (Boston)	Connecticut, Maine, Massachusetts, New Hampshire, Rhode Island, Vermont
Region 2 (New York)	New Jersey, New York, Puerto Rico
Region 3 (Philadelphia)	Delaware, District of Columbia, Maryland, Pennsylvania, Virginia, West Virginia
Region 4 (Atlanta)	Alabama, Florida, Georgia, Kentucky, Mississippi, North Carolina, South Carolina, Tennessee
Region 5 (Chicago)	Illinois, Indiana, Michigan, Minnesota, Ohio, Wisconsin
Region 6 (Dallas)	Arkansas, Louisiana, New Mexico, Oklahoma, Texas
Region 7 (Kansas City)	Iowa, Kansas, Missouri, Nebraska
Region 8 (Denver)	Colorado, Montana, North Dakota, South Dakota, Utah, Wyoming
Region 9 (San Francisco)	Arizona, California, Hawaii, Nevada, Trust Territories
Region 10 (Seattle)	Alaska, Idaho, Oregon, Washington

Source: *Enforcement Accomplishments Report for FY91* (1992a).

CHAPTER FOUR

Prosecutorial Decision Making and the Environmental Prosecutor: Reaching a Crossroads for Public Protection

Donald J. Rebovich

Among criminologists and other criminal justice scholars, it has been recognized that one of the most influential positions in the criminal justice system is that of the criminal prosecutor. Whether on a federal, state, or local government level, the prosecutor is the possessor of a latitude of discretion unparalleled by any other single professional position within the criminal justice system. As the center of the adjudicative and enforcement functions, the prosecutor is vested with discretionary powers that are rarely encumbered by external supervision or review and, consequently, permit fairly unfettered decision making in criminal charging processes and plea negotiations. With this power comes a great deal of responsibility. The prosecutor is not only responsible for enforcing the law but is also responsible for protecting the public *and* ensuring that justice is done. Based upon factors such as strength of evidence, extent of harm resulting from the offense, and public sentiment, the prosecutor may be compelled to take a "tough stance" or make certain concessions like reduction of charge, dismissal of charge, or promise of sentence.

While such prosecutorial decision making is ordinarily subjected to countervailing pressures emanating from various special interest sources, such pressures can be particularly acute in the emerging crime area of offenses against the environment where levels of criminality can be blurred, and where public health can be directly at stake. This reality came to be a sobering one to the young Clinton administration when, in early 1993, then newly appointed Attorney General Janet Reno was forced to first wrestle with the problem of investigating her own department's Environmental Crimes Section (ECS) regarding Congressional committee charges of undue criminal charge/plea bargaining leniency and then to later *defend* her unit against such charges. The ECS affair and the national media coverage it received demonstrates the precarious decision making line prosecutors must tread when taking on environmental crime cases.

This chapter explores a terrain largely untouched by any previous works on the use of prosecutorial discretion; what special decision making issues do environmental crime prosecutors face, and how do they handle these issues. The chapter describes the insight the criminology field has gained over time on prosecutorial decision making in general, discusses the unique nature of prosecutorial decision making involving environmental crime, and offers projections for the future in a prosecution area that promises to continue to test the decision making skills of prosecutors for years to come.

Background

In his work "In Search of a Virtuous Prosecutor: A Conceptual Framework," Fisher (1988) characterizes the prosecutor's great discretionary power as the cardinal fact of the prosecutor's professional life. In a professional world where close organizational supervision of the use of professional discretion is rare, prosecutors enjoy a range of decision making possibilities much wider than that of the average government lawyer serving in an administrative agency. Frase (1980) points out that while all discretion is open to abuse, it is the "discretion to be lenient" that poses the thorniest problems because it tends to be less visible and because its "victims" (e.g., complaining parties, the public at large, other defendants not receiving such leniency) have traditionally not had the means to contest these decisions. Nonetheless, Frase argues that the necessity and legitimacy of selective prosecution can be defended on a number of grounds. Since some offenders are probably unconvictable because of problems of proof, illegal searches, and the like, such cases are legitimately screened out to avoid expensive litigation of what are likely to be unwinnable cases. In other cases, the best interests of justice may be served if some alternative to prosecution, such as restitution, is invoked upon consideration of the special factual situations and mitigating circumstances of the case. Scarcity of resources may also serve as a powerful driving force behind selective prosecution that targets the most serious cases of the prosecutor's office (Frase, 1980).

Moving beyond the initial screening stage, prosecutorial decision making associated with obtaining guilty pleas commands special attention in light of the dominant nature of the guilty plea as a method for criminal adjudication. Charge reduction is the most common concession sought by defendants, typically offering the prospects of a less serious criminal record or a more desirable range of possible penalties (Newman, 1966). Because of continual shortages of resources and courtroom procedures that favor the defendant, prosecutors must frequently resort to concessions on guilty pleas (Grossman, 1970). Some argue that guilty plea concessions based on evidentiary considerations increase the efficiency of the conviction process for factually guilty defendants (Mather, 1979). Adams (1983) asserts that concessions on guilty pleas can only be properly understood in the context of the working environment of the court. The human vagaries of judges, juries, and witnesses can prove to be an incentive for the prosecutor to make concessions for a guilty plea in order to avoid the uncertainty of trial. However, the empirical studies in this area appear to conclude that the strength or weakness of the prosecutor's case becomes the primary factor in the plea negotiation process (Vetri, 1964; Alschuler, 1968; Miller, McDonald and Cramer, 1978). Adams (1983) turns to a marketplace analogy to describe what he characterizes as the "discounting" of current rates of concession for guilty pleas based on the weight of evidence. Although Adams acknowledges that other observational field studies suggest a strong inverse relationship between the strength of the prosecutor's case and concessions offered to the defendant, Adams' study found that the relationship is not as strong for certain types of offenses (e.g., property crimes).

The only study that comes close to representing the decision making dilemma facing environmental prosecutors is Hammet and Epstein's (1993) case study examination of the development of environmental crime prosecution units. In it, they report that the evidentiary requirements imposed on environmental requirements can be of such a technical nature that decision making processes can be hindered by lack of prosecutorial experience/training in the recognition of environmental criminality, lack of access to competent and timely laboratory testing services, and lack of regulatory experts qualified to confidently substantiate evidence of criminal polluting.

This chapter provides a summary of findings from a study of environmental prosecution at the local level (i.e., district, county, and major city prosecutors)[1]. Besides confirming the pivotal roles that evidence presence and quality have in the prosecutorial decision making process in environmental crime cases, the results illuminate how other factors like perception of levels of harm generated by the offense and community pressures can be determinants of decisions made. The associated discussions offer some thoughts on the general implications that findings have for environmental crime prosecution decision making.

Study Findings

In 1992, the American Prosecutors Research Institute conducted a combined national mail survey and case study analysis of environmental crime prosecution at the local level (i.e., survey of 100 local prosecutors' offices in jurisdictions of 250,000 or above and interviews of local prosecution personnel at seven offices coordinating specialized environmental crime control programs). The project sought to survey the field of prosecution to identify the substantive needs and concerns of local prosecutors of environmental offenses.

Decision making processes associated with the decision to criminally prosecute environmental violations were targeted as an important study area by local prosecutors surveyed due to the highly technical nature of determining sufficient harm or threat of harm posed by the pollutants in question, the often uncertain circumstances surrounding the level of criminal intent, and the latitude of discretion that local prosecutors possess in deciding whether to criminally prosecute. Of those surveyed only 13 offices (13 percent) reported that their offices had instituted procedural guidelines for environmental prosecution decision making. Sampled prosecutors were queried on what they believed were the most significant factors in their decision making processes to criminally prosecute environmental offenses.

Table 1: Significant Factors in the Decision to Criminally
Prosecute Environmental Offenses

	Agree	Disagree	No Opinion
Extent of Environmental Harm	92%	4%	4%
Degree of Criminal Intent	87%	7%	6%
Offender's Record	72%	22%	6%
Offender's Cooperation	63%	25%	12%
Offender's Willingness to Remediate	62%	31%	7%

Offices Responding = 96

According to prosecutor responses, the *degree of environmental harm* was considered to be the most important factor (i.e., 92 percent either agreeing or strongly agreeing) followed closely by the *degree of criminal intent* of the offender (i.e., 87 percent either agreeing or strongly agreeing). Although not ranked quite as high, the *offender's record* was said to play a role in the decision to prosecute criminally (i.e., 72 percent either agreeing or strongly agreeing). While cooperation of the offender and the offender's expressed willingness to remediate were also viewed as consideration factors, prosecutors generally agree that these were less influential on the decision to prosecute.

When asked to identify factors critical in the *withholding* of environmental prosecution, the sample reported, overwhelmingly, that *insufficient evidence* was the most significant factor (i.e., 76 percent reporting this being the case). Only 16 percent identified *lack of resources* as an important criminal case rejection determinant. Also noteworthy, is that while 27 percent indicated that *referrals to state/federal agencies* was an important reason for rejection of local criminal prosecution, 17 percent claimed that the *active securing of cases from local prosecutors* by state and/or federal agencies was an important explanation for local criminal prosecution absence. Respondents also supplied information on their *level of willingness to charge* individual officers and employees of corporations, as well as the corporations themselves, as a sign of attaching individual criminal intent to the offenses. Local prosecutors leaned toward the consideration of prosecuting directors/officers (76 percent) and management-level employees (73 percent) to a much greater extent than lower-level employees (45 percent). Prosecutors were found to be split on the granting of immunity to corporate subordinates in exchange for testimony against corporate officers/managers (i.e., 42 percent had granted such immunity while 58 percent had not).

Once prosecutors had decided to move forward with an environmental prosecution, it was discovered that case priority was fundamentally determined by the *level of harm or threat of harm* involved in the respective cases (i.e., 70 percent expressing agreement with this statement). Only 33 percent indicated that the *high profile* of the offender was a factor and only 22 percent of the sample noted the *type of environmental offense* (e.g., hazardous waste, solid waste) as being a factor. In addition, only 22 percent of the sample reported that they had a preference for environmental cases that could be investigated/prosecuted inexpensively.

Traditionally, effective environmental prosecution strategies and programs have been contingent on the amount of system and public support for this relatively new brand of criminal prosecution and the technical expertise and resources available to prosecutors. A series of questions were asked of the sample having to do with the *extent of support* they receive to prosecute environmental crimes vigorously.

As anticipated, the greatest percentage of the sample agreed that sufficient support is received from the DA's office (i.e., 70 percent agreeing with 31 percent of that amount strongly agreeing). Levels of agreement to sufficient support supplied by local government, regulatory agencies and the community were fairly equal (i.e., 61, 58 and 56 percent respectively). The least amount of agreement to support statements involved the assessment of local law enforcement support and local judiciary support (i.e., 48 and 39 percent respectively). Of special importance is the large percentage of those who had *no opinion* for support statements regarding the local judiciary (35 percent) and the community (30 percent). It is assumed that these responses are a result of a lack of awareness of the level of support from these two sources.

For the topic of the local judiciary, this could conceivably be a byproduct of low exposure to criminal trials.

Table 2: Support for Local Prosecution of Environmental Offenses

Local Prosecution of Environmental Offenses Is Strongly Supported By:			
	Agree	Disagree	No Opinion
The DA's Office	70%	12%	18%
Local Government	61%	15%	24%
Regulatory Agencies	58%	24%	18%
The Community	56%	14%	30%
Local Law Enforcement	48%	30%	22%
Local Judiciary	39%	26%	35%

Offices Responding = 99

In addition to canvassing the sample on their perceptions of levels of support by criminal justice and regulatory system components, the survey attempted to gauge the extent of resources available to local prosecutors that would enable them to carry out their duties as environmental prosecutors effectively. Many expressed a general need for additional resources to conduct their work satisfactorily. A full 83 percent of the total sample asserted that more resources are needed for the optimal functioning of their environmental prosecution programs.

In a general assessment of *environmental regulations/laws used* by local prosecutors to prosecute environmental offenses in their jurisdictions, respondents were split on their evaluation of the complexity of environmental regulations (i.e., 36 percent viewing them as overly complex and 34 percent considering them adequate in terms of complexity). Notwithstanding this, 58 percent of the respondents concurred that criminal statutes governing environmental offenses in their respective jurisdictions were effective. Nonetheless, 69 percent of the sample believed that there was a need for the consolidation of environmental laws into more comprehensive statutory schemes.

Other notable findings from the national mail survey include the following:

- Most believe that the appropriateness of alternative civil statutes is a significant factor in the decision to prosecute criminally.

- The vast majority believe they require additional financial support to operate more effectively. Most believe internal competition for funds affects the amount of resources earmarked for environmental prosecutions.

- Almost all indicated a need for increased technical assistance and training to improve the performance of environmental prosecution unit personnel. Less than half believe that training is available now to adequately qualify personnel as experts in environmental investigation/prosecution.

- While few believe that outside pressures from business/labor groups result in environmental charge downgrading, most feel that outside pressures to prosecute, coming from environmental interest groups, community groups, and the media, can result in the filing of environmental offense cases.

Case study interviews conducted at local prosecutors' offices confirmed survey results that there is one decision-making factor that rises above the rest when contemplating factors key to prosecuting environmental offenses criminally; the level of harm and/or the level of threat of harm. In general, prosecutors interviewed equated this with the severity of the offense. Some prosecutors, however, were quick to note that it is important to weigh the level of harm or the threat of harm with the potential cost to criminally prosecute environmental offense cases (e.g., in situations where there is a relatively low level of harm or threat of harm, prosecutors may interpret this balance as a deciding factor in whether to prosecute the case criminally). These prosecutors found it useful to use civil proceedings in these types of cases where criminal intent may not be obvious or may be difficult to prove.

The manner in which local prosecutors initially approach each environmental offense case was found to be quite revealing of the underlying philosophies and subsequent prosecution strategies of the case study sites. Those interviewed typically described every environmental case that comes before them as being treated as if though it were going to trial. As characterized by those interviewed, the local environmental prosecutor takes into account the same elements that would be accounted for in *any* plea negotiations for any other type of case; the nature and severity of the offense, the presence of a victim, and police input. Some interviewed acknowledged that the level of criminal intent and the offender's attitude can play major roles in the determination of plea negotiations and, sometimes, in the use of diversion programs for the accused:

> Often, if somebody is part of an industrial park or if somebody is part of a neighborhood, we'll talk to people out there to see what's good and what's bad about this particular company. We have found interesting things out by doing that, because some people will say "he's a really nice guy, he's just stupid. He runs a shop and he just doesn't know any better." Those are people who you are more likely to try to give a little more to. In this state one of our big issues is not only jail or non-jail, but it's a question of probation versus the diversion program, that's a very big difference because these third and fourth degree offenses have a diversionary program where if you successfully complete a short period of probation all charges against you are dismissed and you don't have a record at the end of it all. People who commit third or fourth degree offenses are likely to be eligible for that program. So, one of the things we look at from the very beginning is how we are going to respond to diversion applications because we know it's coming and there is some cases we know we can stop and some cases we can't stop. The person's attitude and exactly what that person has done play a big role in that and that's why a lot of times we document cases to a great degree just to prove an on-going pollution pattern even though we know we're not going to be able to do anything with it this first time.

Interviewees also concurred that the defendants' ability and willingness to clean up a polluted site also plays a significant role in the charging and plea negotiation processes, particularly in jurisdictions where health department officials work closely with the prosecutor's office as part of a collaborative effort.

With regard to environmental crime *trials*, local prosecutors interviewed argue that the degree to which judges and jurors perceive the seriousness of environmental crime *as* crime is a crucial determinant of the attainment of convictions and penalties that fit the seriousness of the offense. For judges, part of the problem of accepting a criminal connotation for environmental offenses can be traced to a natural comparison of environmental offenses to other offenses that these judges are routinely exposed to. These other offenses may be ones which entail elements of traditional person-to-person violence and involve individual victims who have incurred injuries from the violent acts. In these cases, the cause and effect of injury will be clearer for the judges and will fall into the type of conventional crime that these judges have been accustomed to over time. Compared to these types of offenses, environmental offenses may pale resulting in a lack of empathy by the judges. Some local prosecutors contend that they proceed under the assumption that many judges are going to look at these cases as "major inconveniences."

The overriding problem was seen by these prosecutors as a lack of appreciation of the danger posed by environmental offenses coupled with the dispersal of victimization among many individuals. Because of this, a primary objective in local environmental offense trials becomes the ability of prosecutors to substantiate as much as possible, the gravity of the offenses and to simplify supporting evidence to clarify the serious nature of the threat. Extra effort must be spent in graphically portraying the relationships between the offenses, harm caused by them and criminal profits achieved. As explained by one prosecutor:

> If somebody gets hit over the head and is severely injured, you know immediately that you have a crime. The problem that we deal with is that you can go to a judge and say we found—take a paint can waste case—which may look to the judge like littering. And you tell him that there was a significant level that went into the ground. He says well, okay some paint got into the dirt, who cares? . . .we have a problem dealing with judges who just don't think it's their top priority and we deal with juries who wonder why you're standing there saying this guy didn't have a permit to do this. You're dealing with things which are not necessarily going to be terribly interesting. I think that's something where we need to develop a strategy to make people aware of the fact that these cases should be tried and if they are tried, they should be treated the same way as any other crime. I have to believe that a *local* jury trial with people serving on the jury

who live in the community where the event occurred, is something that could have more impact. You are more likely to get a really responsive, really interested jury.

Overall, those interviewed believed this last point was an essential ingredient for raising the odds that juries will be more receptive to environmental prosecutions. Jurors in *local* trials were described by local prosecutors as being more likely to identify with these cases than are state or federal jurors. Removing a case from its local environment, say local prosecutors, could result in the case being decided by an emotionally detached jury. As one prosecutor stated:

> Local jurors might be more concerned about the case because they know where the case comes from. If you take a case which comes from this county in the middle of the state and you take it to an upstate federal court, you'd be dealing with people who don't even know where your county is and don't even know its demographics. They're likely to take the case less seriously.

Discussion

Through the use of traditional prosecutorial discretion, the local prosecutor is able to decide which cases will be prosecuted and the types of charges to be made. In this way, the prosecutor has the power and responsibility for making public policy; policy that will reflect certain value priorities, such as public health and safety. Use of this discretion influences the way laws are enforced and, in turn, shapes the behavior of individual citizens and is usually reflective of the criminal justice system's needs and goals as influenced by the concerns of the local community. As part of the decision making process to prosecute environmental offenses, local prosecutors must not only be alert to the significance of factors that are commonly accounted for in conventional cases (e.g., criminal intent, reliability of evidence) but also factors that play especially important roles in emerging offense areas that have relatively short histories as being accepted as "true crime" (e.g., potential public reaction, allocation of resources sufficient to prosecute cases effectively).

Respondents to APRI's national mail survey tended to place factors influential in the decision to prosecute environmental crimes into 4 categories: (1) *strength of evidence*, (2) *public threat/harm posed*, (3) *interests of justice*, and (4) *organizational*. The first two factors (i.e., evidence sufficient to prove criminal intent, and the degree of harm posed by the results of the offense) loom large in the decision making process as corroborated by subsequent case study interviews.

Environmental prosecutors must be technically skilled to accurately determine criminal intent associated with activities such as the improper disposal and treatment of hazardous wastes and are, therefore, highly reliant on the abilities of criminal/regulatory investigators and on close interaction with them. Since some offenses are the culmination of criminal directives handed down to lower-level personnel, strong evidence against these offenders may be used as a device to elicit testimony against the upper-level criminal architects. As both the community's attorney against crime and as a protector of public welfare, the environmental prosecutor inevitably injects the *degree of harm or threat of harm* posed by the offense into the decision making process, often resulting in the beneficial byproduct of successfully leveraging the defendant into remediation of the polluted site as part of a plea agreement to a lesser charge.

Interest of justice issues can also be instrumental in the direction that charging decisions take in environmental cases. Case study interviews revealed that the low level of awareness that certain violators may have of the seriousness of their violations (i.e., knowledge of their behavior as improper) may be a deciding factor to prosecute civilly instead of criminally. *Organizational issues* entail the "exchange relationships" among the units of the criminal justice system, the community's political culture, and the resources available to prosecute these cases. By and large, local prosecutors surveyed believe they have now gained sufficient community support as the general public becomes more knowledgeable, through the media, of the immediate and long-term effects of environmental crimes and as they are made aware of environmental prosecutor accomplishments. But accompanying this support, can come a certain amount of attenuated discretion. The extent of harm created by the offense, the pressure of publicity and the influence of complaining victims can all, individually and collectively, limit the prosecutor's discretion in these potentially volatile cases. As seen by local prosecutors, the cumulative affect of these elements *to prosecute* typically serves to neutralize any pressures that may arise from business/labor groups to *withhold* prosecution. Local prosecutors, however, seem to be less optimistic about the level of support received from the judiciary. This professional group is perceived as being devoid of the necessary sensitivity to the gravity of environmental violation consequences.

Resources (or more precisely, the lack of resources) was cited as a factor that may be considered in charging decision making for less serious cases (i.e., downgrading, rejection) to permit the concentration of resources on other offense areas. Despite this, it appears that rejection of prosecution based primarily on this reason is rare. Local environmental prosecutors acknowledge that they sometimes are compelled to compete with other specialized units within the DA's office for fixed amounts of funds. In light of this constraint, the obvious fear is that without the availability of requisite resources to execute their dual public health/law enforcement mandates, local prosecutors will find balancing public harm vs. prosecution costs routine in decision making processes.

Based upon comments from local environmental prosecutors, it can be said they perceive themselves to have something of a moral responsibility to lean in the direction of discounting plea bargaining efforts by defendants to see that the public welfare receives its "money's worth" in health protection. Rejecting the requests for dismissals of defense attorneys if plea agreements can be reached, is viewed, intuitively, as strengthening the general deterrent value of environmental prosecutions by transmitting the unqualified message that local environmental crime is intolerable. However, if a plea agreement is anticipated, experienced environmental prosecutors depend on a tightly prepared environmental case to shift the burden to the defendant to convince him that remediation is the most financially desirable alternative to his legal defense expenses for a trial that would likely demand extensive expert witness assistance.

Upon coming to trial, the environmental crime case can seriously test the communicative abilities of the average prosecutor. The average environmental prosecutor at the local level finds himself/herself responsible for understanding complicated technical aspects of risk assessment, chemical properties, and sampling analysis, *and* "demystifying" all of this to the satisfaction of judge and jurors alike. Compounding the difficulties are the handicaps the average environmental prosecutor can expect to encounter; inadequate funds for laboratory analysis, insufficient training in trial techniques, and deficiencies in effectively identifying those whose testimony could prove to be the linchpin to successful disposition—expert witnesses. In some respects they have become quick studies in the craft of evaluating the sentiment of criminal court judges and, as such, have had to become innovators to counteract judicial ambivalence toward environmental offenses.

When it comes to environmental crime trials, it is the intimacy that local prosecutors have with the local court politics, the immediate community affected by the offenses, and the local public's comfort that the community has with its district attorney that is underscored as an invaluable determinant in gaining satisfying dispositions for the state. Local prosecutors argue that it is their identification with the local community—its customs, hopes, and anxieties—that make local prosecutors ideal for accurately gauging judge/juror levels of understanding of toxic dangers and fears associated with pollution. In turn, local prosecutors argue that to assign these cases to federal courts when prosecutorial expertise is available in the localities, in effect detracts from the familiarity that a local prosecutor brings to the case.

Some Further Considerations

Environmental protection is a field which contains both complex legal principles and unique enforcement and regulatory strategies and techniques. The entire field incorporates lawyers, scientists, and "political appointees" all in high positions of authority. Each person comes from an individualized and unique background, with different attitudes and motives. Yet, they all come together in an attempt to achieve certain policy objectives with regard to the protection of the general public.

Added into this mixture, is the criminal prosecutor. This position can become the focal point of battles between conflicting community interests with regard to pollution violations. Prosecutors can be besieged on one side by environmentalist groups demanding strict interpretation of the law and severe punishment in response to violations against the environment and be pressured by business interests to temper such legal actions against the violators in an acknowledgement of the supposed *noncriminal* nature of the offenses. Compounding the collective effects of these groups can be entities representing the general public (e.g., the media) that openly demand expedient remediation of the polluted site to ward off deleterious effects to public health. The prosecutor becomes the nexus in this swirl of conflicting forces not only because of the power s/he holds with regard to criminal prosecution but also because of the enormous degree of discretion the prosecutor has to work with. Environmental law is written by legislators, interpreted occasionally by appellate courts, but is applied by countless numbers of prosecutors who act according to a variety of factors that can affect their interpretation and use of prosecutorial discretion. How environmental law is applied by prosecutors often outweighs the importance of its enactment or interpretation. The decisions that an environmental prosecutor can make regarding whether to criminally prosecute an environmental violator and if criminally prosecuted, to what extent the violator should be prosecuted, plant the environmental prosecutor in a position where a false step can translate into fierce and persistent criticism by any of a host of special interest groups.

A classic example of the possible ramifications of the use of prosecutorial discretion in environmental cases is in the aforementioned federal government case involving the environmental crime section (ECS) of the U.S. Department of Justice. In this case, a controversy erupted when the investigations subcommittee of the House Energy and Commerce Committee accused the ECS of failing to pursue aggressively a number of significant environmental crime cases. Subsequently, in October of that year, a House judiciary subcommittee issued a consultant's report that stated that the Department of Justice preferred to seek the indictment of corporations rather than individuals and inhibited wetlands prosecutions. Department of Justice officials publicly condemned the criticism and charged that members of Congress were attempting to second guess prosecutorial discretion exercised in legally and factually complex environmental crime cases. DOJ's charges were supported by a number of defenders including *The Wall Street Journal*. After the election of President Clinton, the Department of Justice allowed Representative John D. Dingle's House Energy and Commerce Subcommittee to interview ECS trial attorneys regarding six disputed environmental cases. This was roundly assailed in some quarters as an attack on the use of prosecutorial discretion in the area of environmental crime prosecution. A subsequent report issued by the Department of Justice criticized the Dingle Subcommittee's methods and characterizations, and, while confirming certain ECS management problems, concluded that the outcomes of the specified cases reflected a reasonable exercise of prosecutorial discretion. The report noted that there was no credible evidence that decisions by ECS lawyers were influenced by "improper criteria." While the report appeared to vindicate the Director of the ECS, he announced his resignation from the section shortly after the controversy died down.

The charges lodged by the House Subcommittee in this instance had an undercurrent that was unmistakable: environmental prosecutors were accused of improper use of their prosecutorial discretion in an effort to "go easy" on environmental violators in the political interests of big business and the Bush presidential administration. The inference was that these prosecutors were purposely withholding the means to punish environmental violators, and, by doing so, threatened public health and weakened deterrence of future violators. The prosecutors themselves contended that their use of prosecutorial discretion was appropriate given their personal assessments of the strength of evidence in these cases and, consequently, the probability of conviction. Although a pathfinding agency in the prosecution of environmental crime, the ECS was unable to avoid national scrutinization of their discretionary practices and, instead, fell victim to a public impugning of their professional judgment and conduct. While the environmental violation cases of *local* prosecutors are not as likely to receive the same national attention as those cases investigated and prosecuted by the ECS, local prosecutors who must deal with such violations in their jurisdictions have the potential to step into controversies over the use of prosecutorial discretion in this highly emotional crime area.

In order to fully understand the decision making plight of local environmental prosecutors, it is helpful to consider the problems inherent in the exercising of prosecutorial discretion for environmental cases in the context of strategy options available. The three major legal strategies that can be used for the enforcement of environmental protection laws and regulations are: (1) the civil approach where remedies are injunctions and/or liabilities for damages, (2) the civil related tool of license revocation, which is issued after evaluating the applicant's compliance record, background, and qualifications, and (3) criminal prosecutions under applicable sections in the criminal code and/or environmental statutes. The criminal prosecution, although the least common of these three approaches, receives the most attention because of the potential for severe punishment (e.g., incarceration). There is, no doubt, a critical need for exercising the criminal route because it tackles the worst fraction of environmental offenders and widespread abuses. If the environmental prosecutor is to initiate criminal prosecution, many factors must be carefully evaluated.

For example, fault or culpability becomes an essential element in an environmental crime case and can be discerned from historical patterns of conduct including: (1) the level of supervision over the activity that resulted in the violation, (2) the steps of precautions previously taken to prevent violation of this type, (3) the frequency of past violations, (4) the foreseeability of the violation, (5) the degree of deliberateness, and (6) the nature of the offending agency. In addition, the actors' conduct occurring after the violation may shed light on the level of culpability, for example: (1) steps taken to mitigate the effects of the violation, (2) the speed with which authorities are notified, or conversely, (3) the acts committed to cover up or delay the discovery by authorities. Finally, the effect of or damage caused by the violation should be considered in the decision of whether to prosecute as well as the possible deterrence the case will have on other actors and their potential violations in the future. Once criminal prosecution is decided, the decisions on the length to which the prosecution should go become compounded by a series of other factors. These can include: (1) difficulty in pinpointing individual liability in light of the many "bad actors" who may seem to have assumed relatively equal yet small portions of the diffused criminal responsibility, (2) risk of losing indictment and/or conviction due to public perception regarding the strong moral stigma of a criminal conviction, and the traditional toleration of pollution as the "price of progress," and (3) the possibility of judges imposing minimal sentences on white collar criminals.

Due to what can be marked differences in perceptions of the seriousness of environmental offenses by key players in the criminal justice and regulatory systems, the environmental prosecutor encounters a moral polarization of attitudes toward environmental offenders which represents two diametrically opposed views. Either the environmental violation is not "serious enough" to warrant criminal prosecution, or the violation is viewed, undeniably, as "criminal" where the offender should be penalized to the fullest extent possible. There is rarely any middle ground. Prosecutors who decide to routinely prosecute these types of cases rigorously can expect a rugged battle, especially when facing ambivalence by the judiciary. If prosecutors are successful in their criminal prosecution approach, their actions can serve as a strong deterrent to industries and corporate executives to engage in hazardous waste violations. On the other hand, if unsuccessful, the prosecutor may become the direct target of a backlash engineered by ardent supporters of an unequivocal environmentalist stance.

There can also be an added incentive for criminally prosecuting environmental violations. Environmental cases are usually highly visible and are the source of much publicity. Successful prosecutions in this area can be a feather in the prosecutor's cap. Winning environmental crime cases which impose stiff penalties can be a direct reflection on the legal aptitude of the prosecutor's office and thus can enhance the elected prosecutor's image or reputation. In terms of the elected prosecutor's future career goals, this is usually no small matter. However, because of the high visibility and publicity connected with these cases, criminal prosecution losses can be especially embarrassing for the environmental prosecutor and can be seen by the public and the media as being evidence of the prosecutor's inability to properly assess the "winability" of these cases. But, whether or not the criminal prosecution ends in a conviction or an acquittal/dismissal, the final decision may pale in importance beside the public's view of the efficient remediation of the violated site by the offender. In this way, the prosecutor's role as public health protector against the physical effects of the immediate offense often will take precedence over the prosecutor's role as the agent responsible for specific or general deterrence of offenders. In light of these circumstances, it is not unlikely for environmental prosecutors to seriously consider plea concessions in cases where remediation demands override all others, particularly when questions on evidentiary strength exist.

Toward the Future

As greater numbers of environmental violation cases come before greater numbers of local prosecutors, more will find themselves wrestling with the weighty burden of balancing issues of punishment and deterrence with public health protections. And, there is every reason to believe that these numbers will grow. Through its publication *Enforcement in the 1990's Project: Recommendations of the Analytical Workgroup* (Herrod et al., 1991) the EPA has committed itself to cultivating and supporting proactive environmental prosecution programs locally which should lead to greater environmental control efforts at the local level. Indeed, as evidenced by empirical data drawn from reports of raw numbers of local environmental prosecutions through APRI's national mail survey, such prosecutions have grown dramatically for 100 offices representing populations of 250,000 or over; 381 criminal prosecutions in 1990, 756 in 1991, and 882 in just the first 6 months of 1992.

The decision-making results from the survey illustrate how many local prosecutors who have entered into this relatively new arena of local crime control, have become "quick studies" on the senses needed to successfully navigate through what can be decision making minefields. Some of the local prosecutors' decision making responses mirror similar findings from Gunther's earlier 1990 case studies of environmental prosecution in local prosecutors' offices in California (e.g., concerns with sufficiency of evidence, gravity of violation, potential for harm). But the current study's results also highlight the appreciation that these prosecutors possess regarding: (1) the ethical responsibility *not* to bring criminal charges in cases where there is serious doubt about the ability to prove guilt beyond a reasonable doubt, (2) the importance of strong signals of the likelihood of remediation to the plea negotiation process, and (3) the significance of accurately assessing juror and judicial antipathy toward criminal prosecution of the environmental violator.

As the locus of environmental crime changes in the United States, it can be safely assumed that the decision-making powers of local prosecutors will command greater attention. Since the start of this decade, the crime control world has gained a much more incisive comprehension of key characteristics of the average environmental offender and the offenses he engages in. No longer do we automatically equate environmental crime with the less common, widespread catastrophes like those taking place in Love Canal and Times Beach. We now know that the graver threat can present itself in the form of countless offenses committed by small quantity waste generators at the local level. As the EPA lowers the "cut off" volume level of those hazardous waste generators previously exempt from regulations because of low volumes of waste generation, local prosecutors can expect to see a rise in offenses committed by hundreds of thousands of businesses now subject to EPA regulations for the first time. Furthermore, as enforcement is tightened by those local prosecutors located in highly populated jurisdictions who are seasoned in environmental crime prosecution, it is anticipated that environmental crime spillover into rural and suburban jurisdictions will seriously test the decision making skills of less experienced prosecutors in less populated regions. For this reason, it is important that the APRI survey collecting qualitative data on environmental crime prosecution decision making information only marks the beginning for more intensive analysis of "harder" data on this subject. Only in this manner, can we effectively facilitate the transfer of vital decision making lessons learned from the environmental prosecutors of today to those of the future.

NOTES

1.   This project was supported by Grant 91-IJ-CX-0024 awarded by the National Institute of Justice Programs, U.S. Department of Justice. The Assistant Attorney Generals Office of Justice Program, coordinates the activities of the National Institute of Justice. Points of view expressed here are those of the author and do not necessarily represent the official position or policies of the U.S. Department of Justice.

REFERENCES

Adams, K. (1983). "The Effect of Evidentiary Factors on Charge Reduction." *Journal of Criminal Justice* 11 (6): 525-537.

Alschuler, A. (1968). "The Prosecutor's Role in Plea Bargaining." *University of Chicago Law Review* 36: 50-112.

Fisher, S. (1988). "In Search of the Virtuous Prosecutor: A Conceptual Framework." *American Journal of Criminal Law* 15 (3): 197-261.

Frase, R. (1980). "The Decision to File Criminal Charges: A Quantitative Study of Prosecutorial Discretion." *University of Chicago Law Review* 47 (2): 247-329.

"General Dingell" (1993). *Wall Street Journal (Review and Outlook)* (July 8): A12.

Grossman, B. (1970). *The Prosecutor: An Inquiry into the Exercise of Discretion.* Toronto: University of Toronto Press.

Gunther, A. (1990). "Enforcement in Your Backyard: Implementation of California's Hazardous Waste Control Act by Local Prosecutors." *Ecology Law Quarterly* 17: 803-845.

Hammet, T., and J. Epstein (1993). "Local Prosecution of Environmental Crime." *Issues and Practices*. Washington, DC: The National Institute of Justice.

Herrod, S. L., G. Paddock, S. Patti, H. Holden, G. Lie, and J. Baylson (1991). "Utilizing Local Government." *Enforcement in the 1990's Project: Recommendations of the Analytical Workgroup*. Washington, DC: U. S. Environmental Protection Agency.

Mather, L. (1979). *Plea Bargaining or Trial?* Lexington, MA: D. C. Heath.

McDonald, W., J. Cramer, and H. Rossman (1980). "Prosecutorial Bluffing and the Case Against Plea Bargaining." In W. McDonald and J. Cramer (eds.), *Plea Bargaining*. Lexington, MA: D. C. Heath.

McGee, J. (1994). "Environmental Crimes Controversy Lingers Under Reno." *The Washington Post* (April 7): A25.

Miller, H., W. McDonald, and J. Cramer (1978). *Plea Bargaining in the United States*. Washington, DC: The National Institute of Justice.

Newman, D. (1966). *Conviction: The Determination of Guilt or Innocence Without Trial*. Boston, MA: Little, Brown.

Stevens, L. (1994). "Environmental Crime: Issues Related to Justice's Criminal Prosecution of Environmental Offenses." Testimony before the Subcommittee on Oversight and Investigations, Committee on Energy and Commerce, House of Representatives. Washington, DC: U.S. General Accounting Office (January 11).

Vetri, D. (1964). "Guilty Plea Bargaining: Compromises by Prosecutors to Secure Guilty Pleas." *University of Pennsylvania Law Review* 112: 865-895.

CHAPTER FIVE

Toxic Tragedy: Illegal Hazardous Waste Dumping in Mexico

Valerie J. Cass

> ". . .I can't think of a more heinous environmental crime than dumping toxic waste in a poor country"

> Stephen Mansfield, Environmental Task Force Chief, U.S. Attorney's Office, Los Angeles

> "We're being poisoned here. . ."

> 28-year-old Mexican border vendor

Some officials in the United States predict illegal dumping of hazardous materials will be the international crime of the 1990s (Henry, 1990). The current situation at the United States-Mexican border lends credence to this assertion. There is overwhelming evidence that toxic and hazardous materials in large amounts are disposed of illegally in Mexico. For instance, the New River, which flows from Mexico into the Salton Sea in California, is so polluted that American residents are warned to avoid getting close to the water. Children born near a Tijuana industrial park have high rates of physical abnormalities (Simon, 1993), and various other maladies are attributed to run-off from industry outside of Tijuana (McDonnell, 1991).

This chapter examines illegal hazardous waste dumping in Mexico with a focus on the United States-Mexican border. Examination of specific incidents, laws, and enforcement efforts indicate that responsibility for the problem cannot be placed solely on the shoulders of industry actors. Accountability must be shared by enforcement officials in the United States and Mexico. The environmental laws for each country are sufficient but are not adequately enforced. Many factors contribute to inadequate enforcement: political and economic disparity between the two countries, lack of resources, jurisdictional confusion, difficulty of prosecution, and corruption. The motivations of industry actors to cheat are related to their awareness of the inadequate enforcement. Ultimately, committing environmental crime must be made unattractive. Stepped-up enforcement on both sides of the border is needed before illegal dumping is viewed as "real" crime by those who commit it.

What is Happening in Mexico?

Two primary activities result in illegal dumping in Mexico: (1) the disposal of hazardous wastes by *maquiladora* plants in Mexico, and (2) the transport of wastes across the U.S./Mexico border.

The Maquiladora *Industry*

There are in excess of 6 million people congregated at the border in Mexico (McDonnell, 1991). This population accumulation in so restricted an area can primarily be attributed to the growth of the *maquiladora* industry, which began in 1965 with the Border Industrial Program (Gonzalez & Rodriguez, 1991). A *maquiladora* is a wholly-owned Mexican subsidiary which is incorporated by foreign companies. The parent company enters into an agreement with the *maquila* outlining the terms and fees to be paid to the subsidiary to assemble or process goods as requested by the parent company. There now are approximately 2,000 *maquiladoras* in Mexico. It is estimated that 90 percent have been established by U.S. companies and that 80 percent of these are located along the border. The *maquiladora* is under Mexican jurisdiction although the subsidiary is often completely owned by foreigners (Sanchez, 1990). United States corporations with Mexican subsidiaries are subject to both Mexican and U.S. environmental laws. This leads to jurisdictional problems and ultimately, in practice, to a dilution of enforcement capabilities.

The actual amount of wastes produced by the *maquiladoras* is a matter of contention. A recent study by the University of California, Los Angeles, reports that in excess of 100,000 tons of waste are produced on the Baja peninsula alone. Mexico's environmental ministry, the Secretaria de Desarrollo Urbano Ecologia or SEDUE (also referred to as SEDESOL), reports that no satisfactory estimate exists on the amount of toxic waste produced by the *maquiladoras*, since they refuse to disclose the relevant information (Sanchez, 1990). SEDUE estimates less than 50 percent of those producing toxic wastes probably would qualify for SEDUE-mandated environmental operating licenses (McDonnell, 1991).

The presence of a staggering amount and variety of toxins in border waterways and neighborhoods adjacent to *maquiladoras* strongly supports the belief that wastes are being disposed of illegally. All border waterways when sampled show evidence of toxic substance contamination. In 1990, the National Toxic Campaign Fund (NTCF) spot sampled four waterways in different locations along their course. Two noteworthy findings are: First, xylene, a common solvent and a reported cause of respiratory irregularity, brain hemorrhage, and other internal bleeding, was found in large amounts "just near" the discharge pipes of a General Motors (GM) and a Ford subsidiary (NTCF, 1991). At the Rimir plant (a GM subsidiary) in Matamoros, one of the most, if not the most heavily polluted areas in Mexico, discharges were shown to be greater than 6,000 times allowable U.S. standards. An employee stated company employees regularly washed untreated solvents down a drain which eventually discharged into the Matamoros Canal[1]. Second, toxic pollution in the Nogales Wash was shown to originate with some of the 75 *maquiladoras* in Nogales. This claim is supported by adjacent *maquiladoras'* importation of chemicals detected in the Wash.

In April 1990, U.S. Environmental Protection Agency (EPA) testing of the Tijuana River on the U.S. side of the border found levels of lead to be approximately 100 times allowable U.S. standards (McDonnell, 1991). In a Tijuana run-off stream, EPA discovered a wide range of hazardous chemicals that are used in the *maquiladoras*. The stream, the Rio Alamar, originates at Tijuana's Mesa de Otay atop the neighborhood of Francionamiento Murua. Mesa de Otay is home to dozens of *maquiladoras*. Rio Alamar runs through Francionamiento Murua; testing of Rio Alamar waters found mercury levels approximately five times the maximum freshwater standards allowed by U.S. law. Residents of the settlement report a variety of ailments which they attribute to chemicals washed downstream. Further, evidence of industrial solvent contamination exists in a nearby well (McDonnell, 1991). A separate report indicates that the Tijuana River is so polluted with industrial and municipal wastes that there is fear of outbreaks of malaria and encephalitis (Simon, 1993).

In another settlement near Tijuana, Chilpancingo, the story is much the same. Chilpancingo was built in a canyon 250 feet below one of Tijuana's largest industrial parks. Approximately 100 *maquiladoras* are found in the park. A 1990 analysis of the run-off from the park revealed levels of lead 3,400 percent higher than allowable U.S. standards. Cadmium levels were 1,230 percent higher than U.S. standards allow. Health complaints from the 770 families residing in Chilpancingo range from persistent skin rashes to high incidents of brain-damaged children born in the settlement (Simon, 1993).

Illegal Transport of Wastes into Mexico

In 1990, U.S. industry produced between 60 and 247 metric tons of hazardous wastes (Scramstad, 1991). In 1987, California alone created approximately 16 million pounds of toxic substances (Maes, 1987). The EPA estimated that as much as 90% of such wastes are disposed of improperly (Coleman, 1985). Many believe a significant majority of the wastes are winding up in Mexico. Members of the Los Angeles County Environmental Crimes Strike Force assert that "some unscrupulous American companies and waste haulers were dumping their toxic waste south of the border" (Henry, 1990). William Carter, a

Los Angeles County Deputy District Attorney who specializes in Environmental Crime, receives approximately two reports a week of alleged illegal shipments, and he believes that upwards of tens of thousands of gallons of toxic waste are illegally crossing the border every month (Dolan & Stammer, 1990).

Tijuana provides a telling example of the atrocities committed in Mexico by means of illegal transport into the country. Alco Pacific, a U.S.-owned, California-based company, was hired by Quemetco, a company located in the City of Industry, California, and owned by RSR Inc., an auto battery recycler, to transport lead taken from batteries to the Alco Pacific smelting operation based just east of Tijuana where the lead was to be processed. Any salvageable material was to be returned to RSR (Ford, 1993). In reality, Alco Pacific transported the batteries to its Tijuana subsidiary where the contents were emptied. The acid occasionally was neutralized, but more often it was allowed to seep into the ground without neutralization. The site of the now abandoned "recycler" is saturated with acids. When the company declared bankruptcy, the legacy of approximately 80,000 tons of toxic lead sulfate and a continuously burning underground fire was left for the citizens of Tijuana (Simon, 1993).

U.S. and Mexican authorities worked together to bring a case against RSR. In June 1993, the company pleaded no contest to three misdemeanor counts of illegally transporting hazardous materials and agreed to provide $2.5 million toward the cost of cleaning up the Tijuana site. The actual cost of the cleanup may be ten times the $2.5 million RSR is obliged to contribute. There is speculation that the quick trial and judgement are a result of Mexico trying to establish that it will prosecute environmental crimes. Unfortunately, the rush may have left the government with a substantial portion of the clean up costs. In addition to the charges against RSR, criminal charges were filed against three individuals who allegedly abandoned the waste in Mexico. In December 1993, Morris Kirk, president of Alco Pacific was sentenced to 16 months in state prison and the company was fined $2.5 million for illegally shipping the materials south of the border. The status of the remaining two individuals charged with illegal transportation is yet to be decided.

Laws, Regulations, and Agreements

United States Regulations and Enforcement Authorities

Between 1969 and 1971, environmental issues jumped from tenth to fifth in a U.S. public opinion poll ranking public concerns. In his classic study of white-collar crime, Sutherland (1949) postulated that an organized public outcry can counter industry's political clout. Evidence that Sutherland was partially correct is found in the response by U.S. governmental bodies to the increased concern exhibited by citizens regarding environmental destruction (Barnett, 1993).

Specific Legislation: A surge of environmental legislation began in the late 1960s and continued well into the 1980s. Early legislation imposed primarily civil and administrative remedies for violations of environmental regulations. Most environmental statutes now, however, contain two separate categories of criminal provisions: (1) strict liability, and (2) "knowing" violations. Strict liability requires no *scienter*; it need only be shown that the violation occurred. This provision is reserved for egregious acts. There is a greater degree of moral culpability associated with a knowing violation. Although proving the degree of intent required to convict for a knowing violation is difficult, the courts have allowed as grounds for conviction: (1) "inference" of knowledge, and/or (2) a showing that the accused did not take adequate steps to prevent a violation (Marzulla & Kappel, 1991).

The Resource Conservation and Recovery Act (RCRA), passed in 1976 (42 U.S.C. Sections 6901-6992(i), amended in 1980, 1984, and 1986), was designed to regulate the generation, treatment, storage, and disposal of hazardous waste. In 1980, and again in 1984, RCRA was amended, and it was made a felony for any person to knowingly treat, store, or dispose of hazardous waste without a permit (Section 6928(d)); this addition included any person who knowingly transports wastes to a facility not authorized to dispose of them (Harris, Cavanaugh & Zisk, 1988; Marzulla & Kappel, 1991). The amendment contained the first endangerment offense in federal law. A violation of "knowing endangerment," awareness that certain actions place another individual in "imminent danger" of serious bodily injury or death, carries a fine not to exceed $250,000 or imprisonment for 15 years or both (for an individual). An organizational defendant can be fined up to $1,000,000 (Section 6928 (e)). Due to obvious constraints, no jail time may be imposed on a corporation. The statute has led to prosecutions aimed at a "responsible corporate officer" (Cohen, 1992; Kafin & Port, 1990).

The most significant aspect of RCRA is the "cradle to grave" provision. Potential generators of hazardous materials must (1) obtain a permit from EPA authorizing generation of the wastes and (2) attach a manifest to the materials when they leave the generation site. Generators are responsible for ensuring the wastes are disposed of properly. The requirements allow tracking of the wastes from "cradle to grave."

Responsible Enforcement Authorities: Environmental abuse concerns led to the formation of the Environmental Protection Agency (Clinard & Yeager, 1980). When the EPA was created in 1970, it was mandated to investigate water and air pollution problems, but over the years its specific duties have greatly increased (Coleman, 1985).

In 1981, two significant events occurred: the establishment of the Office of Criminal Enforcement (OCE) in the EPA, and the formation of the Environmental Crimes Unit (ECU) within the Department of Justice (DOJ)[2]. Both units are designed to help increase criminal prosecution for environmental violations. The use of criminal sanctions against corporations for environmental violations is based on the premise that such actions will: (1) deter potential offenders, (2) increase respect for environmental laws, (3) remove the competitive and economic advantage associated with violations, and (4) seek just punishment for the offenders (Moskowitz, 1991). The establishment of the Office of Criminal Enforcement and the Environmental Crimes Unit indicates a perception by enforcement authorities that environmental offenders are real criminals and should be punished by more than a financial "slap on the wrist."

Mexican Regulations and Enforcement Authority

Mexico enacted its first environmental laws in 1971 (Gonzalez & Rodriguez, 1991). Because of ambiguities and too-broad directives in the original legislation and increased attention to environmental problems at the border, these laws have been continually updated. The most recent enactments came in 1988 with the passage of the General Law of Ecological Equilibrium and Environmental Protection (General Law) (Scramstad, 1991). Included in the General Law, based largely on U.S. statutes, is the imposition of criminal penalties on companies which illegally dispose of wastes in Mexico. For a first time violation, Mexican authorities can fine the corporation up to approximately $80,000 U.S. dollars (Gonzalez & Rodriguez, 1991). Further, criminal liability may be brought against responsible managers, and companies can be temporarily or permanently shut down. There is, however, little evidence that such actions have been taken to any significant degree.

The primary responsible authority for enforcing environmental laws in Mexico is SEDUE. A significant difference between RCRA and the Mexican approach to accounting for hazardous wastes is SEDUE's individual authorization scheme for generators, transporters, and handlers of wastes. Where RCRA imposes the "cradle to grave" approach, SEDUE grants rights on a piecemeal basis. Opportunity exists to illegally dispose of materials in Mexico because no tracking system is in place and wastes get "lost" (Scramstad, 1991).

Binational Agreements

The most substantive environmental protection agreement between the United States and Mexico, the La Paz Agreement, was signed in 1983. It calls for joint environmental monitoring and environmental impact assessment (Scramstad, 1991). Further, it formally establishes EPA and SEDUE as the national coordinators for their respective countries. In 1986, annexations to the La Paz Agreement were made. Annex III addresses transboundary shipment of hazardous materials and directs the return of such substances to their site of origin (e.g., when U.S. parent corporations export materials to Mexico to be used in the running of operations, the hazardous by-products must be returned to the U.S.).

Loopholes exist in the language of both the La Paz Agreement generally and Annex III specifically in regard to the final disposition of wastes. For example, SEDUE allows the by-pass of the return to origin clause found in Annex III by stating that treatment and/or dumping can be done in Mexico if authorized by SEDUE. This option can lead to disastrous results as there are only five commercial sites approved for hazardous waste disposal by SEDUE in the entire Mexican nation (Sanchez, 1990). Further, Article 2 of the La Paz Agreement states that both countries are responsible for ensuring that respective domestic laws and regulations are enforced *to the extent practicable*. This statement leaves great latitude in how stringently the laws are enforced on both sides of the border.

Enforcement

Neither country adequately enforces regulations, especially at the border (Sinclair, 1986). Authorities on both sides of the border are accused of not doing their jobs (Rich, 1991). There are several factors that contribute to the inefficient enforcement: political and economic disparities, lack of resources, jurisdictional issues, the difficulty of successful prosecution, and corruption in the Mexican government.

Political and Economic Disparity

Because of the high rate of poverty found in Mexico, government emphasis is on increasing industrialization and raising the level of employment in order to increase the standard of living for Mexican citizens. Unfortunately, as Barnett (1993) points out, these emphases often conflict with environmental initiatives. Rich (1991) maintains that it would be uneconomic to try and clean up the *maquiladora* industry as anywhere from one- to three-quarters of the subsidiaries would be involved in the efforts. Mexico would need to dramatically increase resources for thoroughly investigating and monitoring a large number of the *maquiladoras*.

In line with their economic goals, Mexican officials often are reluctant to risk antagonizing *maquiladora* owners by "overdeterrence" (Cohen, 1992; McDonnell, 1991; Sanchez, 1990). The *maquiladora* industry generates approximately $4 billion annually and is thought to be the healthiest enterprise in Mexico's economy (Sanchez, 1990). Because of the high income generated by the *maquiladoras*, the possible flight of the subsidiaries as a result of tougher enforcement of environmental regulations would not be in the best interests of Mexican industry; it would have significant negative effects on the economy if the companies were to flee (Moor, 1987).

Clinard and Yeager (1980) stress the great influence a corporation may have on the government. In Mexico, the need for industry allows corporations greater latitude in how they run their subsidiaries. The most important factor for the Mexican government is how to attract and keep industry in the country. An example of the high priority placed on attracting business to Mexico (at the expense of environmental standards) is the government invitation to certain industries which produce hazardous materials, including asbestos (Sinclair, 1986). Given the economic and political problems, it appears that environmental standards will remain in the background until more immediate economic concerns can be addressed.

Resources

The lack of resources targeted for environmental enforcement is related to but not synonymous with economic problems (NTCF, 1991; Rich, 1991; Scramstad, 1991; Simon, 1993; Yeager, 1991). According to the La Paz Agreement, both the U.S. and Mexico are to work to enforce the laws satisfactorily. However, no specific resources are allocated by the agreement, and on both sides of the border there has been reluctance to provide the necessary funds. The dearth of inspection officials is evidence of the lack of resources. In 1991, Mexico had approximately 100 inspectors for the total northern area of the country where the overwhelming majority of the *maquiladoras* are located. The EPA has one agent and two investigators to cover four western states (Henry, 1990).

Although little is being spent on either side of the border to address the problem, there is evidence that Mexico is spending significantly less money per capita than the U.S. on environmental protection. In 1991, Mexico budgeted approximately 48 cents per person and the U.S. spent approximately $24.40 per person. The laws on the books are strong, but they lack the economic support needed for satisfactory enforcement (McDonnell, 1991).

Jurisdiction Problems

Substantial controversy exists regarding the issue of jurisdiction. In the United States, governmental agencies involved in the detecting, tracking, investigation, and prosecution of hazardous waste violations include EPA, DOJ, U.S. Customs, the Department of Transportation (DOT), and the FBI. These agencies sometimes have difficulty cooperating and the overlap and confused questions of jurisdictional priorities add to the enforcement chaos.

U.S. Customs, DOT, and the FBI are primarily involved in stopping the illegal flow of hazardous wastes into Mexico. U.S. Customs has independent authority to "stop, inspect, search, seize and detain suspected illegal exports of hazardous wastes" (50 U.S.C. App. 2411 (1969)). Inspections of Mexico-bound vehicles are rarely conducted however; more attention is paid to incoming traffic from Mexico (Henry, 1990; Maes, 1987). The DOT, in overlapping authority with EPA, has the power to regulate the transportation of all materials under the Hazardous Material Transportation Act (49 U.S.C. Sections 1802-1813 (1988)) (Scramstad, 1991). The FBI can become involved if EPA solicits its help. In a Memorandum of Understanding dated March 1982, the FBI agreed to work on at least 30 cases each year if so requested by EPA.

It can be difficult for agencies to apply provisions of the La Paz Agreement since there is little consensus as to who is responsible for what (Shavelson, 1989). For instance, when questioned whether it has authority over Mexican territory, EPA's answer is a defensive no. EPA claims that U.S. Federal law prohibits employees other than those of the State Department from dealing with Mexico and declares that authority rests with the International Boundary Water Commission (IBWC, formerly the International Boundary Commission) established by the 1944 Water Treaty on Water Utilization (Glickman, 1985; Glover, 1987). Although the IBWC is the only institution formally specified to handle U.S. and Mexican environmental cases at the international level, it continually has refused to address hazardous waste problems and lacks any real enforcement power (Sinclair, 1986). If neither EPA or IBWC is monitoring the *maquiladoras*, then who is keeping watch? As of 1989, the EPA had never investigated a *maquiladora* (Shavelson, 1989), although the La Paz Agreement calls for joint inspections by

EPA and SEDUE and although it is unclear how an inspection, if in fact carried out, differs from an investigation.

The increasing problem of jurisdiction in international law regarding subsidiaries has led to further enforcement difficulties. Which country has jurisdiction: the country of the incorporated subsidiary or the country of the parent company? The country where the subsidiary resides often objects to extraterritorial U.S. jurisdiction, insisting that the subsidiary is shielded from U.S. control (Thompson, 1983). Transnational companies minimize control by playing the laws of one country off the other (Clinard & Yeager, 1980). This can be done through law evasion or law violation. "For example, a multinational may shift its operations to a subsidiary in a country that has lax pollution or worker safety standards" (p. 41). Although Mexico's laws are based largely on those of the U.S., the lack of enforcement amounts to approximately the same thing as lax standards.[3]

The Mutual Legal Assistance Cooperation Treaty (1987) between Mexico and the U.S. is designed to foster more coordination between the two countries although no jurisdictional authority is stated. The Treaty established DOJ and the Procuradaria General de la Republica as the operative bodies (Moskowitz, 1991). Whether the treaty has resulted in increased detection and/or prosecution of environmental crime has not been publicized.

Difficulty of Prosecution

The question of prosecutorial powers of both the U.S. and Mexico is closely related to the issue of jurisdiction. It is generally difficult, costly, and time consuming to prosecute for regulatory violations (Coleman, 1985). This problem is further exacerbated by the barrier noted above: jurisdiction. And what of liability? Who should be liable for transboundary environmental damage on both sides of the border caused by the *maquiladoras* (Simon, 1993)? EPA could prosecute for pollution coming into the U.S. The difficulty in amassing the necessary evidence tying one or more operations to specific illegal activities, however, seriously undercuts this option. Better coordination is needed between SEDUE and EPA for successful enforcement. There is some evidence that U.S. and Mexican officials are learning to cooperate, as illustrated by the joint investigative and prosecutorial efforts by the Los Angeles District Attorney and Mexican authorities on the Alco Pacific case.

Corruption

As a form of occupational crime according to the definition by Clinard and Yeager (1980), political corruption, primarily in the form of payoffs, is a prime factor behind illegal behavior in Mexico. U.S. officials acknowledge that political corruption has complicated a number of joint investigations (Simon, 1993). There are reports of corruption in the enforcement system (Moskowitz, 1991), including *maquiladora* inspectors (Simon, 1993) and border officials who accept bribes (Dolan & Stammer, 1990). Although not acknowledged as an instance of bribery, there is evidence that SEDUE entered into enforcement "agreements" with *maquiladora* plant operations under which no inspections would be conducted for a period of one to two years (NTCF, 1991). These agreements allegedly were made so that the industries could work toward achieving some semblance of compliance. This raises suspicions as to statistics reported by officials who claim that companies send their wastes back to the U.S. although U.S. authorities have no knowledge of such shipments.

Industry Motivation

Illicit dumping is said to be carried out in a systematic fashion by "sophisticated corporate officials" (Maes, 1987: 42). Many companies enter into agreements with Mexican subsidiaries to avoid strict U.S. environmental regulation and to take advantage of cheaper labor (Frank & Lynch, 1992; Sanchez, 1990). Further, U.S. companies are believed to exploit the absence of monitoring and enforcement in Mexico when there is little chance of getting caught (NTCF, 1991).

There is no question that the enforcement mechanisms currently in place are inadequate and foster illegal behavior. But how this is connected to the motivations of responsible actors in the industry has not been addressed. The white-collar crime literature offers overlapping theories related to motivations and rationalizations of criminal actors. Of primary interest are: (1) Sutherland's (1949) view on corporate rationality about illegal behavior, (2) Clinard and Yeager's (1980) models to explain business crime, and (3) Macey's (1991) schema for corporate criminal activity. The theories and models are applicable to the current discussion.

Sutherland (1949) states that "violations of law by corporations are deliberate and organized crimes" (p. 239). He identifies three aspects of the rationality of a corporation: the rational corporation (1) selects crimes with very little chance of detection, (2) commits crimes which are difficult to prove, and (3) "fixes" cases when necessary; this last includes preventing adequate implementation of various regulations and political interference in prosecution. Each facet is relevant in some degree to the current situation in Mexico. First, the illegal dumping is difficult to detect and to trace to any particular party. This is true for both illegal transportation across the border and for *maquila* industry dumping. Further, even if the offense is detected, the penalties are minimal if caught in Mexico compared to discovery, and possible prosecution, in the U.S. (Sanchez, 1990). Second, the chances of gathering the requisite proof for prosecution are slim. Third, the corporations, via their subsidiaries, are in a position to thwart enforcement on either side of the border because of their political and economic clout.

Clinard and Yeager (1980) provide two models which suggest what paths corporations will take in business operations: the Rational Goals Model and the Economic and Political Environmental Model. The Rational Goals Model (RGM), which focuses on the primacy of profit, is most applicable in the current situation. Many companies claim that government rules are unjustified because the cost of complying cuts into reasonable profits. Green (1979), however, asserts that the costs are "overstated." Regardless of the actual costs, companies use the primacy of profit as a chief rationalization for breaking laws. The prime motivation of companies illegally disposing of wastes in Mexico appears to be profit and, taken to the extreme, greed (Henry, 1990; Sanchez, 1990). Disposal of one barrel of hazardous substances can run anywhere between $200 and $2,000 in the U.S. whereas in Mexico it rarely costs more than $200 per recycled barrel. To dispose of the wastes illegally costs next to nothing. Many companies find it easier (and cheaper) to pay a fine if caught than to obey the law (Moskowitz, 1991). Maes (1987) claims such market incentives encourage businesses to dispose of their wastes unsafely if not illegally (see also Yeager, 1991).

Another possible explanation for illegal behavior by corporations is the corporate culture in an industry (Macey, 1991). This possibility undoubtedly is involved to some extent in the violation of environmental regulations in Mexico. For example, in Mexicali 42 percent of the subsidiaries produce mechanical auto parts (Sanchez, 1990). This industry may have a culture which leads to a greater tendency to violate environmental standards than other industries.

Conclusion

Although companies responsible for the illegal disposal of hazardous wastes should be held accountable, officials charged with adopting and enforcing regulations are guilty of exacerbating the problem. The lack of seriousness exhibited by both the U.S. and Mexico on this issue enables industries to continue the illegal behavior with very little threat of prosecution or sanction. Lack of resources, prosecution difficulty, and jurisdiction confusion greatly aid and abet industry involved in environmental white-collar crime.

The North American Free Trade Agreement (NAFTA) focused attention on the environmental degradation observed primarily at the U.S.-Mexico border. The NAFTA will allow corporations to move operations deeper into Mexico. Although it is claimed that this will reduce border pollution in the long run, there will be a "profound" increase of pollution at the border during the first 10 years of implementation (Stammer & Pasternak, 1992). Whether the borderlands can reasonably tolerate such an increase is questionable, given the current state of the environment.

In response to the increased concern over environmental impact with the NAFTA, the Clinton Administration called for negotiations of a side accord dealing specifically with the environment. The talks (and subsequent agreement) between representatives of Canada, Mexico, and the United States were completed during the latter part of October 1993. The finalized agreement gives alleged violators at least one year before any significant action can be taken. Further, nothing concrete for alleviating the current environmental problem exists in the agreement. The issue of hazardous waste cleanup is not identified as a priority in the NAFTA (Senator B. Boxer, CSPAN2, October 19, 1993). This suggests that few resources will be designated and little action will be taken to clean up the hazardous waste situation. Additionally, where the enforcement resources will be allocated remains a source of speculation. In 1991, SEDUE's Director General, Rene Altamirano, stated: "I'm concerned now and if it's possible to be more concerned, I will be after [a free trade agreement] is signed. . .we can't work any harder" (*Los Angeles Times*, November 17, 1991). If less than adequate funds are pledged toward enforcing the current regulations, the problem will only increase as more companies relocate and/or incorporate in Mexico.

Before deterrence can be achieved, it is necessary that a message be sent to the responsible parties that criminal disposal of hazardous wastes will not be tolerated. Further, there is a need for the establishment of enforceable international regulations. The Basel Agreement[4] addresses the international transport of hazardous materials. Signed by 53 countries and later ratified by 25 countries, including the U.S. and Mexico, the Agreement entered into force on May 5, 1992 (Russel & Shearer, 1993). The restrictions imposed by the Basel Agreement are similar to those established by the La Paz Agreement and later Annexes to the Agreement (Scramstad, 1991). Therefore, no significant changes or increased hardship should result. Genuine enforcement of the current regulations and/or the Basel regulations would reduce the convenience and profit currently associated with transferring hazardous wastes to less developed countries. Further, the illegal traffic in hazardous wastes is defined as criminal under Basel (Moskowitz, 1991). The increased stigma from possible criminal prosecution might push those previously disposed toward violating environmental regulations to reconsider. Unfortunately, no enforcement authority exists with the Basel Agreement and it is questionable whether significant changes will occur.

A Foreign Environmental Practices Act also has been proposed to increase the reach of U.S. jurisdiction over the activities of subsidiaries abroad. The act would be based on the Foreign Corrupt Businesses Act and would extend the reach of U.S. environmental laws outside of U.S. territory. This would be an important step toward holding multinationals increasingly responsible for their actions abroad.

If corporations do not see compliance as necessary and in their best interests, they will simply move to another, more poverty-stricken Third World nation and continue their behavior there. At some point, these actions should come to be defined as international crimes and then possibly, corporations will be more attentive to pressures to conform. These pressures must originate with stepped-up enforcement and increased government action before industry actors come to appreciate that illegal hazardous waste dumping is criminal behavior.

NOTES

1.	In April 1991, Mexican inspectors briefly closed a different General Motors subsidiary in Matamoros for improper handling of their wastes (McDonnell, 1991).

2.	Clinard and Yeager (1980) state corporate crime, though punished in a non-criminal fashion, still should be viewed as criminal behavior. This is meaningful in the current context because environmental crime is often perceived as non-criminal behavior; offenders are merely violating regulations, not breaking the law.

3.	In its favor, SEDUE reports heavy fines were going to be levied against a number of Fortune 500 companies which have subsidiaries in Mexico, including AT&T, General Motors, and a U.S. subsidiary of Union Carbide.

4.	Basel Convention on the Control of Transboundary Movements of Hazardous Wastes and their disposal opened for signature March 22, 1989, S. Treaty Doc. No. 5, 102d. Congress, 1st Sess. 28 I.L.M. 649 (1989).

REFERENCES

Barnett, Harold (1993). "Crimes Against the Environment: Superfund Enforcement at Last." *Annals of the American Academy of Political and Social Science* 525: 119-133.

"Can Mexico Clean Up Its Act?" (1991). *Los Angeles Times* (November 17): A1.

Clifford, Frank (1993). "Executive Gets Prison Term in Pollution Case." *Los Angeles Times* (December 16): A3.

Clinard, Marshall, and Peter Yeager (1980). *Corporate Crime.* New York: Free Press.

Cohen, Mark A. (1992). "Environmental Crime and Punishment: Legal/Economic Theory and Empirical Evidence on Enforcement of Federal Environmental Statutes." *Journal of Criminal Law and Criminology* 82: 1054-1108.

Coleman, James W. (1985). *The Criminal Elite: The Sociology of White Collar Crime (1st Ed.)* New York: St. Martin's Press.

Dolan, Maura, and Larry Stammer (1990). "Clandestine Toxic Waste Exports to Mexico on Rise." *Los Angeles Times* (May 9): A1.

Ford, Andrea (June 16, 1993). "Firm To Help Pay for Tijuana Site Cleanup." *Los Angeles Times*, D1.

Frank, Nancy, and Michael J. Lynch (1992). *Corporate Crime, Corporate Violence: A Primer.* Albany, New York: Harrow and Heston.

Glickman, Nina (1985). "Note--Keep Your Pollution to Yourself: Institutions for Regulating Transboundary Pollution and the United States-Mexico Approach." *Virginia Journal of International Law* 25: 693-727.

Glover, Nancy (1987). "The New River: The Possibility of Criminal Liability for Transnational Pollution." *Criminal Justice Journal* 10: 99-119.

Gonzalez, Daniel, and Elaine Rodriguez (1991). "Environmental Aspects of *Maquiladora* Operations: A Note of Caution for U.S. Parent Corporations." *St. Mary's Law Journal* 22: 659-700.

Green, Mark J. (1979). "The Faked Case Against Regulation." *Washington Post* (January 21): C1.

Harris, Christopher, Patrick Cavanaugh, and Robert Zisk (1988). Criminal Liability for Violations of Federal Hazardous Waste Law: The 'Knowledge' of Corporations and Their Executives." *Wake Forest Law Review* 23: 203-236.

Henry, Sarah (1990). "The Poison Trail: How Environmental Cops Tracked Deadly Waste Across the Border." *Los Angeles Times Magazine* (September 23): 22.

Kafin, Robert, and Gail Port (1990). "Criminal Sanctions Lead to Higher Fines and Jail." *National Law Journal* (July 23): 12.

Macey, Jonathan (1991). "Agency Theory and the Criminal Liability of Organizations." *Boston University Law Review* 71: 315-340.

Maes, Denise (1987). "Transboundary Waste Dumping: The United States and Mexico Take a Stand." *Natural Resources Journal* 27: 941-948.

Marzulla, Roger, and Brett Kappel (1991). "Nowhere to Run, Nowhere to Hide: Criminal Liability for Violations of Environmental Statutes in the 1990's." *Columbia Journal of Environmental Law* 16: 201-225.

McDonnell, Patrick (1991). "Foreign-Owned Companies Add to Mexico's Pollution." *Los Angeles Times* (November 18): A1.

Moor, C. A. (1987). "Taming the Giant Corporation? Some Cautionary Remarks on the Deterrability of Corporate Crime." *Crime and Delinquency* 33: 379-402.

Moskowitz, Adam (1991). "Comment—Criminal Environmental Law: Stopping the Flow of Hazardous Waste to Mexico." *California Western International Law Journal* 22: 159-186.

National Toxic Campaign Fund (1991). *Border Trouble: Rivers in Peril.* Boston: Author.

Rich, Jan (May/June, 1991). "Bordering on Trouble." *Environmental Forum,* 26-33.

Russel, C., and H. Shearer (1993). "Comparative Analysis of the Basel and Bamako Conventions on Hazardous Wastes." *Environmental Law* 23: 141-183.

Sanchez, Roberto (1990). "Health and Environmental Risks of the *Maquiladora* in Mexicali." *National Resources Journal* 30: 163-186.

Scramstad, Barbara (1991). "Transboundary Movement of Hazardous Waste from the United States to Mexico." *Transnational Lawyer* 4: 253-290.

Shavelson, Lonny (1989). "Acid River." *California Lawyer* 9: 24-25.

Simon, Joel (1993). "Dirty Work." *California Lawyer* 13: 41.

Sinclair, Mark (1986). "The Environmental Cooperation Agreement Between Mexico and the United States: A Response to the Pollution Problems of the Borderlands." *Cornell International Law Journal* 19: 87-142.

Stammer, Larry B., and Judy Pasternak (1992). "Mexico's Pollution Cleanup Tied to Trade Pact." *Los Angeles Times* (February 27): A3.

Sutherland, Edwin H. (1949). *White-Collar Crime: The Uncut Version.* New York: Drydent Press.

Thompson, Robert (1983). "United States Jurisdiction Over Foreign Subsidiaries: Corporate and International Law Aspects." *Law and Policy in International Business* 15: 319-400.

Yeager, Peter (1991). *The Limits of Law: The Public Regulation of Private Pollution.* Cambridge, GB: Cambridge University Press.

CHAPTER SIX

A Native American Criminology of Environmental Crime

Mark Seis

Recognizing a problem is the first step in creating solutions. This chapter explores a mode of thinking that reexamines our view of nature. Preventing ecological crime requires that first, we change the way we perceive our relation to nature and, second, it requires we restructure our laws to accommodate this new way of thinking about our relation to nature.

An eco-critical criminologist perspective assumes environmental crime and the failure of our laws to improve the quality of our environment are attributable to our collective beliefs. Durkheim (1972) once wrote "[w]e must not say that an action shocks the conscience collective because it is criminal, but rather that it is criminal because it shocks the conscience collective" (p. 123). Durkheim's point is humans formulate their ethical conscience by presupposing it in the collective beliefs of their social structure. Environmental crime does not appear to shock our collective conscience, because the social construction of our beliefs presuppose exploitation in our relationship to nature (e.g., human dominion, progress, industrialization, and mechanistic science and technology).

To illustrate how contemporary society presupposes exploitation of nature, this chapter examines a Native American criminology of environmental crime based upon the concept of bioregionalism. The Seneca Indians[1], who occupied the Western portion of New York State from 1650 to 1750, are explored as a culture basically free of environmental crime. The Seneca Indians lived a unique interactive, affirmative, and self-fulfilling existence with their bioregion.

Bioregions are highly complex geographical regions where complex interactions take place between climatic conditions, biogeochemical systems, and living organisms (i.e., plants, animals and people). Examples of bioregions are deserts, plains, arctic regions, tropical rain forests, and mountainous areas. Each one of these bioregions represents a unique set of conditions in which, prior to industrialization, many human civilizations built their cultures around and in conjunction with.

This chapter should not be construed as romanticizing a time gone by, nor should it be perceived as advocating contemporary society revert to forms of life that existed centuries ago. Bioregionalism is explored not as a panacea for contemporary society but as a model for rethinking ways in which we can bring nature back into our everyday lives. Unlike the culture of the Seneca, most aspects of contemporary industrial culture cloak from consciousness an awareness that we are a part of nature. Acknowledging our interconnectedness with nature provides us with the essential starting point from which to think and act differently within our particular bioregions.

We argue that contemporary United States society functions out of sync with nature. This means that many of our environmental crimes and ills stem from inadequate understanding of our dependence on and interrelationships with our designated bioregions. Next, an argument is put forth stating the Seneca Indians living from 1650 to 1750 maintained a fairly ecologically crime free society within their bioregion, which can be demonstrated through eclectic ethnohistorical accounts.

The Ethical Problem of Environmental Crime

Before we can understand alternative discourses on environmental crime, it is imperative we identify the cultural sources responsible for environmentally harmful behavior. To grasp fully the gist of a Native American criminology of environmental crime, we need to identify aspects of our culture that are counter-ecological. This section begins by discussing environmental crime as a problem of understanding our interconnected relationship to the earth.

Contemporary industrial society has come to view pollution as an inescapable byproduct of our culture. We often cast the problem of pollution into dichotomies where the spotted owl is pitted against our need for paper or clean air is pitted against the need for jobs. Take for example, the response of the people from Tacoma, Washington, when they were faced with the problem of illegal amounts of arsenic in the air:

> . . .the administrator of the EPA, William D. Ruckelshaus. . .asked the local residents to choose between increased unemployment and environmental quality. They opted for jobs over environmental quality. . .a choice that was nullified when Asarco Inc. in 1985, faced with falling copper prices, decided on its own to close the plant after all (Commoner, 1990: 83).

Because both work and clean air are necessary for human survival an ideological structure that creates choices of this nature must be flawed. Choices like those above are not really choices and framing our environmental problems as such suggest that he have simply misconstrued our relationship to nature.

Humans, unlike any other species, have an innate ability to radically transform nature. Contemporary industrial society's ability to transform nature in the last 100 years has been unprecedented in human history. In many respects we have truly achieved a sort of dominion over the planet. On the other hand, however, we are still subject to nature's dominion with respect to climate, earthquakes, wildfires, volcanoes, hurricanes, deluges, and drought. Thus no matter how hard we try we can never transcend our basic dependence on the earth's ecosystems to function with some predictability.

The bottom line is that humans are a part of nature; humans can alter aspects of nature and nature can alter aspects of human lives. Whole human civilizations have risen and fallen based upon their relationships with specific bioregions (e.g., Mesopotamians and Mayans). Ancient history is full of such tales but so is modern history. In fact, we may be witnessing such a story right now around the world as pollution becomes more pervasive in our everyday reality, changing such behaviors as the very way we eat, consume water, transport ourselves, and dispose of our waste.

Because of our profligate behavior, we are having to confront aspects of our belief system head on. We are beginning to realize we cannot continue to grow in what are inevitably finite ecological regions comprising a finite global system. Simply put, the earth can sustain only so much abuse, violence, and degradation before our actions boomerang back in the form of major global problems like global warming, ozone depletion, acid rain, water pollution, air pollution and soil depletion. It can be argued that these problems stem from what Aldo Leopold referred to back in the late 1940s as a society grounded in taking without any sense of restraint or giving back.

Aldo Leopold ([1949], 1987) contends modern industrial society lacks an environmental ethic. We have ethics regarding how individuals should act towards one another and ethics regarding how the state and the individual should act, but we have no ethic to tell us how to relate to the earth which provides us with the essentials of living (e.g., air, water, soil, plants and animals). Unlike the Seneca, our social construction of reality has attempted to extricate itself from our inevitable dependence on nature.

Leopold (1987) argues that "[t]here is as yet no ethic dealing with man's [sic] relation to land and to animals and plants which grow upon it. . . The land relation is still strictly economic, entailing privilege but not obligation" (p. 203). Ethics, according to Leopold, rest on the assumption that "the individual is a member of a community of interdependent parts" (p. 203). An environmental ethic "changes the role of Homo Sapiens from conqueror of the land community to plain member and citizen of it. It implies respect for his [sic] fellow-members, and also respect for the community as such" (Leopold, 1987: 204). In its simplest form, then, an environmental ethic is "limitation on freedom of action in the struggle for existence" (Leopold, 1987: 202). An environmental ethic is "a mode of guidance for meeting ecological situations so new or intricate, or involving such deferred reactions, that the path of social expediency is not discernible to the average individual" (Leopold, 1987: 203).

While many contemporary philosophers and concerned environmentalists have struggled and continue to struggle with the structure of an environmental ethic for modern society (Berry, 1988; Carson, 1987/1962; Callicott, 1989; Hargrove, 1989; Hynes, 1989; Kealey, 1990; Nash, 1989; Rolston, 1988; and Wenz, 1988), most are in agreement an ethic will need to incorporate some basic understanding of ecological principles. Environmentalists have been aware of these principles for some time, and Barry Commoner has simplified these principles in rudimentary but precise language. The first principle reads "everything is connected to everything else" (Commoner, 1990: 8). This principle simply means there are no independent parts in an ecosystem. The diversity of species and their function within the intricately woven food webs suggest each living thing has many functions. For example, a bird is not just a bird but a parent, a natural insecticide, food for other species, an organic fertilizer, and when it dies it becomes the life sustaining substance for microorganisms.

The second principle reads "[e]verything must go somewhere. . . everything that is produced in part of the cycle goes somewhere and is used in a later step" (Commoner, 1990: 9). Commoner goes on to point out that:

> The technosphere, in contrast, is dominated by linear processes. Thus, in the technosphere goods are converted, linearly into waste: crops into sewage; uranium into radioactive residue; petroleum and chlorine into dioxin; fossil fuels into carbon dioxide. In the technosphere, the end of the line is always waste, an assault on the cyclical process that sustains the ecosphere (pp. 9-11).

Contemporary society fails to understand that in nature everything is functional and that which does not provide a valuable service to the functionality of nature does not belong. If it is not biodegradable, then it does not belong on this planet. As we will see shortly, these two ecological principles seem to be implicit in the Seneca's understanding of nature.

The third principle reads "Nature knows best" (Commoner, 1990: 11). This is simply to acknowledge nature as a self-sustaining and co-evolutionary process of interactive life. Commoner explains:

> It is an unbroken rule that for every organic compound produced by a living thing, there is somewhere in the ecosystem an enzyme capable of breaking it down. Organic compounds incapable of enzymatic degradation are not produced by living things. . . This arrangement is essential to the harmony of the ecosystem (pp. 11-12).

The earth, in order to strike a balance among the millions of diverse life forms, has produced a unique system where everything living eats something that has lived or is living. This unique balance produces little waste. Synthetic chemicals, plastics, and styrofoam have no place in the physical environment because there are no living organisms that can consume them. These pollutants are non-biodegradable and thus their creation by humans is, in many respects, criminal.

Incorporating an environmental ethic grounded in ecological principles into the discourse about environmental crime aids us in our quest to define environmentally harmful behavior as well as providing a platform for law creation. Behaviors that violate the integrity of ecosystems should be defined as criminal, and environmental law should compel human behavior to conform to the principles of ecology. Reconceptualizing our relationship to nature enables us to better understand the causes of environmental crime and some possible solutions for reconciling our destructive behavior. Let us now turn to a discussion of how Seneca culture prevented environmental crime by an intuitive understanding of their ineluctable dependence on nature.

Native Americans and the Intuitive Land Ethic

Environmentalists have for some time realized the intuitive nature of a land ethic and ecological principles in Native American cultures and have attempted to shed light on these particular attributes (Berry, 1988; Booth & Jacobs, 1990; Bowers, 1993; Collier, 1947; Hughes, 1977; McLuhan, 1971; and Callicott, 1989). Most of these articles or books, however, have presented their cases in an eclectic and synthetic fashion; that is, these authors have drawn from a variety of indigenous native American cultures and have arrived at the conclusion that Native Americans "tended to preserve biological integrity within natural communities. . ." (Booth & Jacobs, 1990: 31). Although these are all excellent writings and immensely helpful in understanding the diversity in which Native Americans coexisted in a variety of natural settings, they do not provide the holistic context in which an ecological awareness was nurtured and facilitated in a particular culture within an everyday context.

The Seneca are explored as a society whose integration with the biotic community made it virtually inconceivable at one time in their history to act in ecologically harmful ways. Whether the Seneca had the technological means to exploit the earth is an irrelevant question. Every human society has the ability, regardless of its mode of production, to take from nature without giving back. At one time in their history, the Seneca did not take without presupposing an obligation to give. Then they met the Europeans. After the Seneca's encounter with the Europeans their relationship with their bioregion began to undergo incremental changes as early as the seventeenth century and was completely altered by the beginning of the nineteenth century. The entire concept of profit markets, trade, and ownership of property were completely unknown to the Seneca, and unequivocally their introduction into the Seneca way of life greatly altered the culture. The European fur trade is an example of introducing animals as commodities; a concept once inconceivable to the Seneca. Accordingly, the Seneca men began to hunt for pelts (e.g., beaver) rather than for subsistence (for a discussion of this topic, see Wallace, 1989: 99-107). For the first time in their history they experienced the effects of land/market exploitation which resulted in the exhaustion of many game animal populations.

Because the Seneca society was mainly agrarian, the interactions with the Europeans did not directly affect their religious, economic, family, and community structures until after the American Revolution. At this time, their culture had significantly changed its locus of being in the world from nature centered to a quasi-Euroamerican value system. Through conquest and exploitation, Euroamerican cultural values eventually coerced indigenous people away from living within the confines of ecological systems to embracing a value system of profligate and exploitative behavior. What is it about our culture that encourages environmental crime? What could we have learned from the Seneca about living with and within ecological systems?

The Framework of Bioregional Analysis

To acknowledge bioregionalism as a form of study is to understand that the earth produces different integrated systems involving climates, landscapes, plants and animals, in which human cultures are inextricably intertwined. Jim Dodge states that bioregionalism "has been the animating cultural principle through ninety-nine percent of human history and is at least as old as consciousness" (cited in Devall & Sessions, 1985: 21). The study of bioregions includes the hydrological cycle, flora, fauna, landscape and climate. It also includes an assessment of the meaning ascribed to these most fundamental components of life by human cultures. The use of the bioregion concept in this paper is focused on asking how cultures reflect their relationship to the geographical area which provides the essential components of life for them.

Bioregionalism is a concept more familiar to the nomenclature of the ecologist than the criminologist. One of the most lucid conceptualizations of what bioregions are stems from the writings of Thomas Berry (1988). Berry's thematic conceptualization is used as the framework for understanding a Native American environmental criminology of a particular bioregion and for contrasting aspects of contemporary society's use of the same bioregion. Berry (1988) defines bioregion as follows:

> A bioregion is an identifiable geographical area of interacting life systems that is relatively self-sustaining in the ever-renewing process of nature. The full diversity of life functions is carried out, not as individuals or as species, or even as organic beings, but as a community that includes the physical as well as the organic components of a region. Such a bioregion is a self-propagating, self-nourishing, self-educating, self-governing, self-healing, and self-fulfilling community. Each component life system must integrate its functioning within this community to survive in any effective manner (p. 166).

The key words in Berry's definition are "self-propagating, self-nourishing, self-educating, self-governing, self-healing, and self-fulfilling community." According to Berry, the future of human civilization lies in understanding and integrating culture around these key concepts of bioregionalism.

Understanding the earth as a living and a self-governing system provides the foundation for the criminalization of environmentally harmful behavior. Imposing counter-ecological technologies on a self-governing system is a violent act, not only against the natural environment but in many cases against fellow human beings which must reside within that community. Just as human society cannot survive by capricious acts of violence committed against its members, a bioregion cannot sustain human life by random assaults against its integrated systems. What needs to be criminalized are those actions that do not conform to the self-sustaining and renewal function of the bioregion.

The Seneca had no problem with serious environmental crime, nor did they have formalistic criminal codes defining acceptable interactions with their natural environment. Seneca culture embodied an implicit environmental ethic that encompassed an understanding of ecological dependency, cooperation, and integration. Unlike contemporary society, the Seneca understood their relationship with their bioregion and integrated their culture around its life-giving attributes and also its constraints, which made environmentally harmful acts virtually inconceivable.

Bioregionalism: A Native American Environmental Criminology

Self-Propagation

The first phase in understanding a Native American environmental criminology of environmental crime and bioregionalism requires an awareness and recognition of other species' rights to exist. Berry (1988) writes, "a bioregion is the domestic setting of the community. . .the community continues itself through successive generations. . .for humans to assume rights to occupy land by excluding life forms from their needed habitat is to offend the community in its deepest structure" (p. 166). When the deepest structures (i.e., moral community) of human society are offended we call this a crime. Grounding ourselves in our relation to a bioregion augments our conception of crime to include those actions that offend non-human inhabitants as well. Because humans are inextricably linked to the survival of other non-human inhabitants, it only makes sense that laws should protect that which human society is dependent upon. Self-propagation, then, goes beyond just human survival to assuring the survival of all aspects of nature that are inextricably intertwined with human survival.

The Seneca realized this obligation in very important ways. The same may be said about all the nations of the Iroquois Federation with whom the Seneca are linked politically through a shared set of cultural beliefs[2]. Whenever the Federation opened a council meeting it was with the following words: "In our every deliberation we must consider the impact of our decision on the next seven generations" (Nollman, 1990). Decisions were made not only for those living but also for those that would follow for seven generations guaranteeing that every generation would think of the next. Presupposing an obligation to future generations serves as a check on the types of decisions and actions that are made on behalf of one's culture, and it assures the preservation of the bioregion which serves as the basis of one's culture.

One of the unique ways in which Seneca culture reflected self-propagation of the ecological community was in their clan structure. The Seneca clan structure was divided into animal and bird affiliations known in anthropological terms as moieties. The animal clans consisted of the Bear, Turtle, Wolf and Beaver; while the bird clan affiliation consisted of the Hawk, Heron, Snipe, and Deer (Francello, 1980: 58-59). Apparently the Deer clan was associated with the bird clan because of the deer's swift and flight-like grace. Nevertheless, each clan represented important animals that were recognized by the Seneca as having unique qualities. In fact, each clan had their own decree, obligations, and forms of recreation which celebrated some unique aspect of the animal or bird (Nitsch, 1979). While the Clans were functional in preventing incestual relationships, they also served as cultural representations of a shared sense of community with other occupants of the bioregion.

Contemporary society, on the other hand, does not think in most cases beyond the economic quarters that divide one fiscal year. In short, we produce massive amounts of waste that are not environmentally friendly (e.g., radioactive waste, toxic waste, and plastic) and will be a problem for a thousand generations in the future. Our mode of economics is not future oriented; rather it is based upon a philosophy of infinite resource exploitation and continued growth. Thus our philosophy is a short-term form of self-propagation which is always at the expense of other non-human occupants of our bioregions; witness the controversies regarding the spotted owl, the Alaskan wolf, or the snail darter. The problem with our short term economic philosophy is that it does not concern itself with long-term self-propagation. Our economic system is designed to satisfy immediate needs at the expense of future needs and future generations. Unfortunately, ecosystems are finite systems with limits, and an economic system that does not take this into consideration will destroy an ecosystem's ability to sustain future generations.

When we trade off air, water, and various living species for temporary jobs, are we thinking even one generation ahead? When we bury radioactive and toxic waste, which have life spans for thousands of centuries, in containers that last for fifty years are we thinking at all? Is contemporary society thinking clearly about the air, water, soil, and natural environment that our grandchildren will inherit? Producing pollution for future generations is simply criminal if we mean by criminal dangerous and harmful behavior.

Self-Nourishment

The second phase in understanding a Native American environmental criminology of environmental crime and bioregionalism is to understand the need for self-nourishment. That is, "the members of the community sustain one another in the established patterns of the natural world for the well being of the entire community and each of its members" (Berry, 1988: 166). This is simply to acknowledge that the earth "carries out its operations with an economy and productivity far beyond that of human institutions" (Berry, 1988: 167). Nature produces nothing that is not in some way nourishing to itself.

The Seneca possessed no such technologies that did not reflect the integrity of the natural world. In short, the Seneca produced very little or no non-recyclable waste. To say that the Seneca did not have the means to exploit their surroundings beyond its carrying capacity is to deny the fact that they were aware of birth control and soil depletion and that they fished and hunted seasonally without governmental regulations (Hughes, 1977: 4). Until Euroamerican intervention, the Seneca structured their culture around a knowledge of bioregional self-nourishment and restraint.

Contemporary society has violated this self-nourishment dimension of the bioregion—witness massive deforestation, species extinction, top soil depletion, toxic landfills, strip mining, water and regional air pollution. Most modern technologies operate against nature not in conjunction with it. They seek to conquer rather than work within self-nourishing cycles of nature. Our creation of waste is linear and destructive; it does not enter back into the self-nourishing cycle of life.

Our technologies cause disease and cancer, which do not perpetuate life
as we are beginning to find out more and more every day.

Self-Education

Another way of understanding a Native American environmental
criminology of environmental crime and bioregionalism is through their
mode of education, which entails participatory observation of natural
patterns. Bioregions, according to Berry (1988), are self-educating:

> The third function of a bioregion is its self-education through
> physical, chemical, biological and cultural patterning. Each of these
> requires the others for its existence and fulfillment. The entire
> evolutionary process can be considered as a most remarkable feat of
> self-education on the part of the planet Earth and its distinctive
> bioregional units. Thus the self-educational process observed in the
> natural world forms a model for the human (p. 167).

Observation is the essential component of science, but a science that
sequesters its observations to a laboratory setting severs the
phenomenon's interconnected relationship to the community. For
example, pesticides are made and tested in a laboratory and then applied
to natural settings where pests reside. When the pesticide enters the
ecosystem, however, it does not just kill the pest but enters a complex
food web and inevitably finds its way into our food. Once these
pesticides enter our body, they concentrate in fat cells, increasing our
risk of acquiring cancer. In short, creating technology in a sequestered
laboratory and applying it to complex interactive bioregions could be
considered criminal because it fails to consider the risk imposed on the
whole bioregion.

The Seneca on the other hand, watched and learned patiently from
the interactions that took place in their bioregion and then acted
accordingly. They learned their technologies from watching the natural
science of living ecosystems rather than creating counter-ecological
technologies in a laboratory and imposing them on natural self-
sustaining ecosystems. For example, the Seneca knew about fertilizer,
crop rotation, and natural pesticides through participant observation
within the natural setting. They used fish to fertilize their main staples

of corn, beans, and squash, and they knew that planting these three crops together served not only a practical function but a natural one as well. The corn stalk provided a natural stake for vining beans, while the beans provided a natural enzyme which washed down the corn stalk and acted as a natural pest control (*Iroquois Food Data Sheet 6*, 1989). The Seneca obviously did not realize the chemical interaction of beans and corn; they did, however, realize that they grow together symbiotically through observation. They explained this natural relationship in the myth of "the three sisters."

Lewis Morgan, whose pioneering anthropological work on the Iroquois is quite famous, offers this description of the three sisters and their significance to the Seneca culture. Morgan (1954) writes:

> Perhaps the most beautiful conception in the mythology of the Iroquois is that in relation to the Three Sisters, the spirit of Corn, the spirit of the Bean, and the Spirit of the Squash. These plants were regarded as the special gift of Ha-wen-ne-yu; and they believed that the care of each was entrusted, for the welfare of the Indian, to a separate spirit. They are supposed to have the forms of beautiful females, to be very fond of each other, and to delight to dwell together. This last belief is illustrated by the natural adaption of the plants themselves to grow up together in the same field, and perhaps from the same hill (pp. 152-153).

The Seneca discovered this interactive relationship through observation of natural patterns in nature and gave this miraculous discovery a unique place in their culture by preserving its significance in myth.

Conversely, contemporary society approaches nature as an object that needs to be conquered. We do not observe how things work in nature; rather we seek to find ways to make nature function the way we want it to. We seek to control nature rather than harmonize with it. For example, we are not deterred by the fact that certain plants do not live in the desert because of the heat and dryness. Rather, we think of ways in which we can subvert the desert ecosystem by channeling water from its natural course, by growing vegetation that does not naturally belong there, and by placing huge human populations in areas not designed for them. The Seneca, on the other hand, respected the wisdom of a five billion year old planet and chose to perceive themselves as members of the Earth rather than its controllers. Thus answers to problems of living were found in nature's patterns, not in purely egocentric human wants and ambitions.

Self-Governance

The fourth aspect of a Native American environmental criminology of bioregionalism is self-governance. Berry (1988) writes:

> An integral functional order exists within every regional life community. This order is not an extrinsic imposition, but an interior bonding of the community that enables each of its members to participate in the governance and to achieve that fullness of life expression that is proper to each. . . Humans have traditionally inserted themselves into this community process through their ritual celebrations (p. 168).

Berry (1988) goes on to suggest that these ritual celebrations "are not simply human activities, but expressions of the entire participating community" (pp. 167-168).

The Seneca understood the self-governance of the bioregion and celebrated this through the rituals of Thanksgiving, which were expressions of gratitude and a plea for continued nurturing from nature. There were six of these rituals practiced in conjunction with the seasons and the harvest of various subsistence gifts of nature. Each ceremony:

> proceeded to give thanks to the pantheon in the standard Thanksgiving Prayer, starting with the spirit forces on earth. . .in the lower pantheon the people (categorized as civil chiefs, religious chiefs, ordinary men and women, and children), the waters, the herbs, grasses, and other small plants, the saplings and bushes, the trees, the staple agricultural foods (corn, squash, and beans), the game animals, and the birds; in the middle pantheon, the thunders (who made the rain), the winds, the sun, the moon and the stars; and in the upper pantheon, the major deities and the Creator (Wallace, 1970: 51).

This prayer treated human life as part of the community of life dependent on flora and fauna and took nothing perceived as living for granted.

The first of these ceremonies was the celebration of the new year which was called the Mid-Winter Ceremony celebrated in January or February. The theme of this ceremony "was a testimonial to the creator, of thankfulness for the blessing and indulgences of the last year, and of a supplication to Him to permit man to enjoy yet another spring" (Wallace, 1970: 52). This ceremony "took place five days after the first new moon following the Zenith of the Pleiades" (Wallace, 1970: 52). The ceremony lasted for nine days with each day scheduling a variety of rituals consisting of naming of the children, the acting out of dream revelations, a variety of Thanksgiving dances, medicine rituals, and games (Wallace, 1970: 52-54).

The second ceremony in the calendar year was a Thanksgiving to the Maple for its sap. The event took place toward the end of February or late March and lasted for one day; the ritual included tobacco burning, dance and song (Wallace, 1970: 56).

The corn planting ceremony was the next Thanksgiving ritual which took place in May or early June for one day. This ceremony was marked by the soaking of the seeds of the three sisters and other garden vegetables in the community longhouse. Along with the traditional prayer of Thanksgiving, special thanks was given to the thunder for its rain, and a special plea was made to the sun not to burn the crops with its rays. Also in June, Thanksgiving was offered to the Strawberry for bearing fruit another year. This festival also lasted one day and involved a purification ritual of the village to rid itself of disease, pestilence, and witchcraft (Wallace, 1970: 56).

The Green Corn Festival marked the Seneca midyear and usually occurred sometime in late August or early September, lasting for four days. It was a festival to give thanks for the ripening of the corn for another year. This ceremony also included the naming of the babies born after the new year and the various rituals of dance, song, the women's rites, and stories of war exploits (Wallace, 1970: 50). The Harvest festival came after all the vegetables were harvested and stored away for winter. This festival was a one-day celebration giving thanks for the harvest and an open-armed welcome of fall, the hunting season (Wallace, 1970: 58-59).

While some rural American communities celebrate aspects of their bioregion in festivals of certain vegetables or fruits (e.g., garlic, cherries, apples, etc.), most do not. In fact, most people in the United States take food for granted and do not even have any idea of how it is grown or for that matter where it is grown. Because we have been fortunate enough not to suffer extreme shortages of food, we take its presence for granted, often assuming there will be more than enough. Other countries are not so fortunate, and many say (see Berry, 1986; Strange, 1988) if we continue our current methods of agribusiness we will not be so fortunate either.

Food is essential to all life; "everything living eats something living." To take this for granted is a sort of arrogance that has led other civilizations to their doom when food was no longer plentiful. All that it takes is a couple of consecutive summers like that of 1993, where flooding in the midwest and drought in the Southeast led to huge crop losses. There is also some evidence that the changing weather patterns endemic to the 1980s and early 1990s are possibly linked to aspects of global warming in which humans actions play a major role (for a discussion of this topic see Bates, 1990; Gordon & Suzuki, 1990; Leggett, 1990).

In contrast to the Seneca's rituals of Thanksgiving, Americans on a national level have no holidays commemorating the very basics which sustain our life, mainly the land, water, and air. Instead, we have Earth Day where the media bombards us with a barrage of statistics detailing how we have failed in the previous year to improve the quality of the environment. Granted, this token media warning is important given the state of our environment. But if we had a few days throughout the year set aside to focus on an appreciation for the land that feeds us and the water and air that sustains all life, then maybe our environment would not be in such dire straits.

Self-Healing

Another dimension of a Native American environmental criminology of bioregionalism is the concept of self-healing. Berry (1988) writes:

> The community carries within itself not only the nourishing energies that are needed by each member of the community; it also contains within itself the special powers of regeneration. . .healing takes place through submission to the discipline of the community and acceptance of its nourishing and healing powers (p. 168).

To understand self-healing in the community is to envision nature as it is—a living organism. Nature heals itself as humans heal themselves through rest and appropriate medicines.

The Seneca reflected awareness of the community's self-healing practices through their techniques of agriculture. The method of clearing was controlled slash/burn which left natural fertilizer for the crops. It is estimated that a particular field would be used for fifteen to twenty years with crop rotation, and then the Seneca would eventually move the entire village to a new location leaving the old fields to heal and regenerate. The fields ranged from ten to hundreds of acres, and Wallace (1970) estimates that in the eighteenth century the Seneca produced over a million bushels of corn per year (p. 24). This is quite amazing considering they used no pesticides, herbicides, inorganic fertilizers, tractors, or even plow animals, just hoes and digging sticks. The Iroquois were noted for their agricultural skill and volume of food production, which exceeded any of the other Northeastern Native American tribes (*Iroquois Food Data Sheet 6*, 1989).

While family farming at one time in this country was the norm, it has now become an endangered existence. As such, "modern farming practices are being recognized as the number one environmental issue in our society" (Strange, 1988: 202). Industrial agribusiness has produced some of the most abusive technologies that the land has ever had to confront. The depletion of topsoil, overuse of fertilizers, the pollution of drinking water from farm chemical run-off, depletion of groundwater tables, and the genetic alteration of seeds is undoubtedly posing serious environmental problems that are threatening the future of our bioregions' abilities to heal (see Berry, 1986, for a discussion of these issues). The current mechanistic technology employed on the land does not show any concern nor understanding of the process of self-healing and the need for regeneration. It only thinks of ways of taking more by circumventing the process of healing. Abuse of the land is a crime that has serious ramifications for future generations.

Self-Fulfillment

The final aspect of a Native American environmental criminology of bioregionalism is self-fulfillment. Berry (1988) explains, "[t]he community is fulfilled in each of its components: in the flowering fields, in the great oak trees, in the flight of the sparrow. . .there are the seasonal modes of community fulfillment, such as the mysterious springtime renewal" (p. 168). Humans find fulfillment through "religious liturgies, in market festivals, in the solemnities of the political assembly, in all manner of play, in music and dance. . ." (p. 168). The concept of self-fulfillment asks us to contemplate how our lives reflect a participatory relationship with nature.

The Seneca understood that nature was the grounding for their biological existence and the only source of knowledge for constructing and patterning culture. They understood their place in the web of being and thus were able to fulfill themselves as members of a bioregional community. They understood that consciousness was conceived in nature, and they constructed their culture in such a way as to never forget their roots. The Seneca celebrated their ties with nature and expressed these ties in the way they produced their food, constructed their culture, and organized themselves politically. The whole culture was built on participating in and celebrating the cycles of life which reflected their linkage to nature.

In contrast, contemporary industrial society is estranged and alienated from nature in the most profound ways. We try to conquer nature and make it work the way we wish it to. For example, our laws treat water and air as if they were stationary phenomena, occupying regions with particular boundaries. Air and water, however, know no boundaries; they circulate around the Earth. Our culture is not built on this understanding; we do not ground our culture in the cycles of nature, rather we attempt to exploit and bend nature to meet the needs of our culture.

Many people do not even know how their food is grown or where it is grown. Food for most Americans comes from the grocery store and that is the end of the inquiry. This estrangement from food is considered progress, but is it? It only takes a couple of very dry summers or very wet summers to deplete food supplies as starvation around the world attests. Food is something that should never be taken for granted or left solely to the "agribusiness experts" to produce. Food is the essential basis of all life and this simple fact should never be forgotten.

Contemporary society makes it difficult to be self-fulfilled in nature because most aspects of our culture attempt to remove us from nature. We drive through "pristine" national parks in our metal boxes which spew out an assortment of highly toxic air pollutants. We do not get out and walk in which case we might actually see, touch, taste, smell and hear the sounds of life. Our contact with nature is secondary and tertiary; it comes to us through filters like television or through the tinted windows of our air conditioned, combustion engine automobiles.

Conclusion

A Native American environmental criminology of bioregionalism was grounded in the knowledge that human beings are a part of nature and hence dependent upon its health. Their criminology of environmental crime started with the assumption that we are interconnected with nature and that all human actions have consequences within ecological systems. Accordingly, it is a criminology that prevented environmentally harmful actions by structuring culture in such a way as to make environmentally harmful actions inconceivable. It was a criminology that realized humans cannot conquer nor control nature, and hence we are much better off constructing our lives within ecological constraints. It was a proactive rather than reactive criminology.

Contemporary environmental criminology is reactive. It starts with the assumption that we are separate from nature, and therefore we can transform nature to our liking through control and command technologies. Pollution is perceived as a natural byproduct of our separateness from nature and our ability to transcend nature through our linear applications of technology. Thus, modern society attempts to control pollution rather than eliminate it—a strategy that has been a failure in most cases (see Barnett, 1988; Block, 1993; Greve & Smith, 1992; Hessing, 1993; Kauzlarich & Kramer, 1993; Seis, 1993; and Yeager, 1987).

Contemporary environmental criminology does not question the premises of a society that is jeopardizing its future with problems like global warming, ozone depletion, acid rain, radioactive and toxic waste, deforestation, topsoil depletion and water and air contamination. While everyone realizes these are serious problems, nobody wants to change the behaviors that create them. To use the old adage, "we want our cake and we want to eat it too." But as Commoner (1990) points out "there is no such thing as a free lunch." Environmental regulation has simply not worked and has only served to undermine the need for industrial culture to reexamine the deeper metaphysical and epistemological issues that underlie our profligate behavior.

We cannot go back in time and act like early Native Americans, but we can study and learn from cultures who tended to live within the restraints of ecological systems. The solution to our environmental problems does not lie in more environmental law as much as it lies in redefining our relationship to nature in general and to our bioregions in particular. Only after redefining our relationship to nature will environmental crime shock our collective conscience and lead to changes in our behavior. It is our culture, values, and perceptions that need to be reexamined if we are going to get at the core of solving environmental crime.

NOTES

1. The Seneca were considered by Natives and white settlers alike as a formidable people, who Wallace (1970: 22) describes as: "the most feared, most courted, and most respected Indian tribe in North America." As a part of the Iroquois Federation, the Seneca tribe had the largest population and supplied the most warriors to one of the strongest Indian empires of North America (Francello, 1980: 116-129). The Iroquois Confederacy was formed with five nations sometime around 1450 A.D.—the Mohawks, Onondaga, Oneidas, Cayugas, and the Seneca.

2. Within the Iroquois nation the political structure was quite sophisticated and emphasized values of equality among individuals and among each tribe's representation in governmental affairs (Fenton, 1986). In fact, at the Constitutional Convention Benjamin Franklin suggested modeling the United States Constitution along the same democratic representative principles as the Iroquois league of nations (Francello, 1980: 200).

REFERENCES

Barnett, Harold C. (1988). "The Extent of Social Regulation: Hazardous Waste Cleanup and the Reagan Ideology." *Policy Studies Review* 8 (1): 15-35.

Bates, Albert K. (1990). *Climate in Crisis: The Greenhouse Effect and What We Can Do.* Summertown, TN: The Book Publishing Company.

Berry, Thomas (1988). *The Dream of the Earth.* San Francisco, CA: Sierra Club Books.

Berry, Wendell (1986 [1977]). *The Unsettling of America: Culture & Agriculture.* San Francisco, CA: Sierra Club Books.

Block, Alan, A. (1993). "Into the Abyss of Environmental Policy: The Battle over the World's Largest Commercial Hazardous Waste Incinerator Located in East Liverpool, Ohio." *The Journal of Human Justice* 5 (1): 82-128.

Booth, Annie L., and Harvey M. Jacobs (1990). "Ties that Bind: Native American Beliefs as a Foundation for Environmental Consciousness." *Environmental Ethics* 12 (1): 27-43.

Bowers, C. A. (1993). *Education, Cultural Myths, and the Ecological Crisis: Towards Deep Change.* Albany, NY: State University of New York Press.

Callicott, Baird J. (1989). *In Defense of A Land Ethic.* Albany, NY: State University Press.

Carson, Rachel (1987 [1962]). *Silent Spring.* Boston, MA: Houghton Mifflin Co.

Chafe, Wallace L. (1961). *Seneca Thanksgiving Rituals.* Smithsonian Institution Bureau of American Ethnology Bulletin 183. Washington, DC: United States Printing Office.

Collier, John (1947). *The Indians of the Americas.* New York: W. W. Norton and Company.

Commoner, Barry (1990). *Making Peace with the Planet.* New York: Pantheon Books.

Devall, Bill, and George Sessions (1985). *Deep Ecology: Living as if Nature Mattered.* Salt Lake City, UT: Gibbs Smith, Publisher Peregrine Smith Books.

Durkheim, Emile (1972). *Selected Writings.* Anthony Giddeons (ed.). New York: Cambridge University Press.

Fenton, William N. (1986). "Leadership in the Northeastern Woodlands of North America". *American Indian Quarterly* 10 (1): 21-45.

Francello, Joseph A. (1980). *The Seneca World of Ga-No-Say-Yeh: Peter Crouse, White Captive*. Washington, DC: University Press of America.

Gordon, Anita, and David Suzuki (1990). *It's a Matter of Survival*. Cambridge, MA: Harvard University Press.

Greve, Michael S., and Fred L. Smith, Jr. (eds.) (1992). *Environmental Politics: Public Costs, Private Rewards*. New York: Praeger.

Hargrove, Eugene C. (1989). *Foundations of Environmental Ethics*. Englewood Cliffs, NJ: Prentice Hall.

Hessing, Melody (1993). "Environmental Protection and Pulp Pollution in British Columbia: The Challenge of the Emerald State." *The Journal of Human Justice* (5) 1: 29-45.

Hughes, Donald J. (1977). "Forest Indians: The Holy occupation." *Environmental Review* (2): 3-13.

Hynes, Patricia (1989). *The Recurring Silent Spring*. New York: Pergamon Press.

Iroquois Food Data Sheet 6 (1989). Seneca Iroquois National Museum: Allegany Indian Reservation, New York.

Kauzlarich, David, and Ronald C. Kramer (1993). "State-Corporate Crime in the US Nuclear Weapons Production Complex." *The Journal of Human Justice* 5 (1): 4-28.

Kealey, Daniel A. (1990). *Revisioning Environmental Ethics*. New York: State University Press.

Leggett, Jeremy (1990). *Global Warming: The Greenpeace Report*. New York: Oxford University Press.

Leopold, Aldo ([1949] 1987). *A Sand County Almanac*. New York: Oxford University Press.

Martin, Calvin (1978). *Keepers of the Game: Indian-American Relationships and the Fur Trade*. Berkeley, CA: University of California Press.

McLuhan, T. C. (1971). *Touch the Earth: A Self Portrait of Indian Existence*. New York: Promontory Press.

Morgan, Lewis H. (1954). *League of the HO-DE-NO-SA-NEE of Iroquois*. New Haven, CT: Human Relation Area Files.

Nash, Rodrick Frazier (1989). *The Rights of Nature: A History of Environmental Ethics*. Madison, WI: The University of Wisconsin Press.

Nitsch, Twylah Hurd (1979). *Wisdom of the Seneca*. Albany, NY: The University of the State of New York, The State Education Department, Bureau of Bilingual Education.

Nollman, Jim (1990). *Spiritual Ecology: A Guide to Reconnecting with Nature*. New York: Bantam Books.

Rolston, Holmes III (1988). *Environmental Ethics: Duties to and Values in the Natural World*. Philadelphia, PA: Temple University Press.

Seis, Mark C. (1993). "Ecological Blunders in US Clean Air Legislation." *The Journal of Human Justice* 5 (1): 58-81.

Strange, Marty (1988). *Family Farming: A New Economic Vision*. Institute for Food and Development Policy, San Francisco: University of Nebraska Press.

Wallace, Anthony C. (1970). *The Death and Rebirth of the Seneca*. New York: Alfred A. Knopf.

Wallace, Paul A. W. (1989). *Indians in Pennsylvania*. Harrisburg, PA: The Pennsylvania Historical and Museum Commission Anthropological Series #5.

Wenz, Peter S. (1988). *Environmental Justice*. Albany, New York: State University of New York Press.

Yeager, Peter C. (1987). "Structural Bias in Regulatory Law Enforcement: The Case of the U. S. Environmental Protection Agency." *Social Problems* 34 (4): 330-344.

CHAPTER SEVEN

An Ecofeminist Critique of Environmental Criminal Law

Nanci Koser Wilson

Ecofeminism is an environmental movement that draws attention to the parallels between the victimization of women and the victimization of the environment. To date, ecofeminism has not addressed the specifically *criminal* aspects of environmental harm. This chapter attempts to fill that gap by considering the parallels between women's *criminal* victimization and the *criminal* victimization of "the environment." Let us begin by first discussing the general nature of ecofeminism and ask: how does an ecofeminist critique differ from other ecological critiques?

The Ecofeminist Critique

"The major difference between ecofeminism and the field of environmental ethics is that none of the latter's paradigms succeed in integrating a social analysis" (Salleh, 1992: 196). Ecofeminism does so because its central insight is that femininity and nature share a joint oppression. Female human beings, or conceived more generally, the feminine portion of human nature,[1] has been suppressed, submerged, and denigrated by the masculine portion of human nature. This oppression of feminine human nature is directly linked to the exploitation of the "natural" (i.e. non-human) world. "Nature" is typically conceptualized as feminine, the "other," the "to-be-used," a free "resource." "Culture" is seen as masculine, the necessary controller, the entitled exploiter of the natural world.

Ecofeminism sees that these two forms of exploitation sustain one another. While social ecology also challenges the nature/culture dualism, "Ecofeminism finds misogyny at the root of that opposition" (King, 1989: 19). Hence, we cannot heal our relationship with the "natural world" unless we simultaneously heal our relationship to the feminine aspect of our human nature.

By definition then, while feminism critiques human interrelationships and the ecological perspective critiques human/non-human relationships, ecofeminism proceeds by critiquing the two together. This is a significant advantage in that it recognizes ecology as a *social* science. Flowing from this critique is a vision of justice which links social and environmental justice.

Because the ecofeminist critique focuses specifically on the nature/culture split typical of Western thinking (Griffin, 1989), it aids us in avoiding the mistake of pitting human interests against "nature's" interests, as is typical of contemporary policy. Instead of seeing "man's" defining characteristic as culture (conceived as unnatural) and posing it in opposition to some imaginary wild, natural "state," this perspective skirts the entire culture/nature split in proposing for us a vision of human self as transcendent self identified with all of nature. It thus converts such difficult choices as "spotted owls vs. logger's jobs" into false dilemmas.

Considering our relationship to the land, we may make the following contrasts between a "feminine" model (one based on those aspects of human nature that have been socially constructed as feminine) and a "masculine" model (those aspects of human nature that we have traditionally thought of as masculine).

Within the masculine model, the natural world is seen, just like the female human, as "other," an object to exploit, a free resource. The feminine model, in contrast, seeks sustainability as the goal of both social and natural interaction. Sustainability works within nature's limits, allowing her to self-renew; exploitation works against nature. Since the latter model does not respect limits to "resources," it comes to see all of nature and her "products" as scarce.

Traditional Aspects of Human Nature

MASCULINE MODEL	FEMININE MODEL
Exploitation	Sustainability
Competition	Cooperation
Aggression	Harmony
Dualism	Holism
Homogenization	Diversity

This, of course, leads to a model of competition for these scarce resources rather than cooperation; it features aggressive moves rather than the seeking of harmony. Emphasizing the competitive aspects of nature, seeing evolutionary process as a "struggle of the fittest" meant that "the power and privileges of the powerful, the elimination of the weak and powerless, could be rationalized by appealing to the universal laws of nature" (D'Souza, 1989: 31).

The masculine model is strongly marked by dualism; it starts by separating the human from the natural world, creating, epistemically, two oppositional forces. Nature is opposed to culture, body to spirit or mind. Woman is defined as all natural, man as mostly cultural. The dualism is hierarchical; the first term in each pair is the valued, the second that which is to be contained, controlled, and exploited. A holistic model, in contrast, respects and nourishes diversity, leading toward harmonious interrelationship among diverse parts rather than homogenization (which ultimately is a distortion).

This masculine model has been highly successful during the Industrial Age. It helped humans to exploit to the fullest the resources of the natural world; it rewarded individual humans who adopted this stance in business, professional, and personal life. It is the model some feminists thought they had to adopt to gain equity with men and the model some onlookers feared would succeed so well for women that there would be no femininity left in the world. It is the model that, exported by the Northern hemisphere to the Southern, or Third World, threatens to destroy Earth, our only home.

Understanding the nature/culture split and the hierarchy it created to achieve effective domination provides us with a standpoint from which to critique contemporary environmental law.

Current Environmental Law

Few would disagree that our environmental law is ineffective, but most critiques do not reach to the heart of the matter. The central problem with our law is that it is a-ecological, that is, *it fails to recognize its own subject matter.* The ecological perspective is one of interconnectedness, in which "everything is connected to everything else" (Commoner, 1990) and where everything is interdependent. This interdependence means that the health of all the natural "objects" of each ecosystem is dependent upon other natural objects and upon the health of the whole.

But, as we have seen, in its dualism, the Western tradition conceives the natural as separate from the human. Our law follows suit and splits off various kinds of law and policy making. That we have one law for "the land" and another for business results in ugly, non-real choices within a competitive context in which only the most aggressive can survive. It pits loggers against spotted owls, dairy farmers and poultry ranchers against cows and chickens and, ultimately, the human consumers of their products. It pits various kinds of humans against one another, for example, in the disposal of toxic waste in inner-city ghettos, on Indian reservations, and in the Third World, as in policies which subsidize highways and oil companies thus further polluting the common global air while proposing to Brazil that she refrain from cutting her rain forests in order to protect that same common air.

Because American environmental policy fails to recognize nature's interconnectedness and basic circular nature, it stimulates conflict among a variety of human users of environmental resources. As natural damage progresses, access to life sustaining pure resources becomes more and more limited. Eventually, to deal with these conflicts, the most potent sanction available, the criminal law, is brought to bear on the problem.

Use of the Criminal Sanction in Environmental Law

Let us first consider the unique role of the criminal sanction. The distinguishing characteristic of the criminal law is its movement to prohibit and command. Environmental criminal law, however, is simply a harsher sanction attached to a regulatory process in which little, if any, destruction is forbidden, and little, if any, ecologically-conscious action is commanded. Thus our environmental law's use of the criminal sanction is perverted. Under current environmental law, the criminal sanction is used as a tack-on to the regulatory process (Adler et al., 1991: 299 ff.). When consent decrees, stop and desist orders, and even substantial civil fines no longer work to regulate the worst of the destruction, then corporate officials may perhaps be given a sentence of imprisonment or a criminal fine (Hammett & Epstein, 1993).

The force of criminal law is normally achieved through its protection of the sacred. For example, laws forbidding murder are underlain by a sentiment for the sacredness of human life. Because we do not view the land as sacred but rather as a resource for human use, criminal law in the environmental arena currently tends to be arbitrary, meaningless, ambiguous, and thus ineffective.

But a more vigorous use of the criminal sanction is possible. I want to suggest that consideration of the manner in which criminal law has been recently reshaped to provide protection to human females may point the way toward a more effective criminal environmental law.

The Women's Liberation Movement and the Environmental Movement

Both the Women's Movement and the Environmental Movement engage in attempts to criminalize previously permissible behavior. In this regard, two changes are of fundamental importance; the alteration toward perceiving crime where people did not perceive it previously and the process of beginning to value formerly free resources.

The latter may be the more problematic change. American experience with drug policy demonstrates the rapidity with which citizens are capable of changing their ethical attitudes toward behaviors. In just one century we have alternately allowed and criminally prohibited the use of a variety of chemical substances. We may just as rapidly change our view of environmental damage toward seeing it as truly criminal.

In any case, the process of valuing "free" resources is fundamental to, and logically prior to, the process of criminalization. Until exploitation is recognized, effective criminalization cannot proceed.

Valuing "Free" Resources

The American economic system and American psychological predispositions are deeply built upon a refusal to value nature's "resources" (Barnett, 1994; Waring, 1988). As with the women's liberation movement, the difficult change is in relinquishing dependence upon free inputs.

When the Industrial Revolution pulled men out of the household, women continued to perform their traditional tasks and took on men's traditional household tasks as well. One result was feminized child rearing, which some criminologists saw as a source of male juvenile delinquency.

When women, too, left the household for paid work in the commercial labor market, much traditional "women's work" required rearranging. Many women simply took on two jobs, resulting in the stress and fatigue of a double day. Some household work has been industrialized, as in the case of fast food and commercial day care. And, slowly, some husbands have begun to share in household tasks.

But attempts to allocate household work more fairly have met with strong resistance. Women's unpaid labor made up such a large proportion of the domestic national product that its removal threatened to create a collapse. Waging housework seemed equally impossible; who would pay this wage? the government? husbands? the market? Reallocation of this labor seemed the only solution, but male jobs were premised upon free female labor. Women's work in home maintenance and care of the helpless (e.g., the elderly, sick, children) allowed men to work full time outside the home. If husbands were to take on more housework, the nature of their paid labor and/or their leisure time would change, too.

The Women's Liberation Movement also advocated changes in the nature of women's paid labor. When they entered the commercial labor market, women were treated very much like traditional housewives. Though they were waged, they earned less than men (generally around 2/3 of the male wage), usually worked under the direction of men, and performed tasks related to their sexuality and/or their nurturing capacities (Sokoloff, 1980). Frequently they were confined to the so called "pink ghetto," to jobs that combined all of these characteristics; they were elementary school teachers, nurses, waitresses, and secretaries. While at work they were subject to sexual harassment, an offense which operated either to reaffirm male access to female sexuality (in the workplace as well as the home) or to announce woman's unfitness for "male" jobs. As the Women's Movement rose in response to the increased exploitation, resistance took the form of alternately denying that any exploitation existed or blaming women for abandoning their "natural" duties.

Similar to its tendency to heighten an exploitation that was already present as regards women's work, the Industrial Revolution increased human exploitation of nature. More and more resources, irreplaceable ones like coal and oil and items like forests which require long-term growth, were gobbled up by the "industrial machine." And more and more dangerous byproducts (ordinary garbage, nonbiodegradable human-made chemicals) were dumped into nature's sinks.

Similarly too, proposed legal changes designed to protect nature seemed to threaten the American way of life. Thus, as the Environmental Movement rose in response to this increased exploitation, it too, brought forth resistance and a tendency either to deny that there was any exploitation going on, or to argue that exploitation was nature's way. Just as it was said to be woman's biological destiny to nurture, it is said that nature exists solely to serve mankind. In a strong parallel to the Women's Movement, a reaction has been to blame nature and, more particularly, nature's contemporary guardians, the Environmental Movement organizations.

Recognizing Criminal Behavior

Criminal law enforcement had always had a role to play in protecting scarce resources like game, forests, and wilderness areas. Under newer environmental law, this has expanded to include the protection of air, water, wetlands, and so forth; thus formerly free resources are valued. The change requires a sense that air and water provide a valuable service to human beings and that they can be victims in the classic sense.

At this point in the Women's Movement, the criminal law became important in the struggle to value woman's labor and to protect women from what was increasingly defined as exploitation. There are strong parallels in the new environmental criminalization movements.

One very strong parallel, frequently drawn by ecofeminists, is rape. While the criminal law had long recognized rape as a crime, it had a limited effect. It seemed that only physically violent rapes committed by strangers upon previously chaste victims were prosecutable. Most events that women recognized as rape were seen by others as ordinary sex; that is, coercive sex was normal.

Feminists insisted that rape was not a sexual crime but an assaultive crime. They wanted the law to perceive the coercion in it and to recognize force as the defining element. They asked for changes in the operation of the law, changes in legal reference materials that did not, in effect, categorize particular kinds of women as rapable, as free resources to exploit for self-gratification.

They also pointed out that rape was a consequence of the rapist's tendency to see himself as disconnected from other human beings and from his own sexuality, to see sex as an object "out there."

It was not so much that feminists pushed for the creation of a new crime, but that they attempted to widen its definition. They attempted to persuade their fellow citizens that coercing a date or a wife into sex was real rape. It was said that rape was easy to charge and difficult to prove. But men could be called to account for it. Marital rape was not seen as rape; as one observer noted "if you can't rape your wife, who can you rape?" But husbands could be called to account for this form of assault, and many states adopted laws criminalizing it.

Similarly, environmental crimes committed by large corporations have been treated as regulatory matters and even as "ordinary business."

But these can be redefined so that ordinary business methods don't involve damage, just as consensual sex rather than coercive sex can become the norm. That is, the ordinary way of doing things can be changed.

The process of criminalizing certain uses of nature meets with strong resistance because it is the same net-widening process we have seen in re-conceptualizing much "ordinary sex" as rape. In the environmental arena too, "rape" of the land had always been recognized as wrong; the green movements are attempts to reconceptualize much ordinary land usage as criminal. It had long been an offense to damage that portion of land that belonged to another human being as his property. To see unowned land, earth generally, as "rapable" is an important shift. So, too, is the shift toward prohibiting certain forms of land use, even for owners. In the resistance to laws protecting wetlands on private property, we can hear a deep echo of the resistance toward defining marital rape as real rape.

Another strong parallel is in wife battery. This crime was formerly perceived as a domestic quibble with no serious consequences or as a social problem in which law enforcement had no legitimate role. It was a private family problem.

But it could be addressed as a crime, using ordinary criminal law enforcement tools. Many police departments have adopted presumptive arrest policies for wife battery. This has been accompanied by a change in police perception of the behavior. Rather than seeing battery as an unfortunate extension of the husband's legitimate right to control his wife's household labor and her sexuality, the new policies encouraged officers to define the event as a criminal battery. Rather than counsel the wife to obey her husband's demands and the husband to find some other way of controlling her, officers sent a message that his behavior was prohibited.

Similarly, damage done to the environment in the process of production has been seen as a private matter. If the damage was done to one's own property or upon one's own property, it was perceived as a private matter in which property rights take precedence. Underlying this is the presumption that humans have a right to dominate and control the natural world. But just as women can be redefined as persons in their own right who can be criminally victimized rather than as property to be treated however its owner wishes, the criminal sanction can be applied to those who victimize the environment. The environment, too, can be recognized as existing in its own right and deserving of protection from crime. Rather than seeing environmental damage as an unfortunate by-product of our "masculine" right to control a "feminine" nature's labor, such damage can simply be prohibited.

A final parallel is sexual harassment. This is not only a newly defined offense, it is a relatively new behavior. It consists in using rape-like techniques to obtain a valued end from women. For many, sexual harassment has been seen as ordinary behavior, as mere flirting behavior. Its coercive aspect was ignored because women were not valued outside their sexuality and because some see male access to female sexuality as a right. The parallel to humans' masculine access to a female world's free resources is very strong.

Sexual harassment is sometimes used to keep women out of the workplace or to keep them from advancing within the workplace. Generally its purpose is to maintain access to free resources, to maintain hegemony over those resources. Environmental crime also constitutes an attempt to maintain control--in this case, of the earth and earth's resources.

When sexual harassment was first defined as an offense, reaction was strongly negative. To many, it seemed natural that women existed almost solely as sexual and nurturing beings whose purpose was to serve men in the workplace as well as in the home. Failing to separate out the consensual from the coerced, some expressed fear that sexual relationship itself was threatened. Workplaces have struggled to define policies that would allow for consensual relations while prohibiting coerced sexuality. Strongly marking the sense of male prerogative, many men saw no wrong in Clarence Thomas' alleged treatment of Anita Hill or in the Tailhook scandal but clearly perceived the opportunity for such wrong when the prospect of having homosexuals as commanding officers in the military arose.

The change in perception of these three offenses against women is instructive. Until very recently, while rape was a crime, effectively, it could be committed only against certain kinds of women. Because it was assumed that there was a male entitlement to particular women, wives could not be legally raped. Nor in many cases was a successful prosecution possible where the woman knew the man, had previously had sexual relations with him, or even dated him. Prostitutes were unrapable, and a defense attorney could make a parallel argument for any "unchaste" woman; they were often seen as "open territory" victims (Clark & Lewis, 1977). In effect, though rape was a real crime, only certain women were rapable.

Wife battery was wrong but only because it went a little beyond the bounds of acceptable husbandly control of a wife's labor and her sexuality. Sexual harassment was not even defined as a wrong until very recently.

It is possible that similar changes in perception and in criminalization will occur concerning environmental matters. Ecofeminism will be useful in that process because it is an environmentalism which combines a feminist insight with an ecological insight. These two movements support one another because:

- They both urge the valuing of formerly free resources.

- They both see humans less as isolated atoms competing with one another and more as interconnected parts of a whole. Ecofeminism sees men connected to women, and to their own sexuality (the older, more "masculine" view saw sex as an object to be obtained). It sees humans connected to the environment, the feminine portions of our human nature to the masculine portions.

- In both cases, the central change involves giving up a sense of entitlement and replacing it with interconnectedness. Rather than stressing power/over as a defining human adult characteristic, these movements seek joint empowerment—of women and men, of the environment, and the human being.

- In both cases criminal sanctions will be resisted. And in both cases criminal sanctions will be effective if and only if the object to be protected is valued for itself rather than simply for its services to ego. But, paradoxically, criminal sanctions will aid in this process of valuing.

As Durkheim (1933; 1938) argued, the criminal law tends to create social solidarity around shared values. Thus, the valuing of formerly free resources and the criminalization of damaging behavior constitute a two way street, albeit a rocky and uneven one.

Conclusion

We see, in environmental crime, not an exotic legal creature but instead the familiar face of ordinary crime. We see profit motives, theft of resources, and fraud. The only new thing is a new object to be protected.

But that itself is a major change. Existing power relations will have to be altered. Changing the power that men have over women is not easy; at stake is the entrenched power of 50 percent of the population. In environmental crime, the power base is even stronger. In that case, humans as a class maintain power over all non-humans.

This power is often used in a way that some humans can exert power over other humans by "locking up" valuable "resources" as in the attempt to foist garbage onto poor minority groups or Third World nations. Ecofeminism attempts to address the needs of humans and nature as parts of an interconnected whole, thus avoiding this tendency.

As with crimes against women and the power of men over women, the weak are not totally powerless. They can resist domination. Unlike women, nature cannot resist consciously. Like women, however, nature does resist purposefully; that is, in the sense of achieving self-protection. With nature, the processes are more nearly "automatic." The natural systems will attempt to cleanse themselves of pollutants and to protect the integrity of the whole through adjustment, as the Gaia hypothesis suggests (Thompson, 1987). But as that hypothesis cautions, these adaptations achieve the effect of maintaining earth as a total system, and it may not be such that the system can sustain human life.

Another strong parallel to women's oppression is central, however. At the base of every power structure is the deep dependence of the powerful upon the services of the exploited. To the extent humans recognize their ultimate dependence upon the health of natural systems, protection for these systems will gradually arrive. Whether this recognition will come in time to "work" for us is, as yet, unclear.

In the process of attempting to value formerly free resources, the criminal law will play a pivotal role. Lessons learned from the Women's Movement and its use of the criminal sanction will be especially important.

NOTES

1. Ecofeminism proceeds from an understanding that "feminine" and "masculine" are *socially constructed* aspects of human nature. While biologically female human beings may perhaps contain in their nature a greater proportion of "feminine" traits than do biologically male human beings (because of their differential socialization and social position), both males and females may develop their "feminine" portion, or alternately, neglect and devalue it. "Ecofeminism, specifically, is about a transvaluation of values, such that the repressed feminine, nurturant side of our culture can be woven into all social institutions and practices" (Salleh, 1992: 203). See also Shiva, 1989.

REFERENCES

Adler, Freda, Gerhard O.W. Mueller, and William S. Laufer (1991). *Criminology*. New York: McGraw-Hill.

Barnett, Harold C. (1994). *Toxic Debts and the Superfund Dilemma*. Chapel Hill, NC: The University of North Carolina Press.

Cheney, Jim (1987). "Ecofeminism and Deep Ecology." *Environmental Ethics* (9).

Clark, Lorene, and Debra Lewis (1977). *Rape: The Price of Coercive Sexuality*. Toronto: The Women's Press.

Commoner, Barry (1990). *Making Peace with the Planet*. New York: Pantheon Books.

Daly, Mary (1978). *Gyn/Ecology: The Metaethics of Radical Feminism*. Boston, MA: Beacon Press.

D'Souza, Corinne Kumar (1989). "A New Movement, A New Hope: East Wind, West Wind and the Wind from the South." In Judith Plant (ed.), *Healing the Wounds: The Promise of Ecofeminism.* Philadelphia: New Society.

Durkheim, Emile (1933). *The Division of Labor in Society.* Translated by George Simpson. New York: The Free Press.

Durkheim, Emile (1938). *The Rules of Sociological Method.* Translated by Sarah Solovay and John H. Mueller. New York: The Free Press.

Gray, Elizabeth Dodson (1981). *Green Paradise Lost.* Wellesley, MA: Roundtable.

Griffin, Susan (1989). "Split Culture." In Judith Plant (ed.), *Healing the Wounds: The Promise of Ecofeminism.* Philadelphia, PA: New Society.

_____ (1978). *Woman and Nature: The Roaring Inside Her.* New York: Harper and Row.

Hammett, Theodore M., and Joel Epstein (1993). "Prosecuting Environmental Crime." *NIJ Program Focus* (August).

King, Ynestra (1989). "The Ecology of Feminism and the Feminism of Ecology." In Judith Plant (ed.), *Healing the Wounds: The Promise of Ecofeminism.* Philadelphia, PA: New Society.

_____ (1983). "Toward an Ecological Feminism and a Feminist Ecology." In Joan Rothschild (ed.), *Machina Ex Dea: Feminist Perspectives on Technology.* New York: Pergamon Press, 1983.

Merchant, Carolyn (1980). *The Death of Nature: Women, Ecology and the Scientific Revolution.* San Francisco, CA: Harper and Row.

Ruether, Rosemary Radford (1975). *New Woman/New Earth: Sexist Ideologists and Human Liberation.* New York: Seabury.

Salleh, Ariel Kay (1992). "The Ecofeminism/Deep Ecology Debate." *Environmental Ethics* 14 (3).

_____ (1994). "Deeper Than Deep Ecology: The Eco-Feminist Connection." *Environmental Ethics* 16 (Winter).

Shiva, Vandana (1989). *Staying Alive: Women, Ecology and Development*. London: Zed Books.

Sokoloff, Natalie (1980). *Between Money and Love: The Dialectics of Women's Home and Market Work*. New York: Praeger.

Thompson, William Irwin (1987). *Gaia: A Way of Knowing—Political Implications of the New Biology*. New York: Harper and Row.

Waring, Marilyn (1988). *If Women Counted: A New Feminist Economics*. San Francisco, CA: Harper and Row.

CHAPTER EIGHT

Radical Environmentalism and Crime

Scott Hays
Michael Esler
Carol Hays

Environmental crime is ordinarily associated with violations of criminal laws that protect the environment from polluters. This type of white-collar crime stands in contrast to a blue-collar variety committed by a small but significant group of radical environmentalists. The salient distinction is that while polluters commit crimes against the environment, radical environmentalists commit crimes in the name of the environment. These crimes are justified, at least in part, by the belief that modern society commits far more serious crimes against the environment and the failure of the political process to respond to these abuses has resulted in environmental crisis.

In this chapter, the links between radical environmentalism and criminal activity are investigated. Specifically, the types of criminal activities committed in the name of environmental protection, the world view that justifies these activities, and the impact that these illegal tactics have on the environmental movement are discussed.

Radical Environmentalism and Crime

Committing crimes in the name of environmental protection is not a recent development. Environmental sabotage has occurred since at least the end of World War II, although typically as isolated and unorganized events. Billboards have been felled, survey stakes pulled, and bulldozers disabled as activists responded to society's encroachment on the wilderness. In the early 1970s, militant groups such as the Black Mesa Defense disrupted international conferences on the environment. In Chicago, "the Fox" plugged industrial drains and smokestacks, collected effluent, and dumped it in corporate offices. In Minnesota, the "Bolt Weevils," in Arizona, the "Ecoraiders," in Michigan, the "Billboard Bandits," and in Florida, the "Eco-Commandoes" engaged in similar illegal activities (Bandow, 1991: 255).

Still, "ecotage" or "monkeywrenching" (references to the sabotage of machinery that is used for economic development) has been pursued at unprecedented levels during the last two decades. The primary reason for this growth of ecotage was publication of Edward Abbey's 1975 novel, *The Monkeywrench Gang*. In a case of life following art, radical environmentalists found inspiration for their criminal activities in the exploits of the book's protagonists. For his part, Abbey claimed that "This book, though fictional in form, is based strictly on historical fact. Everything in it is real and actually happened" (Abbey, 1975: dedication page). Others report that the novel was based on the activities of radical environmentalists operating in the American Southwest during the 1960s and 70s (Foreman, 1991a: 119).

The novel also played a role in the formation of Earth First!, one of the organizations most often associated with environmental sabotage. Formed in 1980 by five individuals who had become dissatisfied with the tactics of mainstream environmental politics, Earth First! dedicates itself to "direct action" in defense of the environment.

In fact, Earth First! has no officers, professional staff, bylaws, policy statements, centralized control, or criteria for membership beyond the belief that the protection of earth is of the highest priority (Foreman, 1991a: 20). To the extent that the group has any organization at all, it consists of the editors and writers of the journal that bears its name. The journal regularly publishes articles, editorials, and letters to the editor about ecotage.

In 1985, one of the co-founders of Earth First!, Dave Foreman, co-authored *Ecodefense: A Fieldguide to Monkeywrenching*. As its title suggests, the book is a manual for conducting environmental sabotage. It provides details on how to destroy power line towers, flatten the tires of logging trucks, spike trees, destroy billboards, block timber cuts and road building, and disable bulldozers and other machinery. Similarly, in 1990 Earth First! member Christopher Manes published *Green Rage: Radical Environmentalism and the Unmaking of Civilization*, which, among other things, argues that these tactics are effective ways to combat development projects.

Although Earth First! is willing to justify its illegal activities in various forums, it was founded as and continues to be primarily an action oriented movement (Abbey, 1991: 248; Foreman, 1991a: 20). During the 1980s, members of Earth First! practiced what they preached. Co-founder Mike Roselle reportedly began toppling billboards around Yellowstone Park after reading *The Monkeywrench Gang*. Later, Roselle and three others were arrested for disorderly conduct when they blockaded a logging operation in the Siskiyou National Forest. Another co-founder of Earth First!, Howie Wolke, was arrested and jailed for pulling survey stakes at a Chevron Oil Company road project in a national forest.

Foreman has been arrested six times for his illegal activities. In the most notorious case, Foreman and four others were arrested on an assortment of charges, including destruction of property and conspiracy. The defendants pleaded guilty to reduced charges in a series of plea bargain arrangements. Foreman avoided a prison sentence, but co-defendant Mark Davis was sentenced to six years in prison and fined $20,000 for his role in vandalizing a ski resort in Arizona.

Earth First! helps to organize and otherwise inspire numerous acts of environmental sabotage by radical environmentalists who are only remotely connected to the group. These include road-blocking operations in the Kalmiopsis Wilderness of Oregon in 1983, destruction of hundreds of thousands of dollars' worth of seismic equipment used by oil companies in Wyoming's Bridger-Teton National Forest in the late 1980s, firebombing a $250,000 wood-chipper in Hawaii in 1985, releasing two dolphins held in captivity in Hawaii in 1985, and cutting power lines in Moab, Utah in 1981. Members of Earth First! and those inspired by the group have also participated in spiking trees, blockading forest roads, chaining themselves to bulldozers, climbing trees scheduled to be cut, and raiding labs to release animals.

While most of these crimes are undertaken to directly halt or at least slow development projects, others are designed primarily as theatrical displays to gain media attention. One of the first actions taken by Earth First! was the "cracking" of Glen Canyon Dam over the Colorado River in 1981. With other activists, the media, and the local sheriff looking on, five members of Earth First! unfurled a large sheet of black plastic down the side of the dam to create the appearance of a growing crack in its structure.

Although Earth First! engages in, writes about, and inspires others to commit environmental sabotage to a greater degree than other groups, it is not the only group that has violated laws in the name of environmentalism during the last two decades. Greenpeace has engaged in such actions since its inception in 1969. While Earth First! focuses most of its attention on the protection of wilderness areas, Greenpeace and its spin-off organizations concentrate most of their activities on protecting air and sea environments (Hunter, 1979). Greenpeace has become famous for its highly publicized actions to curtail pollution of waterways, stop nuclear testing, and to save whales and harp seals. It has sent boats to nuclear test zones near the Aleutian Islands. It has challenged Russian, Japanese, and Icelandic whaling operations on the high seas. Often with media in attendance, Greenpeace members have risked their lives by maneuvering small crafts between whalers' harpoons and their prey.

In a highly publicized effort to prevent the killing of harp seals, valued for their white fur, Greenpeace members dyed the seals' coats, thus rendering their pelts economically worthless (and, ironically, more susceptible to attack from their natural predators). Greenpeace also has engaged in actions such as plugging radioactive waste dumps in England and chemical-effluent pipes in New Jersey, hanging banners on polluting plants in Tennessee, and parachuting off smokestacks emitting acid rain in Ohio.

The Sea Shepherd Conservation Society was founded by Paul Watson, a co-founder of Greenpeace who, with other activists, left Greenpeace in a dispute over the use of illegal tactics. Referred to as "Earth First!'s Navy," Sea Shepherd vessels have committed numerous criminal acts in the name of defending whales, dolphins, and seals (Watson, 1991a: 33). They have cut nets, and rammed and disabled fishing vessels on the high seas. In Reykjavik in 1985, members of the Sea Shepherd society sunk two ships of the Icelandic whaling fleet, and heavily vandalized a nearby whale processing plant (Watson, 1991b: 28). In 1993, Watson was arrested for forcing cod fishing boats out of the Grand Banks in Newfoundland.

Beyond these documented cases, it is difficult to assess the frequency with which environmental sabotage is used. Reliable records on the extent to which ecotage takes place are difficult to find. And not all recorded acts of environmental sabotage are committed by radicals pursuing environmental goals (Foreman, 1991a: 153). The most comprehensive record appears in *Earth First!*, which includes coverage of monkeywrenching in virtually every issue. Based on a regular reading of the journal, ecotage appears to be quite extensive. On the other hand, the Forest Service, conservative think tanks, and various timber associations claim that the practice is not common (Law Enforcement Division, U.S. Forest Service (CM), 1994: 257). Of course, since Earth First!, the Forest Service and these other organizations have an interest in promoting their respective positions, each claim must be viewed cautiously.

Justifying Illegal Action to Protect the Environment

It is paradoxical that radical environmentalists take pride in their image as action oriented, counter-cultural (even anti-cultural) "warriors" for the environment while simultaneously providing thoughtful justifications for their illegal activities. Indeed, adherents of radical environmentalism have been prodigious in their writings. This is particularly true of members of Earth First!, such as Foreman. Their writings, therefore, provide valuable insight into the belief system that leads this subculture of the environmental movement to commit crimes in the name of the environment.

Radical environmentalists who engage in ecotage share a common set of beliefs about the relationship between the environment and society that serves to justify their illegal tactics. These include an environmental ideology that, ultimately, devalues humans; a belief that the environment is in crisis; that the political process is incapable of producing necessary changes to end the crisis; and that committing crimes is an effective and useful tactic in the struggle to save the environment.

The Deep Ecology World View

Radical environmentalists who engage in illegal activities share a belief in "deep ecology" or "biocentrism." The twin axioms of deep ecology are the rejection of anthropocentrism, the idea that human interests are the measure of all value, and the acceptance of biodiversity, the idea that maintaining diversity of life is the highest value to pursue (Naess, 1991: 169). Aldo Leopold, whose work serves as an important inspiration for deep ecology, opined "[a] thing is right when it tends to preserve the integrity, stability, and beauty of the biotic community. . ." (Naess, 1991: 171).

According to this viewpoint, humans are a part of nature, but have no greater claim to the environment than other living things. Foreman (1991a) states, "[a] Grizzly Bear. . .has just as much right to life as any human has, and is far more important ecologically. All things have intrinsic value, inherent worth. Their value is not determined by what they will ring up on the cash register of the gross national product, or by whether or not they are good. They are good because they exist" (p. 3).

In theory, this applies to humans as well as other life forms. However, several implications of the deep ecology world view actually serve to devalue humans. Since wilderness produces the greatest amount of biodiversity, deep ecologists place the highest value on protecting wilderness areas. For them, wilderness is the essence of natural life and holds a spiritual as well as material significance: "[Wilderness areas] are the places that hold North America together, that contain the genetic information of life, that represent the eye of sanity in a whirlwind of madness" (Foreman, 1991a: 111).

It follows that human society becomes increasingly separated from nature as it develops. Human traits associated with development—material self-interest, and the powers to reason, develop technology, and transform nature—are seen as unnatural and ultimately destructive of nature (the idea that humans in developed societies are alienated from nature is reflected in deep ecologists' references to wilderness as the "Big Outside"). From a biocentric perspective, then, humans in developed societies are less valued than other forms of life because their culture poses a major threat to biodiversity (Manes, 1991: 128; Naess, 1991: 170).

The devaluation of humans is further promoted by deep ecology's failure to develop a theory of social development. In fact, some deep ecologists dismiss the need for social theory as overly "humanist." In an outline of the principles guiding Earth First!, Foreman calls for going "beyond the tired, worn-out dogmas of left, right, and middle-of-the-road. These doctrines, whether blaming capitalism, communism, or the devil for all the problems in the world, merely represent internecine squabbles between different factions of humanism" (Foreman, 1991a: 30). For deep ecologists, going "beyond" social doctrines often means developing a relatively theoretical, action-oriented program to protect the environment. As Foreman puts it, "We are warriors. Earth First! is a warrior society. We have a job to do" (p. 33).

This approach to the relationship between society and the destruction of nature distinguishes deep ecology from the approaches of other radical environmentalists. For instance, when ecofeminists situate the roots of environmental degradation in the organization of a patriarchal social order or green socialists locate it in the workings of a capitalist culture, they identify a particular organization of society as the root cause of environmental problems. On the other hand, lacking a developed theory that accounts for the social forces that drive humans to degrade nature and how society might be transformed to become more compatible with nature, deep ecology concludes that humanity itself is to blame: "Our environmental problems originate in the hubris of imagining ourselves as the central nervous system or the brain of nature. We're not the brain, we are a cancer on nature" (Botkin et al., 1990: 48).

It is hardly surprising, then, that deep ecology gives rise to chants of "Down with Human Beings" around Earth First! campfires (Bookchin & Foreman, 1991: 19), Earth First! bumperstickers that read, "Visualize Industrial Collapse" and "Pregnancy: Another Deadly Sexually Transmitted Disease," statements that AIDS and famine are desirable because they reduce human population without destroying the environment, or calls for reducing the world population to one hundred million.

Many in Earth First! have distanced themselves from these positions (Dawn, 1993). Moreover, deep ecologists consistently denounce violence against humans when practicing environmental sabotage. Abbey (1984), for instance, distinguishes between "ecotage" (or "ethical" monkeywrenching) and terrorism in that the former does not involve violence against humans, only their property (p. 18). While the distinction may be lost on some, it serves an important role in justifying sabotage for environmental radicals. As long as no one is hurt, the practice is seen as consistent with the deep ecology axiom that diversity of life (including human) is more important than the integrity of inanimate objects, especially objects that are used to diminish diversity of life (Foreman, 1991a: 121).

Still, it is disingenuous for radical environmentalists who engage in sabotage to profess their belief in non-violence. The core assumptions of deep ecology and their implications for developed societies are no more inconsistent with a program of violence against humans than they are with the destruction of property. Moreover, radical environmentalists certainly understand that even the most well-intentioned efforts to avoid harming people may eventually result in accidental injuries and death. Indeed, without the threat of such accidents, environmental sabotage loses much of its force.

The flippant defenses that radical environmentalists use to respond to these criticisms also belie their calls for non-violence against humans. For instance, in a chapter titled "In Defense of Monkeywrenching," Foreman (1991a) dismisses charges of being an "ecoterrorist" by countercharging that the "true" ecoterrorists are the despoilers of nature (p. 124). Further, Foreman simultaneously denies that environmental sabotage has injured anyone and blames the opposition for injuries when they do occur from ecotage. For instance, in discussing injuries that result from tree spiking, he blames the Forest Service and mill operators for not heeding warnings when trees are spiked and for not maintaining band saws in proper operating condition. He concludes, ". . .it becomes a matter of debate as to who is responsible if a saw encounters a spike" (p. 154).

The apparent inconsistency between deep ecologists' calls for non-violence and basic features of the deep ecology world view dissolves upon close examination of the context in which calls for non-violence are made. That is, non-violence is supported for practical reasons, not for reasons that inhere in the deep ecology world view itself. For deep ecologists, non-violence is a tactic in appeals for popular support (Wolke, 1991: 251; Foreman, 1991a: 114, 124, 128; this point is advanced later in this chapter).

Given the perspective that wilderness is the essence of nature, that humans in developed societies are artificial and destructive of wilderness and lacking a social theory that accounts for these destructive propensities, deep ecology devalues humans and thus creates a context in which committing crimes in the name of the environment loses much of its stigma. In conjunction with other aspects of radical environmentalism, such as the assumption of environmental crisis, the futility of mainstream politics, and the utility of sabotage as a tactic, it becomes, for some, a moral imperative.

Environmental Crisis

Radicals who commit crimes in the name of environmental protection perceive the environment to be in crisis. Manes (1990) writes, "[Radical environmentalism] is based on one simple but frightening realization: that our culture is lethal to the ecology that it depends on" (p. 22). Similarly, Foreman states, "We live in perilous times. The peril is of our own making, and many of us probably deserve it. But the children, and the native peoples of this world, and most important, all the other species sashaying around in this great dance of life don't deserve the peril we have created" (Foreman, 1991a: viii).

The opening sentence of *Confessions of an Eco-Warrior* states, "We are living now in the most critical moment in the three-and-a-half-billion-year history of life on Earth" (Foreman, 1991a: 1). Later he states, "Human beings have stepped beyond the bounds; we are destroying the very process of life" (p. 4), and "In the space of a few generations we have laid waste to paradise" (p. 110). Wolke (1991) writes, "Once wilderness is gone, in most places geologic time will be needed for nature to restore it. And once the living organisms that depend on wilderness become extinct, they're gone forever. . ." (p. 247).

The depths of the perceived crisis are revealed in the metaphors used to describe it. Radical environmentalists refer to the "blitzkrieg" of logging operations (Thomas, 1991: 22), the "war" on animals (Foreman, 1991a: 1), and the "battle" for life (Foreman, 1991a: 2). The destruction of wilderness is likened to matricide (Mills, 1991: 167). Wolf-control policies are compared to Hitler's Final Solution (Foreman, 1991a: 90), and the loss of species to timber harvesting is called a "more heinous holocaust" than the Nazi actions during World War II (Sayen, 1991: 94).

Given the magnitude and immediacy of the crisis, extraordinary measures are required. As Foreman (1991a) states, ". . .there isn't time for me to achieve perfection before trying to save the Earth. It's got to be done now" (p. viii). He continues: "Why shouldn't I be emotional, angry, passionate? Madmen and madwomen are wrecking this beautiful blue-green living Earth. Fiends who hold nothing of value but a greasy dollar bill are tearing down the pillars of evolution a-building for nearly four thousand million years" (p. 5). Perhaps most telling is the analogy used by Foreman in justifying extreme measures in defense of the environment: "You walk into your house, there's a gang of Hell's Angels raping your wife, your sister, your old mother. You don't sit down and talk balance with them, you go out and get your twelve-gauge shotgun and come back in and blow them to hell" (Killingsworth & Palmer, 1992: 217).

Failure of the Political Process

Radical environmentalists who engage in sabotage do not rely only on illegal methods to meet their goals. Typically, they encourage participation in political campaigns, lobbying, filing lawsuits, and other forms of mainstream political activity as well as in civil disobedience. Nevertheless, radical environmentalists who participate in sabotage fundamentally distrust the political process. As political outsiders they believe that the process is deeply flawed and that exclusive participation in conventional politics co-opts radicals.

Much of the radical environmental critique of the political process is based on the failure of government to stop the illegal activities of those who harm the environment (Watson, 1991b: 28). Government itself is frequently charged with violating the law. Thus, Congress is accused of an "end-run" on the Endangered Species and the National Environmental Policy Acts (Foreman, 1991a: 123); the practice of attaching riders to legislation is viewed as a "veiled attempt to circumvent the democratic and legal process" (Carlton, 1991: 105); the Forest Service, Bureau of Land Management, Park Service, the Fish and Wildlife Service, and the FBI are denounced as "outlaw" agencies that engage in "criminal acts" (Thomas, 1991: 16, 20; Czolgosz, 1991: 27; Kincaid, 1991: 44; Carlton, 1991: 107; Jacobson, 1993: 29; Bookchin & Foreman, 1991: 44); and court rulings are dismissed as "clearly unconstitutional" (Thomas, 1991: 20).

Some of these references are to violations of natural law or crimes against nature (Watson, 1991a: 28; Watson 1991b: 36; Foreman, 1991a: 121). These references are rooted in a legalistic approach to environmentalism that favors assigning rights to nature (Foreman, 1991a: 143; Nash, 1989). Government is also criticized for ignoring the will of the people when majorities favor stronger environmental protection (Foreman, 1991a: 141). Government thus violates the spirit of the law even when it follows the letter of the law. Still other references to the illegal actions of government are quite clearly in regard to violations of the letter of the law. Here, radical environmentalists usually criticize one branch of government (often an agency such as the Forest Service) for violating laws duly established by another branch (such as Congress or the courts).

It is surprising that radical environmentalists place so much emphasis on legal aspects of the political process. Given their obvious lack of respect for certain types of law, it seems incongruous for them to criticize others for violating the law. More fundamentally, it is difficult to think of concepts that are more anthropocentric than those of "law" and "rights." Law serves to rationalize the basic institutions of any society. Given their critique of this culture, it seems out of place for radical environmentalists to adopt legalistic concepts as standards for evaluation. If nothing else, it places them in the difficult position of justifying their violations of law in the name of enforcing the law (Watson, 1991b: 28-32; Watson 1991a: 39).

Environmentalists who support environmental sabotage share a deep sense of pessimism that mainstream politics can ever work to protect the environment. Foreman (1991a) states, ". . .the political process is stacked in favor of those who are gobbling up fragile natural areas for a fast buck" (p. 122). Much of the pessimism stems from radical environmentalists' hostility to compromise, which, of course, is central to the political process. This hostility is enunciated in the Earth First! motto, "No Compromise in Defense of the Earth." It is manifested most powerfully in the disdain that radical environmentalists hold for "reformist" groups that participate in conventional politics.

A number of environmental radicals who promote the use of sabotage began their careers as members of mainstream environmental organizations but departed when they became disenchanted with the reformist approaches of these groups (Watson, 1991a: 38; Foreman, 1991a: 13-18). For these radicals, reformist organizations inevitably become "professionalized" and thus more concerned with the viability of the organization than the cause (Foreman, 1991a: 201-206) or, worse, get co-opted by the forces that the organization was originally organized to fight (Watson, 1991b: 32). Wolke avers, "By submerging ourselves in the process; indeed, by making an effort to exhaust the process prior to conducting illegal but moral resistance, we guarantee more fodder for the dragon" (Wolke, 1991: 254).

Given the limitations of working within the system and the inconsequential, even counterproductive, results produced by mainstream environmental organizations, radical environmentalists turn to more unconventional tactics. Abbey (1991) argues, "It is not enough to write letters to Congressmen, deliver sermons, make speeches, or write books. The West we love is under violent attack; the Earth that sustains us is being destroyed. . . We must continue to take part in political action, to reason with our adversaries, to think and mediate and develop a philosophy that gives moral justification to what we believe. But we must also be prepared to put our bodies on the line. Philosophy without action is the ruin of the soul" (Abbey, 1991: 248).

Environmental Sabotage as a Tactic

For some radical environmentalists, sabotage is an act of desperation, an effort to lash out at a system that they see as destructive and beyond their control (Mills, 1991: 167). Others view sabotage as a way of reclaiming their identity as natural, spiritual beings in an increasingly artificial world (Foreman, 1991a: 115-146). For most, however, environmental sabotage has strategic value as one of a number of tactics that can effectively help protect the environment.

Environmental radicals who engage in sabotage for tactical reasons believe that it serves short- and long-term goals. In the short-term, they believe that sabotage can raise the cost of development projects, discourage developers, and thereby slow or even halt specific projects (Foreman, 1991a: 113, 132). The strategy is to protect as much nature as possible from destruction before more fundamental social changes can be made (Foreman, 1991a, 144). Or, more darkly, it is promoted as a means for preserving as much of the natural environment as possible before the "inevitable demise of today's biological aberration" (Wolke, 1991: 256). Environmental sabotage is also seen as a useful tactic for the long term transformation of society toward the principles of deep ecology. Most acts of ecotage are designed to generate favorable publicity for the cause as well as to end specific projects. Greenpeace and the Sea Shepherd Society are especially adept at generating publicity for their actions. They carefully document the illegal activities of their targets and regularly distribute the results to the media (Watson, 1991a: 40-41). Sometimes arrangements are made for the media to be present while the sabotage takes place. Moreover, some activities are staged purely as media events, often with good humor, such as the "cracking" of the Glen Canyon dam.

The care that radical environmentalists take to nurture an image of themselves as non-violent, selfless heroes of the environmental movement is part of the effort to generate positive publicity for their cause. The image of Greenpeace volunteers risking their lives by positioning themselves between harpoon boats and whales is a classic example. Environmental radicals generally situate their actions in the long tradition of civil disobedience in the United States. Thus, they associate themselves with the rebels of the Boston Tea Party and American Revolution, Henry David Thoreau's civil disobedience, the Underground Railroad, Martin Luther King's civil rights activities, the labor movement, and the protests against the Vietnam War (Foreman, 1991a: 119-136).

Radicals also portray their tactics as a form of "bearing witness," the Quaker tradition of standing forth and setting an example for others (Killingsworth & Palmer, 1992: 196; Devall, 1992: 59). They also invoke conservative images when justifying their activities. They play on the "right to life" movement by suggesting that pro-life forces should extend their concept of life to include non-human forms. However, they also suggest that a biocentric right to life movement might entail abortion as a means for reducing human population, thereby promoting biodiversity (Flowers, 1991: 145).

Radical environmentalists also believe that their extreme positions and tactics add legitimacy to the activities of reform-oriented environmental organizations. By taking extreme positions and engaging in controversial tactics, radical environmentalists allow liberal reform groups to appear to be more moderate than they otherwise would. By the same token, radicals hope to transform the terms of the environmental debate and in the process move the entire environmental movement closer to their biocentric perspective (Dawn, 1993; Killingsworth & Palmer, 1992: 227).

The Impact of Environmental Sabotage

It is difficult to assess the impact of environmental sabotage on the environment. Ecotage has not stopped development in wild areas or ended the exploitation of the seas, as some optimistically predicted (Foreman, 1991a: 133). Arguably, ecotage has played a role in stopping or slowing a number of specific projects (Killingsworth & Palmer, 1992: 216; Foreman, 1991a: 133). However, since more conventional tactics were also used to fight these projects, it is not clear precisely what role sabotage played in any of them.

The impact of environmental sabotage can be measured in other ways, however. The Association of Oregon Loggers estimates that the average monkeywrenching incident costs $60,000. Earth First! figures the cost to top $100,000 when investigative, security, legal, and insurance costs are included. Earth First! further estimates that ecotage costs industry and government from $20-25 million annually (C.M., 1991: 258).

Ecotage has also resulted in injuries, although documented cases are relatively few in number. One serious injury to a sawmill worker has been attributed to tree spiking; however, since arrests were never made it is not known what motivated the action (Bandow, 1991: 257). Radical environmentalists are as likely to be the victims of violence as they are the perpetrators of it. In 1990, two members of Earth First! were injured when a bomb exploded in their car. It is not clear whether it was a bomb that they intended to use for sabotage, as police originally suspected, or whether they were the intended victims. The case has never been solved. In 1985, the Greenpeace ship *Rainbow Warrior* was sunk in the South Pacific, reportedly by French commandoes, after the ship interfered with French nuclear testing in the region. A crew member was killed.

Local, state, and federal police agencies and prosecutors take environmental sabotage seriously as evidenced by the aggressive manner in which they typically prosecute those accused of environmental crimes. State and local jurisdictions often seek and receive maximum fines and jail sentences for convicted ecoteurs. The FBI actively investigates groups such as Earth First! and Greenpeace (Devall, 1992: 60; Manes, 1990). In its 1989 case against Foreman and others, the government based its case on information generated by FBI infiltrators and 806 hours of conversations recorded by wiretaps. The government recorded 1,356 phone calls to and from the home of one of the defendants alone. Moreover, Congress added an anti-monkeywrenching rider to its 1988 Drug Act, making environmental sabotage a federal offense (18 USCA, Sec. 1864). Oregon has passed similar legislation and other states are considering it (C.M., 1991: 259).

Environmental sabotage has met with strong reaction from industries involved in logging, mining, cattle grazing, and other activities that are the targets of ecotage. Logging associations and other conservative organizations in western states have formed alliances to monitor and control acts of sabotage and to counter favorable publicity that radicals might receive from their activities (Devall, 1992: 60; C.M., 1991: 257; Freedman, 1991: 101; Bandow, 1991: 259).

Environmental sabotage has had, perhaps, its most significant impact on the environmental movement itself. Moderates in the environmental movement are divided in their response to the use of these tactics. Some acknowledge the utility of illegal methods for increasing awareness of environmental issues (Bandow, 1991: 259). Arguably, attention created by acts of ecotage has helped persuade mainstream groups such as the National Audubon Society and the Wilderness Society to make ancient forest protection a priority (Foreman, 1991a: 215). Arguably, too, environmental sabotage has generated attention for the deep ecology world view amongst people who otherwise would not have considered it. Undoubtedly, the radical positions taken by deep ecologists have allowed moderate groups to take bolder positions on environmental issues without the fear of being marginalized in the political process (Killingsworth & Palmer, 1992: 206).

Other environmental moderates believe that environmental sabotage is counterproductive. They describe these acts as "ecoterrorism" and decry the use of violence for any purpose. They criticize other mainstream environmental organizations and liberal politicians for not distancing themselves from these radical tactics. They fear that ecotage will bring the entire environmental cause into disrepute (Bandow, 1991: 254-260).

The use of illegal tactics has also driven a wedge between radical environmentalists. As early as the late 70s, Greenpeace purged a number of activists over a dispute about tactics. The result was the formation of The Sea Shepherd Society. The two organizations have been hostile to each other ever since (Watson, 1991b: 32, 38). In 1983, the first editor of *Earth First!* resigned over a dispute about the publication of monkeywrenching tips in Foreman's "Dear Ned Ludd" column (Foreman, 1991b: 8). More recently, Foreman and other former members of Earth First! left the organization to form Wild Earth. The split was precipitated by concerns that Earth First! was becoming too much of a social movement, and by the fallout over criminal prosecutions for environmental sabotage (Foreman, 1991c: 262; Davis, 1993: 3).

More fundamentally, the use of environmental sabotage is related to a major division that has emerged between "deep ecologists" and "social ecologists." Although both can be fairly described as radical environmental movements, social ecologists criticize deep ecology for its general devaluation of humans. It is noteworthy that while they share many ideas about the causes of and solutions to environmental problems, social ecologists are significantly less enthusiastic about the practice of environmental sabotage (Bookchin & Foreman, 1991).

In the end, radical environmentalists who engage in sabotage in the name of the environment share a common worldview that gives emphasis to the environmentally destructive propensities of humans, the idea that the environment is in crisis and the political process is incapable of responding to it, and that extreme tactics have strategic value. While other environmentalists share aspects of this worldview, those who engage in sabotage generally adhere to all of its components. Although environmental saboteurs represent a small proportion of all environmentalists, their impact has been greater than their numbers would suggest. Due as much to their willingness to publicize their activities as the activities themselves, these radicals have generated attention to and discussion about a wide range of environmental values that otherwise would not have received the same level of attention.

REFERENCES

Abbey, Edward (1975). *The Monkey Wrench Gang.* New York: Avon.

_____ (1984). "The Plowboy Interview: Slowing the Industrialization of Planet Earth." *Mother Earth News* (May/June): 17-24.

_____ (1991). "Ed Abbey to Earth First!" In John Davis (ed.), *The Earth First! Reader* (pp. 247-249). Salt Lake City: Peregrine Smith.

Bandow, Doug (1991). "Radical Activism Cannot Help Protect the Environment." In Neal Bernards (ed.), *The Environmental Crisis: Opposing View Points* (pp. 254-260). San Diego, CA: Greenhaven.

Bookchin, Murray, and Dave Foreman (1991). *Defending the Earth.* Boston: South End Press.

Botkin, Daniel, Dave Foreman, James Lovelock, Frederick Turner, Robert D. Yaro, and Michael Pollan (1990). "Only Man's Presence Can Save Nature." *Harpers* 280: 37-48.

Carlton, Jasper (1991). "Of Politics, Extinctions, and Ecological Collapse." In John Davis (ed.), *The Earth First! Reader* (105-117). Salt Lake City: Peregrine Smith.

C. M. (1991). "Monkey Wrenching: An Appraisal." In John Davis (ed.), *The Earth First! Reader* (pp. 256-262). Salt Lake City: Peregrine Smith.

Czolgosz, Leon (1991). "Late Texas News." In John Davis (ed.), *The Earth First! Reader* (pp. 27-28). Salt Lake City: Peregrine Smith.

Davis, Mark (1993). "An Open Letter to Susan Zakin, Author of Coyotes and Town Dogs." *Earth First!* 14: 1,3.

Dawn, Kimberly (1993). Staff/Editor of *Earth First!* Personal Interview (October).

Devall, Bill (1992). "Deep Ecology and Radical Environmentalism." In Riley Dunlap and Angela Mertig (eds.), *American Environmentalism* (pp. 51-62). Philadelphia: Taylor and Francis.

Flowers, R. Wills (1991). "This is Pro-Life?" In John Davis (ed.), *The Earth First! Reader* (pp. 143-149). Salt Lake City: Peregrine Smith.

Foreman, Dave (1991a). *Confessions of an Eco-Warrior.* New York: Harmony.

_____ (1991b). "Foreword." In John Davis (ed.), *The Earth First! Reader* (pp. 7-11). Salt Lake City: Peregrine Smith.

_____ (1991c). "Good Luck, Darlin' It's Been Great." In John Davis (ed.), *The Earth First! Reader* (pp. 262-268). Salt Lake City: Peregrine Smith.

Foreman, Dave, and Bill Haywood (1985). *Ecodefense: A Field Guide to Monkey Wrenching.* New York: Harmony.

Freedman, Mitch (1991). "Old Growth vs. Old Mindsets." In John Davis (ed.), *The Earth First! Reader* (pp. 96-105). Salt Lake City: Peregrine Smith.

Hunter, R. (1979). *Warriors of the Rainbow: A Chronicle of the Greenpeace Movement.* New York: Holt, Rinehart, and Winston.

Jacobson, Mat. (1993). "Forest Service Sabotages Clinton Directive to End Logging Subsidies." *Wild Earth* 3 (2): 29-32.

Killingsworth, M., and Jacqueline Palmer (1992). *Ecospeak: Rhetoric and Environmental Politics in America.* Carbondale, IL: Southern Illinois University Press.

Kincaid, Clive (1991). "The BLM." In John Davis (ed.), *The Earth First! Reader* (pp. 45-50). Salt Lake City: Peregrine Smith.

Law Enforcement Division of the U.S. Forest Service (1994). Interviews with staff members in the office of Al Truillo, Washington, D.C. (June).

Manes, Christopher (1990). *Green Rage: Radical Environmentalism and the Unmaking of Civilization.* Boston: Little, Brown and Co.

————— (1991). "Technology and Mountain Thinking." In John Davis (ed.), *The Earth First! Reader* (pp. 128-132). Salt Lake City: Peregrine Smith.

Mills, Stephanie (1991). "Thoughts from the RRR." in John Davis (ed.), *The Earth First! Reader* (pp. 164-168). Salt Lake City: Peregrine Smith.

Naess, Arne (1991). "Deep Ecology and Conservation Biology." In John Davis (ed.), *The Earth First! Reader* (pp. 168-172). Salt Lake City: Peregrine Smith.

Nash, Roderick Frazier (1989). *The Rights of Nature.* Madison, WI: University of Wisconsin Press.

Sayen, Jamie (1991). "Developers Take the Lead in the Northeast 10 Million." In John Davis (ed.), *The Earth First! Reader* (pp. 80-96). Salt Lake City: Peregrine Smith.

Thomas, Chant (1991). "Return to Bald Mountain." In John Davis (ed.), *The Earth First! Reader* (pp. 20-25). Salt Lake City: Peregrine Smith.

Watson, Paul (1991a). "Raid on Reykjavik." In John Davis (ed.), *The Earth First! Reader* (pp. 28-33). Salt Lake City: Peregrine Smith.

————— (1991b). "Tora! Tora! Tora!" In John Davis (ed.), *The Earth First! Reader* (pp. 33-42). Salt Lake City: Peregrine Smith.

Wolke, Howie (1991). "Thoughtful Radicalism." in John Davis (ed.), *The Earth First! Reader* (pp. 249-256). Salt Lake City: Peregrine Smith.

CHAPTER NINE

Monkeywrenching: Practice in Search of a Theory

Thomas C. Shevory

"It ain't junior high anymore."

Dave Foreman

The following chapter involves an attempt to analyze and criticize "monkeywrenching" as a mode of political action. While the radical environmental movement has been the subject of much journalistic commentary and has provided a fair body of writing, the practices of monkeywrenching have not been systematically examined as part of broader historical traditions of disobedience and dissent. The first part examines various practices that could be said to constitute monkeywrenching. Next, monkeywrenching within broader traditions of resistance to civil authority—liberal and what I call "republican." The chapter addresses some traditional justifications of disobedient activity and attempts to place monkeywrenching within them.

Theoretical justifications of the practices of monkeywrenching are found in patchwork form in the writings mostly of Edward Abbey and Dave Foreman. These writings place a heavy reliance on action at the expensive of theory. This is a mistake. For monkeywrenching to be a successful or even legitimate feature of the struggle for environmental preservation, it must weave itself into the broader movement of "radical ecology."

"Self-defense against attack is one
of the basic laws not only of human
society but of life itself, not only of
human life but of all life."

Edward Abbey

Monkeywrenching as a Practice

The practice of monkeywrenching is usually associated with
radical environmentalists. Radical environmentalism is a disparate
political movement that developed largely in response to perceived
failures of conventional environmental politics. (Dave Foreman, for
example, founder of Earth First!, began as a lobbyist for the Wilderness
Society.) Since radicals were disenchanted with the results achieved by
routine political practices (like lobbying), they have been generally
hostile to attempts to centralize control within the radical movement
itself.

Earth First!, which is the largest and most visible radical group
(estimated to have a membership of roughly 12,000) (Short, 1991: 175),
hardly represents a unified political force. Earth First!'s Dave Foreman,
having been convicted, along with several others, in federal court of
cutting powerlines to the Palo Verde Nuclear Power Plant, has now
disassociated himself from the group. (For a discussion of the Palo
Verde case, see Zakin, 1993.) Foreman's disaffection has stemmed, it
seems, partly from his legal troubles, partly from his disenchantment
with the group's move toward institutionalization, and partly from Earth
First!'s associations with the more traditional left (Foreman, 1990:
219).[1] Other radical groups include Greenpeace (which Rik Scarce has
termed the "bridge to radicalism"), Sea Shepherds (the "navy" to Earth
First!'s "army" according to its director Paul Watson (Parfit, 1990: 185),
the "somewhat tamer" Earth Island Institute (Scarce, 1990: 28) and even
the "more rambunctious side of the Sierra Club" (Foreman, 1990, 217).

Radical environmentalism in the U.S. has tended to be a western movement, much of its attention being focused upon the preservation of the few remaining wilderness lands. The movement is essentially defined by its philosophy of direct action. Monkeywrenching, then, is a form of direct political action undertaken for environmental protection.

Radical environmentalism can be distinguished from radical ecology. Radical ecology, a term coined by Carolyn Merchant (1992), connotes a broad-based set of intellectual and political responses to the contemporary environmental crisis. Radical ecology connects various forms of environmental action through an array of theoretical re-envisionings. Radical ecology includes radical environmentalism, social ecology, eco-feminism, and various ecological sciences. Radical ecology is, in other words, highly diverse and multifaceted. Radical ecology reveals that theoretical and political inconsistency and multiplicity are inevitable in the face of the crises that we confront. Radical ecology provides a matrix (or maybe a "web") from within which we can rethink and remake the world, recognizing that theory and practice are interwoven. Thus, radical ecology implies theoretical and practical responses to continued environmental deterioration.

The term "monkeywrenching" as applied to radical environmental action was coined by Edward Abbey in *The Monkeywrench Gang*, published in 1975. Abbey's characters—the most memorable of whom was George Washington Hayduke, Vietnam vet and borderline psychopath—cut down billboards, blew up bridges, pulled up survey stakes, burned road building equipment, and dreamed of destroying the Glen Canyon Dam. Abbey (1975) delighted in the anti-intellectualism of his characters, especially Hayduke, whose response to intellectual problems was more often than not: "what the fuck who gives a shit" as he would "grab the tab snap the cap from another can of Bud, buddy, pop the top, Pappy, from another can of Schlitz" (p. 101).

Abbey's emphasis on action set the tone for much of the radical environmental movement. As one character, Doc Sarvis, put it, "Let our practice form our doctrine thus assuring precise theoretical coherence" (Abbey, 1975: 65). Abbey's only allusion to previous radical traditions involved the Luddites. "They called him lunatic but he saw the enemy clearly. Saw what was coming and acted directly. And about the wooden shoes, *les sabots*. The spanner in the works. Monkey business. The rebellion of the meek" (Abbey, 1975: 65). Abbey, in fact, dedicated the book to Ned Ludd. But the references to Luddism, as noted below, rest on a misinterpretation. Thus, while Abbey's characters seem "anti-capitalist" or even "anti-civilization," it is difficult in the end to make complete sense of what their purposes are.

The list of actions taken by various radical environmental groups that could reasonably be considered as "monkeywrenching" is long and varied and at times looks like the working out of Abbey's script. In 1981, Earth First "cracked" the Glen Canyon Dam, unrolling a three hundred foot banner down its face. Edward Abbey is reported to have been on hand for the unveiling of an act which symbolically fulfilled a fantasy of his fictional monkeywrenchers (Scarce, 1990: 37-38). In 1982, Foreman and Mike Roselle pulled up survey stakes on a road built by Getty Oil into the ecologically sensitive Granite Creek area near Yellowstone (Scarce, 1990: 63-65). In 1983, Earth First! blockaded the entrance to Bald Mountain and the North Kalmiopsis wild area (Scarce, 1990: 68). Large tree spiking operations have been conducted on the border of the Bull Run Watershed (source of Portland, Oregon's drinking water) and on the Measres Islands, off the coast of British Columbia (Scarce, 1990: 25). In 1986, Rod Coronado and David Howitt attacked the Icelandic whaling station and sank half of its fleet of ships (pp. 187-200). In 1989, $187,000 worth of logging equipment was destroyed at a worksite in Washington State. In July 1989 a road grader was set on fire in Washington State's Okanogan County (Parfit, 1990: 184). It has even been reported that Earth First! has engaged in sabotage of ski resorts (Rose, 1991: 23).

If *The Monkeywrench Gang* provided the inspiration for direct environmental action, *Ecodefense*, a book that became a best-seller in the Northwest (Parfit, 1990: 184), authored by Foreman and Bill Haywood, provided the basic methodology. Foreman and Haywood gave instructions on how to engage in acts of environmental sabotage, including detailed advice regarding tools to use and even articles of clothing to wear (e.g., the "well-dressed tree spiker" wears "cheap cloth gloves," "running shoes," "lightweight jacket in forest colors," and carries bolt cutters and a "felt tipped pen") (Foreman & Haywood, 1990: 29). In spite of the book's "Standard Disclaimer,"[2] it was obviously designed to incite action, much of it illegal.

Foreman and Haywood (1990) instruct their readers on the intricacies of an assortment of operations, including:

- Destroying mining claim markers in wilderness areas (especially federal property) (pp. 68-74).

- Cutting power lines (pp. 74-75).

- Disabling seismographic equipment used in drilling operations.

- Road spiking. "With this technique you can cure an ORV problem or make a logging or mining operation unprofitable" (p. 92).

- Flattening tires. "Suppose your neighborhood is infested with off-road vehicle scum, or you chance upon an unattended muscle wagon where it shouldn't be. A quick slash job is in order" (p. 100).

- Disabling motor vehicles of all kinds. "The classic act of monkeywrenching is messing with a bulldozer. . . The 'dozer is a tool of destruction. But like David and Goliath, a little ingenuity and chutzpuh can go a long way toward stopping a monster" (p. 116). Or, "In some cases, burning a target is the most effective way of decommissioning it" (p. 143). Moreover, helicopters and other aircraft also "are useful tools for the large scale Earth raper" (p. 145). These, too, should therefore at times be disabled.

- Animal defense. Destroying traps and cutting fences (pp. 157-187).

- Miscellaneous deviltry, including, smoke and stink bombs in corporate headquarters (pp. 195-196), computer sabotage (pp. 213-218), and "condo trashing. . .for use against environmentally objectionable projects such as condominiums, shopping centers and the like" (p. 219).

Tree-spiking, the most notorious form of monkeywrenching, is given special attention by Foreman in both *Ecodefense* and his *Confessions of an Eco-Warrior*. In *Ecodefense*, Foreman and Haywood defend careful tree spiking in which the spikes are placed "well above the area where the fellers will cut" with the intent of disabling sawmill blades, "a much more devastating loss to a timber company" than simply wrecking the blades of individual sawyers. According to them, the chances of worker injury are minimal in larger milling operations, because workers operate from a control booth or from behind a plexiglas shield. These larger operations should, according to Foreman and Haywood, be the usual targets of a tree spiking operation, since "[l]ocally owned and operated sawmills are seldom a major threat to the wilderness" (Foreman & Haywood, 1990: 26-27). Also, sites for spiking should, they state, be carefully chosen, and instructions are given as to how to identify areas that are marked to harvest. Areas of special ecological significance are the highest priority (p. 33).

Foreman defends tree-spiking even in the face of a well-publicized incident in which a mill operator, George Alexander, was seriously injured when a saw shattered in a Louisiana-Pacific mill in Coverdale, California. Foreman discounts the incident as one that was: (1) not undertaken by Earth First! and (2) the result of improper and dangerous working conditions in the plant (Foreman, 1990: 152).

It is in his defense of tree-spiking that Foreman's version of biocentricism reveals itself. While giving some consideration to worker safety, it is obviously not his highest priority. Earth First!'s internal fracturing, in fact, occurred right along the lines revealed by tree-spiking. Judi Bari, leader of the "red" faction of Earth First! and herself a carpenter, has denounced tree-spiking: "What you have to understand," she has stated, "is, these timber corporations are not just anti-forest or anti-life—they don't treat the workers any better than they treat the forests" (Bari & Kohl, 1991: 74). Attempts to synthesize traditional worker radicalism with radical environmentalism encouraged Foreman to split from Earth First!

Given the actions that Foreman has either been associated with or advocated, it is unsurprising that Earth First! and other radical groups have been roundly denounced in the mainstream press. As with other radical movements, it has been suggested that the monkeywrenchers have done the cause of environmentalism more damage than good (Carpenter, 1990: 50-51). They have been labeled as "terrorists" (they have been treated as a "case study" in the journal *Terrorism*; see Badolato, 1991: 237-239). Radicals have been the subjects of bomb attacks, and they been treated as criminals on more than one occasion. Foreman compares federal actions against Earth First! with the COINTEL program of the 1960s, which successfully destroyed the Black Panthers, assassinating many of its leaders. Given the government's actions in the Palto Verde case, the comparison seems to have merit.

> "[T]he term "civil disobedience". . .has been used to describe everything from bringing a test case in the federal courts to taking aim at a federal official."
>
> Marshall Cohen

Monkeywrenching Defended

Many monkeywrenching activities constitute violations of the criminal law, and some are obviously quite serious ones. But lawbreaking is often considered legitimate for certain ends, whether those actions are relatively unintrusive and involve minor legal violations (like sit-ins or unauthorized demonstrations) or major ones, involving violent revolutionary activity. All kinds of radical political actions, some violent (the American Revolution) and some not so (the civil rights movement) have been incorporated to and celebrated within the American political tradition. Given the record established by radical environmentalists, it seems useful to consider how monkeywrenching fits into various traditions of radical political practice. Is it an environmental form of "civil disobedience" that will someday be legitimized alongside various strands of abolitionism, civil rights, women's, and gay rights movements? Or perhaps the often-covert direct action approach of Earth First! marks it as a revolutionary or guerrilla movement? These questions cannot be fully answered here, but some preliminary observations can be made.

Foreman's writings are of limited usefulness (but still some usefulness) in answering the above questions, because he is inconsistent in his analysis of monkeywrenching's purposes. For example, while he distinguishes monkeywrenching from civil disobedience, he also seems perfectly willing to draw implicit connections between the environmental and civil rights movements of the 1960s (Foreman, 1991: 177). And while, he echoing Abbey's Doc Sarvis, says that "actions" ought to "set the finer points of our philosophy" (p. 20), he also speaks of "*conscientiously* disobeying the law" (emphasis added) (p. 167). Moreover, radicalism's defenders, like Rik Scarce, in his highly sympathetic account of various radical groups, invokes Gandhi as well as Ned Lud (pp. 11-13). While not worked out in a detailed or systematic way, radical environmentalists appeal to a variety of traditions to legitimate their nominally criminal behavior.

In *Confessions of an Eco-Warrior*, Foreman (1991) sets forth his most systematic defense of monkeywrenching. He makes a variety of claims: First, Foreman contends, monkeywrenching is "non-violent," since it is "never directed toward harming human beings or other forms of life. It is aimed at inanimate machines and tools that are destroying life. Care is always taken to minimize any possible threat to people, including the monkeywrenchers themselves" (p. 113). The destruction of property is thus not considered to be a "violent act." Foreman also claims that it is "not organized," even though it constitutes a "widespread movement across the United States." It is, he says, "targeted" and "timely," not "[m]indless, erratic vandalism," which is "unethical" and "leads to loss of popular sympathy" (p. 114).

Monkeywrenching is, according to Foreman "fun" and it gives "a sense of accomplishment, and unparalleled camaraderie from creeping about in the night[.]" It is not "revolutionary," since it is not designed to overthrow any "social, political, or economic system. . . It is merely aimed at keeping industrial 'civilization' out of nature areas and causing its retreat from areas that should be wild." Overall, then, Foreman considers monkeywrenching to be "deliberate and ethical." Monkeywrenchers are "thoughtful and not cavalier" (p. 115).

Foreman distinguishes monkeywrenching from civil disobedience on two grounds. First, civil disobedience, "appeal[s] to the public and reasonably fair authorities with the rightness of one's cause and personal integrity," (Foreman, 1991: 130) while monkeywrenching does not. Second, civil disobedience seeks to "reform" a social, economic, or political system, while monkeywrenching is merely designed to "thwart destruction" (p. 131). But neither of these distinctions seems to hold given other statements made by Foreman. For one thing, he, like Scarce and other radicals, justifies the activities of radicals in terms of making the "Gang of Ten's" (mainstream organizations') demands seem more moderate (in a "bad cop," "good cop" sense) to policy-makers and the public. "Publicity" seems an important part of what he is about. (He has participated in writing three books and has been a legendary performer on the lecture circuit.) Also, it seems odd, given his agenda, for him to say that he does not seek either revolution or "reform." At the very least, Foreman would presumably like to reform the National Park Service. Also, Foreman's appeals to law's overall legitimacy have clear associations with traditions of civil disobedience. He states, "the more one becomes involved in conscious lawbreaking, whether nonviolent civil disobedience or monkeywrenching, the more one needs to be scrupulously deliberate about doing so. . . When we break unjust political laws to obey higher ethical laws, we must guard against developing a laxity toward standards in general" (p. 170). Given these tensions, it seems warranted to take a look at civil disobedience within the traditions of American political dissent and consider monkeywrenching in relation to them.

Traditions of Civil Disobedience

Scholarly analysis of and justifications for civil law breaking reached something of a peak in the 1960s in response to the activities of anti-war and civil rights dissenters. (See, for example, Cohen, 1969; Pennock & Chapman, 1970; Walzer, 1970; Zashin, 1972.) In the American context, discussions of civil disobedience have tended, sooner or later, to invoke Thoreau's famous essay (see, for example Adams, 1975: 294). This makes sense, not only because Thoreau was an American writer but because his justifications of civil disobedience tap into liberal and Protestant strains of American *political* culture. But Thoreau's approach to justifying civil disobedience is not the only one available. Another tradition, that of "republicanism," offers an alternative means for justifying dissent, one that I will argue better fits some aspects of environmentalist monkeywrenching but which also reveals the approaches of radicals like Dave Foreman as problematical. Thoreau couched the legitimacy of disobedient actions in the individual conscience. Individualism is a clear and consistent theme of his essay. "Can," Thoreau asked, "there not be a government in which majorities do not virtually decide right and wrong, but conscience?-- Must the citizen ever for a moment, or in the least degree, resign his conscience to the legislator? Why has every man a conscience, then? I think that we should be men first, and subjects afterward" (Thoreau, 1967: 32-33). Like other liberals, then, Thoreau was suspicious of any sort of political action. Thus, he says that, "There is little virtue in the action of masses of men" (p. 37). Politics corrupts, and the only truly moral response is detachment. Thoreau even advised abolitionists to abandon the political arena in favor of passive resistance. "I do not hesitate to say," he states, "that those who call themselves Abolitionists should at once effectually withdraw their support, both in person and property, from the government of Massachusetts, and not wait till they constitute a majority of one, before they suffer the right to prevail through them. I think that it is enough if they have God on their side, without waiting for that other one" (Thoreau, 1967: 41).

In *On Civil Disobedience*, then, Thoreau (1967) expressed more concern with the rightness of his actions and the condition of his conscience than with the state of the world. As he says, "I came into this world, not chiefly to make this a good place to live in, but to live in it, be it good or bad" (p. 40). The night that he spent a night in jail, before his aunt paid his fine for tax evasion, seems to have been enough to assuage his conscience, and to encourage him to instruct others on how to proceed against slavery. As Hannah Arendt has noted, "Thoreau did not pretend that a man's washing his hands of [unjust public actions] would make the world better or that a man had any obligation to do so." Thus, "[h]ere as elsewhere, conscience is unpolitical" (Arendt, 1972: 60). In other words, Thoreau "argued his case not on the ground of a *citizen's* moral relation to the law, but on the ground of individual conscience and conscience's moral obligation" (p. 60).

"Republicanism" has become a ubiquitous political term over the last couple of decades, at least in academia, especially among scholars of American history. The beginnings of "republican" revisionism as a phenomenon can be traced, at least partly, to Arendt's writings. She drew on classical ideas regarding citizenship and political action to develop a critique of Western liberal and Marxist theory. Arendt's analysis of civil disobedience, then, questioned the intense reliance on individual conscience or intuition as the grounding for legitimately disobedient action as manifested in Thoreau's writings. Rather than focusing on fragile individual intuition as the basis for disobedience, Arendt, and Michael Walzer as well, attempted to place it in wider political contexts. "Disobedience" is, according to Walzer, "almost always a collective act, and it is justified by the values of the collectivity and the mutual engagements of its members" (Walzer, 1970: 4). Walzer thus expressed suspicion toward conscientious objection insofar as it reflects only an individual act based in conscience. "I do think," he states, "that conscientious objection has and probably ought to have greater weight in the eyes of the larger community when it has as its basis a smaller community, within which some degree of responsibility, mutuality, and social discipline is likely to exist" (p. 131).

Arendt (1972) makes the same point in a somewhat different way: "The greatest fallacy in the present debate seems to me the assumption that we are dealing with individuals, who pit themselves subjectively and conscientiously against the laws and customs of the community—an assumption that is shared by the defenders and the detractors of civil disobedience. The fact is that we are dealing with organized minorities, who stand against assumed inarticulate, though hardly 'silent,' majorities, and I think it is undeniable that these majorities have changed in mood and opinion to an astounding degree under the pressure of the minorities" (p. 99).

The shift in emphasis from individual to collective judgement and action reflects a commitment to political action that is generally absent from liberal thinking. Politics, while offering many opportunities for compromise and corruption, still offers the only satisfactory response to social injustice. Politics involves action and thought, not simply withdrawal and passivity (or even passive resistance).

Arendt's arguments on civil disobedience parallel her analysis of revolution. Revolutionary activity, like civil disobedience, is marked by the formation of voluntary associations (which are carefully and importantly distinguished, she says, from "interest groups," the purpose of which is to further a set of private interests). In this vein, Arendt states, "It is my contention that civil disobedients are nothing but the latest form of voluntary association, and that they are thus quite in tune with the oldest traditions of the country" (p. 96). One implication of the comparison is that the line between disobedience and revolution is not a bright one. Both are versions of political action, and both need to be evaluated in terms of means and ends in a given context.

Civil disobedience is often confronted with two means-related issues. First, what is "violence," and when, if ever, is it justified? Second, what burdens does disobedience place on a dissenter in terms of accepting responsibility and making public disclosure? Republican perspectives offer some interesting insights on both these questions in terms of how they could apply to monkeywrenching.

Civil disobedience has a long association with non-violence. A commitment to non-violence is often grounded in both strategic and moral considerations, as it was, for example, in the case of Martin Luther King, Jr. (see, for example, Branch, 1988). The problem of political violence obviously cannot be examined in the depth that it deserves here. In terms of monkeywrenching, a crucial issue involves whether the destruction of property, in which humans are neither injured nor threatened, constitutes a form of "violence." Gandhian disobedience, for example, forswears the destruction of property. Foreman doesn't consider the destruction of machinery to be an act of violence. Some radicals even propose that equipment destruction is actually property "enhancement." (Scarce, 1990: 11).

The law, it seems, cuts both ways here. Obviously, the destruction of property is a crime in every American criminal jurisdiction. On the other hand, "property crimes," like theft, are generally distinguished from "violent crimes" and treated more leniently. "Vandalism" is usually not deemed a violent crime, although "sabotage" is certainly a serious one. And violence can, in some instances, be defined quite broadly as in labor law. (See *Esco Operating Corporation v. Kaplan*, in which violence in labor disputes "is not limited to physical contact or injury, but may include picketing conducted with misleading signs, false statements, publicity, and veiled threats by words and acts").

Along with its emphasis on citizenship and political action, republicanism tends toward a distinct analysis of entitlements to property. During the eighteenth and early nineteenth centuries republican interpretations of property emphasized its public character. In social custom and courts of law, property was often treated as a creature of the public realm. Contracts and debts were modified by juries, and powers of eminent domain were often exercised without offering compensation. Property was treated as public good held in individual trust which could be altered or even confiscated under appropriate circumstances. The language of "rights," in other words, was not as fully imbedded into legal consciousness as it is today (see Meidinger, 1980; Schultz, 1991; Treanor, 1980).

If one applies this perspective to issues of disobedience, it seems to create possibilities for treating actions against property as having political legitimation even if outside the law. From this perspective then, actions against property ought to be judged in terms of broad political purposes and not on the moral distinction between violent and non-violent behavior. In other words, property's meaning is socially constructed, and actions resulting in its destruction need to be judged within an historical and political context. From this view, the sabotaging of equipment in sensitive (public) wilderness lands would be entitled to greater legitimacy than random tree spiking or "condo trashing." Republicanism, thus, demands a contextual and historical analysis of the circumstances in which direct action might be considered. A republican analysis of disobedience then tends to support Foreman's understanding of monkeywrenching, especially insofar as he emphasizes its "conscientiousness." Republicanism, then, like radical environmentalism, deliberately obscures the distinction between private and public, violent and non-violent, civil and uncivil, and even reformist and revolutionary.

If then, a republican approach to disobedience and direct action requires a commitment to public purposes, does it demand public disclosure of one's individual acts of wrongdoing? Since monkeywrenching is covert, almost by definition, it would seem that the requirement to accept responsibility would subvert, if not entirely destroy, its effectiveness as a tool of direct action. It is argued that public purposes do not require public disclosure. While the conscientious monkeywrencher needs to take political contexts into account, he or she should not have to and should not reveal his or her identity in all circumstances. Demands to do so summon a liberal framework in which the acceptance of punishment reflects moral worthiness and evidence of commitment to a cause. But insofar as disobedient activity is specified as political and collective, requirements for the purity of individual actions diminish. Republicanism reflects an understanding of what Michael Walzer once referred to as the problem of "dirty hands." Moreover, depth of commitment doesn't necessarily indicate the validity of one's claims, since, as Arendt notes, it can simply signal fanaticism or dementia: "For if accepting punishment were what distinguished civil disobedient actions, then accepting punishment for rape and murder could legitimate. . . Intensity, moreover, might simply be the mark of a fanaticism that is neither laudable nor rational" (Arendt, 1972: 66-67).

Acceptance of punishment is also warranted only if the system of political power being challenged represents legitimate authority. Important theoretical approaches to law in the twentieth century, including, Legal Realism, Critical Legal Studies, and feminist legal theory, cast considerable doubt on the legitimacy of Western systems of legal order. While there is no singular understanding of law that captures these perspectives, especially one that can be explicated in detail here, a useful summary is contained in David Kairys's simple statement that "Law is simply politics by other means" (Kairys, 1982: 17). Law, according to Kairys and other Critical theorists is not grounded in either natural right (the conservative view) or social utility (the liberal view). Rather law is an expression of political power. Law, then, is historically contingent. It does not embody a long and messy march toward expanding rights, nor does it capture and implement immutable ethical prescriptions. This does not mean law never accommodates the interests of subordinate groups, nor that it is wholly illegitimate. But changes in the legal order, both large and small, do reflect the attempts on the part of the powerful to maintain their positions, while making the necessary accommodations that must at times be made to maintain social stability. A good example here is the development of labor law in the United States, which has been far from progressive in sanctioning expanded rights for unions and in fact represents only the most grudging acquiescence to labor's demands as the result of long and protracted direct political actions (see Forbath, 1991). What Critical Legal Studies teaches is that law is political and that it needs to be evaluated and addressed in terms of broad historical and political purposes. Historically, changes in the legal system that have accommodated dispossessed groups have done so often only because of disobedient and even violent expressions of political resistance.

If a republican perspective on civil disobedience assists a positive appraisal of some kinds of monkeywrenching, a brief examination of Luddism, a chief source of inspiration for Foreman, Abbey, and company, helps to further specify monkeywrenching as a form of political activity. In considering the relation of eco-tage to Luddism, however, serious flaws are exposed in the approaches of Foreman and some other radicals to direct action. While Ned Ludd may or may not have been a "Leicestershire youth who became enraged at his tiresome job one day and took a hammer to his needles" (Scarce, 1990: 12), the Luddite movement was not simply an expression of technophobia. Thomis has shown the complex character of the Luddite movement. Specifically, he has revealed its significance as a workers' movement. "These attacks on machines," he states, "did not imply any necessary hostility to machinery as such; machinery was just a conveniently exposed target against which an attack could be made. Just as the Luddism of 1811-16 was to consist of a mixture of coercion of employers by violence and anti-machinery demonstrations, so were both these elements present in the century and a half that preceded 1811." The Luddites attacked machines whose activation often led to the elimination of their employment. As Thomis (1970) notes, "examples have been cited of the unopposed introduction of machinery into the mining and printing industries where improvements did not threaten the position of existing groups of workers" (p. 14).

E. P. Thompson (1963) has shown the historical connections between Luddism and the development of various later English workers' movements. Luddism, in other words, represents some of the germinal seeds of what eventually became English (and European) workers' radicalism. It cannot and should not thus be represented as simply a reaction against technology in favor of simplicity or "nature" (pp. 472-602).

The attempt to draw monkeywrenching into a radical politics of disobedience faces one very serious conceptual difficulty; this has to do with the underlying justifications for radical action, i.e., the bio-centric vision. In fact, bio-centrism, while attractive and useful as a tool for criticizing the historical Western impulse to dominate the natural world, tends toward an anti-humanism that may be unique in Western history and is ultimately incompatible with other radical traditions.

When Foreman calls humanity a "cancer on nature" (Gabriel, 1990: 62) or suggests that AIDS is "nature healing itself," he moves toward an irrational politics that smacks of fascism. In fact, Foreman's bio-centrism is close in tone and substance to the authoritarian leanings of a variety of neo-Malthusians (for an analysis, see Paehlke, 1989). For monkeywrenching, then, to fulfill its potential as a possible tool for resistance to environmental destruction, along with other forms of political resistance and action, it needs a broader and more sophisticated political orientation than is offered by bio-centrism. Monkeywrenching,

in other words, needs to be placed within the larger web of resistance
to environmental destruction that we can begin to specify under the
banner of "radical ecology."

"The Earth is in the balance."

Al Gore

Radical Ecology

Radical ecology responds to the enormous variety of serious
environmental crises that we now confront. The list of ongoing and
potential environmental catastrophes that threaten us is long and
distressing, and cannot be critically examined in any detail here. But it
is important to realize that the crisis is worldwide, affecting both
advanced industrial populations as well as Eastern European ones,
developing nations along the Pacific rim, and the least industrialized
nations of Latin America, South Asia, and Africa. Therefore, while each
(bio) region of the world has unique sets of problems, some, such as
species depletion and ocean and global atmospheric pollution confront
us all. But, while there is ultimately no escape from the problems, still,
certain sectors of the world population face greater threats to health and
safety than do others. It seems clear that the least well off, whether in
the First World or the Third, are generally those most harmed by
environmental deterioration (see, for example, Bullard, 1993; Hofrichter,
1993). Radical ecology, then, starts from the premise that there is a
connection between environmental preservation and social justice.
Radical ecology, while drawing insights from biocentrism, does not
collapse into Malthusian despondency.
    Radical ecology can thus be distinguished from radical
environmentalism, although the two are obviously not entirely
distinguishable. Radical environmentalism is, in essence, a relatively
narrow political movement with a heavy emphasis on biocentricism,
Malthusianism, and direct action. Carol Smart (1992), in *Radical*

Ecology, defines "radical ecology" as follows: "Radical ecology emerges from a sense of crisis in the industrialized world. It acts on a new perception that the domination of nature entails the domination of human beings along lines of race, class, and gender. Radical ecology confronts the illusion that people are free to exploit nature and to move in society at the expense of others, with a new consciousness of our responsibilities to the rest of nature and to other humans." Through this definition, Merchant indicates obvious parallels to Murray Bookchin's notion of "social ecology." Bookchin has for many years argued that environmental destruction cannot be considered apart from human social systems. According to him, "*all ecological problems are social problems*" (Bookchin, 1990b: 30). Thus, a complete analysis and, ultimately a political program must take into account the multiplicity of social and economic factors that threaten various ecosystems. Bookchin and Foreman then represent two very different versions of environmentalism. Foreman's distaste for the non-biocentric left is reflected in his conflicts with Bookchin (see Bookchin, 1990b).

"Radical ecology," draws from social ecology but extends its analysis in various ways. Merchant has detailed the multifaceted and disparate strands of the ecology movement that promise a fundamental re-envisioning of humanity and our "place in the world." By specifying various aspects of radical ecology, Merchant reveals a mosaic of ideas and movements, which, envisioned together, suggest a reconstituting of the relationships that we have to one another and to the environment, a reconstitution that undercuts human/environment or human/nature distinctions. Thus, radical ecology involves a critique of positivist science that borrows from Marx, Alfred North Whitehead, Aldo Leopold, and feminist thinkers such as Merchant herself (Merchant, 1992: 41-59).

Combined with its epistemological implications, radical ecology has provided the impetus for the reconstruction of ethics that both extends and criticizes traditional liberal rights analysis, drawing on biocentric and other perspectives (Callicott, 1989). Radical ecology also connects with the conventional and unconventional politics of various western Green parties, and with Third World movements, represented by the late Chico Mendez and the Amazonian rubber tappers (see Hecht & Cockburn, 1989). Radical ecology is radical, in other words, because it provides a basis for a thorough and wide-ranging critique of the construction of power in the post-modern world, and it thus opens possibilities for creating a new politics.

Radical ecology provides a means to counterbalance and subvert power as it manifests itself on a multiplicity of levels. Radical ecology points to many paths of resistance. Direct action can be one important aspect of radical ecology. But, like worker movements of the earlier era, it needs to be self-consciously theoretical, and thus self-consciously political. And, insofar as the distinction between theory and practice is diminished, extreme bio-centrism is inevitably moderated—theorizing, after all, is a distinctively human activity (as least so far as we know). Thus, the practice of monkeywrenching needs to be more firmly grounded in past traditions of disobedient activity, whether revolutionary or reformist. Only through this can it free itself from associations with mere vandalism and simple crime, and meet the stated aims of Foreman and others to be "thoughtful" and "deliberate." Thus, Bari's attempts to connect, theoretically and practically, with workers' movements are positive. Insofar as Foreman rejects Earth First!'s attempts to draw connections to other radicals through thought and action, he should be viewed with a good deal of suspicion.

NOTES

1. The split between Foreman and the "biocentric" wing of Earth First! and the "humanist" or "red" wing has been the subject of a fair amount of commentary. Judi Bari and Darryl Cherny (both of whom were injured when a pipe bomb exploded in a their car on the way to organizing an action known as "Redwood Summer") are most responsible for the "leftward" turn of Earth First!, at least on the West Coast. Bari has attempted to draw connections between exploitation of workers and destruction of natural ecosystems by attempting to work with worker organizations (Bari & Kohl, 1991: 71-77).

2. "*Ecodefense: A Field Guide to Monkeywrenching* is for entertainment purposes only. No one involved with the production of this book—the editors, contributors, artists, printers, or anyone— encourages anyone to do any of the stupid, illegal things contained herein" (Foreman & Haywood, 1990: n.p.).

REFERENCES

Abbey, Edward (1975). *The Monkeywrench Gang*. New York: Avon Books.

Adams, James Luther (1975). "Civil Disobedience: Its Occasions and Limits." In Roland Pennock and John W. Chapman (eds.) *Political and Legal Obligation* (pp. 293-331). New York: Atherton Press.

Arendt, Hannah (1972). "Civil Disobedience." In *Crises of the Republic* (pp. 51-102). New York: Harcourt, Brace, Jovanovich.

Badolato, Edward (1991). "Environmental Terrorism: A Case Study." *Terrorism* 14: 237-239.

Bari, Judi, and Judith Kohl (1991). "Environmental Justice: Highlander after Myles." *Social Policy* 21: 71-77.

Bookchin, Murray (1990a). *Defending the Earth: A Dialogue between Murray Bookchin and Dave Foreman.* Boston, MA: South End Press.

_____ (1990b). *Remaking Society: Pathways to a Green Future.* Boston, MA: South End Press.

Branch, Taylor (1988). *Parting the Waters: America in the King Years: 1954-1963.* New York: Simon and Schuster.

Bullard, Robert D. (ed.) (1993). *Confronting Environmental Racism: Voices from the Grassroots.* Boston, MA: South End Press.

Callicott, J. Baird (1989). *In Defense of the Land Ethic: Essays in Environmental Philosophy.* Albany: SUNY Press.

Carpenter, Betsy (1990). "Redwood Radicals: Is Environmental Extremism Doing the Cause More Harm Than Good?" *U.S. News and World Report* 109: 50-51.

Cohen, Marshall (1969). "Civil Disobedience in a Constitutional Democracy." *The Massachusetts Review* 10: 211-226.

Esco Operating Corporation v. Kaplan. 144 Msc. 646, 258 N.Y.S. 303.

Forbath, William E. (1991). *Law and the Shaping of the American Labor Movement.* Cambridge, MA: Harvard University Press.

Foreman, Dave (1991). *Confessions of an Eco-Warrior.* New York: Harmony Books.

Foreman, Dave, and Bill Haywood (eds.) (1990). *Ecodefense: A Field Guide to Monkeywrenching.* Chico, CA: Ned Ludd Books.

Gabriel, Trip (1990). "If a Tree Falls in the Forest, They Hear It." *New York Times* (November 4): 34-62.

Hecht, Susanna and Alexander Cockburn (1989). *The Fate of the Forest: Developers, Destroyers, and Defenders of the Amazon.* London: Verso.

Hofrichter, Richard (1993). *Toxic Struggles.* Philadelphia, PA: New Society Publishers.

Kairys, David (1982). "Legal Reasoning." In David Kairys (ed.), *The Politics of Law: A Progressive Critique* (pp. 11-17). New York: Pantheon.

Meidinger, Errol (1980). "The "Public Uses" of Eminent Domain: History and Policy." *Environmental Law* 11: 1-66.

Merchant, Carolyn (1992). *Radical Ecology: The Search for Livable World.* New York: Routledge, Chapman and Hall, Inc.

Paehlke, Robert C. (1989). *Environmentalism and the Future of Progressive Politics.* New Haven, CT: Yale University Press.

Parfit, Michael (1990). "Earth First!ers Wield a Mean Monkey Wrench." *Smithsonian* 21: 184-204.

Pennock, Roland, and John W. Chapman (eds.) (1970). *Political Obligation: Nomos XII.* New York: Atherton Press.

Rolston, Holmes (1986). *Philosophy Gone Wild: Essays in Environmental Ethics.* Buffalo: Prometheus Books.

Rose, Peter (1991). "Eco-Terrorists Target Ski Resorts." *Ski* 55: 23.

Scarce, Rik (1990). *Eco-Warriors: Understanding the Radical Environmental Movement.* Chicago: Noble Press.

Schultz, David (1991). "The Locke Republican Debate and the Paradox of Property Rights in Early American Jurisprudence." *Western New England Law Review* 13: 155-188.

Short, Brant (1991). "Earth First! and the Rhetoric of Moral Confrontation." *Communications Studies* 42: 172-188.

Smart, Carol (1992). *Radical Ecology.* New York: Routledge, Chapman and Hall.

Thomis, Malcom I. (1970). *The Luddites: Machine Breaking in Regency England.* Hamden, CN: Archon Books.

Thompson, E. P. (1963). *The Making of the English Working Class.* New York: Pantheon.

Thoreau, Henry David (1967). *The Variorum Civil Disobedience.* New York: Twayne Publishers.

Treanor, William M. (1980). "The 'Public Uses' of Eminent Domain: History and Policy." *Environmental Law* 11: 1-66.

_____ (1985). "The Origins and Original Significance of the Just Compensation Clause of the Fifth Amendment." *Yale Law Journal* 94: 694-716.

Walzer, Michael (1970). *Obligations.* Cambridge, MA: Harvard University Press.

Zakin, Susan (1993). *Coyotes and Town Dogs: Earth First! and the Environmental Movement.* New York: Viking.

Zashin, Elliot M. (1972). *Civil Disobedience and Democracy.* New York: The Free Press.

CHAPTER TEN

Environmental Criminal Enforcement: Efforts by the States

Sally M. Edwards

Except for a few highly sensational cases, the criminal prosecution of environmental violations at either the federal or state level is a relatively recent phenomena (Tennille, 1978; Reitze, Jr. & Reitze, 1978; Kelly, 1978; Stone, 1978; Comment, 1985), although since the mid-1980s the federal government has increased its efforts to prosecute environmental violators rather than pursue them civilly (Habicht, 1984; Tejada, 1984; McMurry & Ramsey, 1987; DiMento, 1990; Russell, 1991). However, because the states have primacy in the enforcement of many of the federal environmental statutes and regulatory responsibility for both federal and state environmental statutes (Bowman, 1984; Stanfield, 1984; Bowman, 1985; Crotty, 1987; Crotty, 1988; Ringquist, 1993), any meaningful measure of whether or not a society is serious about the enforcement of environmental statutes has to include an assessment of states' efforts, individually and collectively, with regards to the criminal prosecution of environmental violations.

Unfortunately, evaluating the efforts of the states is not an easy task, given that academic research and/or journalistic reporting on this topic primarily focuses on federal regulatory efforts, next on federal civil and criminal actions, and lastly on the efforts of state and local authorities (Ringquist, 1993). Indeed, even the criminal enforcement efforts of local (city, county, etc.) jurisdictions receive more review than the efforts of the states (Hammett & Epstein, 1993). But as with other, more traditional street crime, if criminal prosecutions of environmental violations are to become effective deterrents, it will be the states leading the prosecution efforts. As is true of current efforts to curtail violent crime, serious attack on environmental crime will fail miserably without stringent enforcement action by the states. After all, environmental concerns, like violent crime, are often local problems that have collectively mushroomed into national issues.

This chapter is an assessment of criminal enforcement activity, at the state level, with regard to utilizing the criminal provisions of environmental laws to pursue violators.[1] If states are, indeed, moving into the criminal prosecution of environmental violations, the two organizations on which to focus an evaluation or assessment of the efforts are the office of attorney general and state police organization. These agencies offer the most logical assessment of state environmental criminal enforcement efforts because: (1) they have traditionally been charged with, and are responsible for, state level criminal investigations and (2) most state "environmental" agencies do not necessarily have the expertise to properly investigate and prosecute criminal violations, since their focus, for the most part, is on regulatory compliance and civil violations.

Methodology and Findings

The empirical data for this article were collected through a survey administered to the state police agencies and a similar survey subsequently administered to the attorneys general of each state[2]. The surveys for both agencies were similar, with only minor adjustments to account for the differences in the mission of the agencies, and contained questions on jurisdiction, organization, personnel, training, facilities, and activities. Both surveys also asked for information regarding the increase or decrease in the level of activity of environmental crimes experienced since 1988 and why, what the agency believed the level of activity would be in the next two years and why; the violations that were the easiest and the hardest to enforce and why, what was the greatest environmental threat to their state and why, and what was the biggest obstacle the agency had to face in investigating environmental crimes.

Jurisdiction over Environmental Crimes

State Police: Forty-one state police organizations responded to the question regarding jurisdiction. Twenty-one reported they had jurisdiction over one or more categories of environmental crime. The environmental crime category over which most state police organizations (both state police and highway patrol) reported jurisdiction was the illegal transport of hazardous materials as is to be expected with an environmental crime related to transportation and highways. For air pollution from vehicles, all of the states reporting both jurisdiction and activity were highway patrol states. Generally, non-vehicle air pollution crimes were rarely investigated, except in Louisiana and Maryland, by state police agencies, who reported they routinely investigate stationary or other air pollution violations. Table 1 reveals the responses to the question regarding jurisdiction.

Considering the vast organizational and operational differences in state police organizations[3], and because a police agency can have jurisdiction, but not exercise authority, a simple "yes" or "no" answer regarding jurisdiction was insufficient to determine the depth and breadth of activity. Jurisdictional authority cannot be equated with actual investigative activity. Therefore, where the state police organizations indicated jurisdiction over a category of environmental crime, they were also asked if they routinely investigated it.

Most state police organizations reported actively and routinely investigating violations related to explosives. Interestingly, there was no clear demarcation between highway patrol and state police agencies. Again, this provides an interesting question for further research; the investigation of this crime is not organizationally driven, as was vehicular air pollution, but the differences among the states for this crime must be driven by state need or some other factors. The only other crime with a relatively high response rate was the illegal disposal of waste and water pollution, where, except for California, the states reporting involvement were all state police agencies. But California's activity is not surprising, given its problems with the transportation of hazardous waste to Mexico for disposal to avoid the stricter and more costly hazardous waste disposal regulations in the United States. Indeed, Los Angeles employs a task force to track and investigate this problem.

Responses regarding jurisdiction and activity relating to fertilizer, herbicide, noise pollution, pesticides, and wetlands violations indicate activity for these crimes appears driven not by the type of agency but rather by other factors, such as states having specific problems with these environmental categories. Since so few state police agencies are involved with the preceding environmental categories (two for herbicides and noise pollution and only one for fertilizers, pesticides, and wetlands), maybe the question should be why are any state police agencies involved at all? The answer will probably lie with each state's institutional capabilities or some sensitivity by these states to these particular problems.

To summarize, although state police organizations are more active in investigating the illegal transport of the various types of hazardous material and the illegal disposal of hazardous and nonhazardous waste, police actions concerning environmental crimes are not confined to these traditionally "highway-oriented" crimes. State police agencies are also investigating many other types of environmental crimes, albeit the number of states involved is low and type of activity being investigated is limited to a relatively few categories of environmental violations.

Attorneys General: The responses by the state attorneys general round out the "big picture" concerning state activity in the enforcement of environmental crimes. The initial question asked of the attorney general was if they prosecuted environmental crimes, and if they did not, to indicate who did within their states. Thirty-eight attorneys general responded to the question regarding jurisdiction to prosecute environmental crimes. Twenty-six attorneys general reported their office had jurisdiction to prosecute one or more of the categories of environmental crime. Table 2 contains the responses to this section of the survey. Indiana consistently answered its office provided legal advice only. And a quick perusal of Table 2 indicates that Indiana was the only state with a consistent answer.

Arkansas, Florida, Georgia, Idaho, Indiana, Nevada, Virginia, and West Virginia all indicated local district attorneys, or the equivalent, are responsible for prosecuting environmental crimes. A comparison of these eight responses with the responses of the state police organizations from the same eight states leads to the conclusion that the two agencies in these eight states may not be coordinating their efforts, for whatever reason, to deal with this problem, since none of the state police organizations from these eight states reported significant activity in environmental crimes either. Conversely, Connecticut's Attorney General responded that the Chief States Attorney had responsibility for the prosecution of environmental crime, reflecting at least some effort by that state to consolidate or focus environmental criminal prosecutions under one centralized state agency.

Oklahoma indicated criminal environmental prosecutions are the responsibility of the Department of Health. Again, vesting the responsibility for criminal prosection of environmental violations in an agency not normally associated with criminal investigation and prosecution, often suggests a relative lack of concern for environmental crime at the state level. Those states yet to establish environmental institutions and who have left the enforcement of environmental laws and regulations to "traditional" institutions with missions other than environmental protection risk weaker enforcement. Within the agencies with traditional goals and objectives, there is much tension among the personnel concerning environmental enforcement, and often environmental concerns get lost among preexisting demands and needs (Ringquist, 1993).

If a state reported it did prosecute environmental crimes, the attorneys general were asked questions concerning jurisdiction, similar to those questions asked of the state police organizations. If the offices responded that they prosecuted environmental crimes, they were further asked to indicate their involvement level. Specifically, the attorneys general were asked if, for a given environmental crime, they prosecuted environmental crimes, provided legal advice only, or were not involved.

As with the state police, the jurisdiction reported by the attorneys general was very "issue specific," albeit more state attorneys general are involved in the prosecution of environmental crimes than state police organizations are in their investigation. However, this is not an unexpected circumstance—attorneys general are often confronted with dealing with non-traditional activities while environmental crimes are a very new issue confronting police. For the most part, the attorneys general are heavily involved in the same environmental crimes as are state police organizations: air and water pollution and the illegal disposal or transport of hazardous waste. Again, although not entirely absent, endangered species, asbestos, fertilizer and herbicide violations do not appear to occupy much of the attorneys' general time.

Finally, the 26 states reporting jurisdiction are comparable to the 29 states reported by Matulewich as having environmental task forces to combat environmental crimes in his report (1991). Also, the states

Table 1: Jurisdiction (State Police Organizations)

Arizona	7,8,9,10,11,14,15,16,17,18
Arkansas	7,8,9,16
California	2,12,14,15,16,17,18
Georgia	2,19
Idaho	14,15,16,17,18
Illinois	7,12,13,14,15,16,17,18,20,21
Kentucky	7,9,12,13,21
Louisiana	1,3,7,8,9,11,12,14,15,16,17,18,21
Maryland	1,3,12,13,14,15,16,17,18,21,22
Mississippi	7,8,9,15,16,17,18
Missouri	2,7,12,13,14,15,18,19
Nebraska	7,8,9
New Jersey	7,12,14,15,16,17,18,21
New Mexico	7,8,9,14,15,16,17,18
New York	7,15,16,17,18
Oklahoma	2,7,9,14,15,16,18
Oregon	4,5,6,7,9,13,21
Texas	2,14,16,17,18
Vermont	15,16,17,18
Virginia	7,8,9,14,15,16,17,18
Wisconsin	15,16,17

1 = Air Pollution (Stationary)
2 = Air Pollution (Vehicles)
3 = Air Pollution (Other)
4 = Endangered Species (Birds)
5 = Endangered Species (Animals)
6 = Endangered Species (Fish)
7 = Explosives (General)
8 = Explosives (Industrial)

12 = Illegal Disposal (Waste)
13 = Illegal Disposal (Non-hazardous Waste)
14 = Illegal Transport (Biological)
15 = Illegal Transport (Chemical)
16 = Illegal transport (Explosives)
17 = Illegal Transport (Nuclear/Radioactive)
18 = Illegal Transport (Other)
19 = Noise

Table 2: Jurisdiction to Prosecute Cases (Attorneys General)*

	Has Jurisdiction	Advice Only	N/A
Arizona	1-3,6-13,19-22		
Colorado	1-3,12,13,21		
Delaware	1-3,7,10-16,18-22		4-6,8,9
Hawaii	12,13,16,21		
Illinois	1,3,7-9,12-15,17,18,21		10,11
Indiana		1-21	
Kentucky	1,7-16,20,21		3,18
Louisiana	1,7,12-18,21		2-6,8-11, 19,20,22
Maine	1,11-15,20-22		3,19
Maryland	1,3,12,14,20,21,22		
Minnesota	1,3,7-16,18,20,21		
Missouri	7-16,18,20,21		1-3
Nebraska	1,3-22		
New Hampshire	1-3,10-18,20,21	4-6	
New Jersey	1-3,7-16,18,20-22		
New Mexico	1,3,9,12,13,15,18,21		20
New York	1,3-6,10-15,18-22		2,7,8,16, 17,19
North Carolina		1-3,14-16, 18-19,22	12,13,17
North Dakota	1,3,12,13,21	2,14-17,19	10,11,17
Pennsylvania	1,3,7,10-15,18,20-22		
South Dakota	4-6,10-13,18,20-22		1-3,19
Tennessee	21,22	3,12	1,14
Texas	1,3-6,12,13,20,21	10,22	
Utah	1,3,12,13,21	2,10,11,20	
Vermont	7-13,16-22		1-3,15
Wisconsin	1,3,4,6,12,13,15, 16,18,21,22		

* For jurisdiction codes, see Table 1

that consistently appear in the state police data in Table 1 also appear in Table 2, with the exception of California. The California attorney general's office responded they were involved in the prosecution of environmental crimes but due to budget constraints they did not fill out surveys or answer questionnaires. Thus, California is omitted from the specifics of this report even if they are active in environmental crimes.

Organization and Origins

The surveys to the state police organizations and attorneys general sought information on when states began investigation and prosecution activity and why as well as whether or not the states had any special organizational arrangements for the investigation or prosecution of environmental crimes. Specifically, the state police agencies and attorneys general were asked whether their respective agencies were the primary investigator/prosecutor or merely supporters in the investigation/prosecution of environmental crimes. We also wanted to know if an environmental task force similar to the marijuana or drug task forces that have been set up among various agencies to fight the "war on drugs" existed in the states. These responses can be clues to answering the question of whether enforcement efforts are substantive or symbolic action by the state. If activity was internally driven, then the problems the state faces may be severe, but the state does not have the will and/or institutional arrangements to deal with the problem (Lester, 1994). However, state agencies involved in the investigation or prosecution of environmental crimes due to legislative, executive, or other agency demand may be indicative of a state with the will but not the resources or institutional arrangements to deal with the problem (Lester, 1994). Finally, there were questions concerning whether or not the environmental enforcement personnel had any special equipment or separate facilities.

State Police: The state police organizations from Alaska, Mississippi, North Dakota, and Wisconsin gave no starting date for their involvement. Arizona, Arkansas, California, Illinois, Kentucky, Maryland, New Jersey, and Vermont reported beginning the investigation of environmental crimes during the 1980s. The only pre-1980's starting dates reported were South Dakota (1938), Oregon

(1970), Indiana (1979), and Texas (1977). Since the environmental era began in the 1970s, the starting dates for Indiana, Oregon and Texas could be understood. South Dakota's date appears at first to be an anomaly; however, it is most likely its organizational date and authority over most, if not all, statutory crimes was probably granted at that time. As one respondent indicated, "technically we have always had authority because when the [agency] was first created. . .we were given investigative authority over any statutory crime."

Statutory jurisdiction, however, clearly does not always translate into agency activity as the other responses by South Dakota reveal. The South Dakota Highway Patrol is not very active in investigating environmental crime, even though they indicated the primary reason they are involved is due to state statute. Kentucky, on the other hand, reported their activity was an agency-initiated decision, even though technically they had always had the statutory authority to investigate all crimes in the state. These responses illustrate the "reading between the lines" necessary in understanding self-reported data. Although Kentucky has always had the statutory authority to investigate all crimes, they more accurately reported the more recent date of their involvement in the investigation of environmental crimes. South Dakota's response to these questions was based on statutory authority, not their actual activity level, as data affirms. Arizona, Indiana, Mississippi, and Texas reported their involvement in the investigation of environmental crimes was due to state statutes.

For the remainder of those states who responded to this question, the primary reason the investigation of environmental crimes was initiated varies. Only Kentucky reported it was an agency-initiated program, and through a follow-up interview we know the agency initiated their activity due to public demand. On the surface, involvement by police organizations due to public demand suggests regulatory enforcement failure by other state agencies with authority over environmental violations. Only further research will reveal whether this deduction is correct.

The other responses relating to why state police organizations became involved do not directly measure public demand or institutional failure. If public pressure led to police activity it may have been filtered through other institutions. In fact, one reason for this research was to ascertain whether the states have become involved in the utilization of the criminal provisions of environmental laws due to grassroots activity or demand, in other words from the bottom up, or whether it was institutionally driven, from the top down. Only Kentucky's response indicated a heavily grassroots-driven policy. For states that answered their activity was due to state statute, governor initiation, the state attorney general, or another state agency, determining whether it was a top-down or bottom-up push was rather difficult. A top-down mandated program may have ultimately been driven by public demand filtered through other agencies. Again, only further research can answer that question.

This initial research effort suggests more of a "top-down" reason for state police involvement in the investigation of environmental crimes. Alaska, California, North Dakota, and Wisconsin indicated their activity was due to federal mandates. Most of the federal environmental laws require the implementation and enforcement of these laws by the states. Thus, a federal mandate on a state could be viewed as state failure to implement and enforce regulatory and/or environmental laws. The responses by California and Wisconsin, indicating they are involved due to federal mandates, are puzzling; both states are popularly known as very progressive toward, or in the forefront of, environmental policy at the state level (Lester, 1994). But once you realize the state police organizations in these two states are classified as "highway patrol" agencies, then the confusion lessens; highway patrol agencies traditionally are not involved in crimes beyond the highways. But even though California, throughout the survey, claimed its involvement was highway related activity, it would still be fruitful to discover why these particular states would claim it is a top-down mandate, considering their progressive environmental stance.

The rest of the states responding to this question also had more of a top down process. Arkansas and Oregon indicated that another state agency was responsible for their involvement in the investigating of environmental crimes. Maryland and New Jersey reported the state attorney general initiated the program. Illinois and Vermont reported state police activity began at the direction of the governor.

Attorneys General: The responses regarding reasons for involvement are similar to those given by the state police agencies. Sixteen states (Arizona, Colorado, Hawaii, Illinois, Maine, Maryland, Minnesota, Nebraska, New Hampshire, New York, North Dakota, Pennsylvania, South Carolina, South Dakota, Texas and Vermont) reported their activity began during the 1980s, specifically, during the latter part of that decade. Only Delaware (1970), New Jersey (1978), and Wisconsin (1973) reported prosecuting environmental crimes earlier. Five states (Louisiana, Kansas, New Mexico, Tennessee, and Utah) reported their programs began in the 1990s. Missouri was the only state that did not indicate when its program began. Four states (Delaware, Missouri, Pennsylvania, and Wisconsin) reported their activity was mandated by state statute. Fourteen states (Arizona, Colorado, Illinois, Louisiana, Maine, Minnesota, New Hampshire, New Jersey, New Mexico, New York, North Dakota, Tennessee, Utah, and Vermont) indicated their involvement was internally driven. Hawaii reported its program was initiated by the state Department of Health; Maryland's by both the Department of Health and the state EPA; South Dakota's by the state EPA; and Texas, by request from district attorneys. Three states (Kansas, Nebraska, and South Carolina) did not indicate the reason they began prosecuting environmental crimes.

One hypothesis of our research was that formal programs for the prosecution of environmental crimes by the state attorneys general would be instituted before activity by state police organizations began. The rationale for this assumption is simple: while prosecuting the first cases prosecutors would soon recognize a need for better investigators. The state police organizations would be one logical place to find such investigators. And for the most part, the data confirmed this. In Arizona, Maryland, New Jersey, and Vermont, attorney general activity in prosecuting environmental crimes preceded investigative action by the state police organizations in these states. For two states, North Dakota and Wisconsin, it cannot be determined which agency began activity first. The state police from these states did not answer this particular question, but these states are two of the four that reported that their programs were federally mandated. The state police in Illinois and Texas reported starting dates as preceding the attorneys general; however, those police organizations said their programs were initiated by state statute. As discussed earlier with the case of South Dakota, statutory authority does not necessarily lead to active programs. Finally, only Kentucky reported its environmental crimes program was an internally developed program. Thus, all the other states answering this question began their environmental crimes investigation at the request of or by mandates from others. Although only further research can provide the definitive answer to which came first, attorneys general activity or state police activity, this data reaffirms a discussion at a recent American Bar Association meeting of the Section on Natural

Resources, Energy, and Environmental Law (SONREEL), that a major problem confronting officials in the prosecution (and defense) of environmental crimes is the dearth of properly trained investigators.

Perceived Roles

State Police: Agencies were asked how they would describe their role in the investigation of environmental crimes. Illinois and Maryland reported they were the only investigators of environmental crimes. California, Indiana, Kentucky, New Jersey, South Dakota, and Texas indicated they were primarily responsible but shared the responsibility with others, while Arizona and North Dakota stated they helped other agencies who were primarily responsible. Arkansas, Alaska, Idaho, Minnesota, Nebraska, New Mexico, Oregon, Vermont, and Washington indicated they only supplied assistance, on request, from other agencies. Again, this information can only be added to the rest of the information to paint a full picture of what the states are doing.

Attorneys General: Six attorneys general (Delaware, Illinois, Maine, New Hampshire, New Jersey, and South Dakota) were the only prosecutors of environmental crimes in their respective states. The meaning of such a closed prosecutorial system is unclear. Are the state attorneys general the only prosecutors of environmental crimes in these states in order to lessen the pressure on local prosecutors by the public and industry representatives when the communities' largest employer is the violator? Or is the reverse true, does the state want to reserve the prosecutorial powers to prevent over-zealous local prosecutors from inflicting damage to the state's major industries? Only further research can determine the answer to these questions, but an educated guess is that it is a little of both.

For the rest of the attorneys general answering this question, the states are approximately evenly divided between the attorney general being primarily responsible with others helping and others being responsible or providing advice only. The differences between these two basic responses are undoubtedly due not only to varying commitment to environmental enforcement but also to different institutional responsibilities of state attorneys general offices. As with most state agencies, the organization and responsibilities vary from state to state.

This is especially relevant in the interpretation of this and othe similar data.

Personnel

State Police: Each state police organization was asked to identify the number of personnel, full and part time, dedicated to criminal environmental enforcement. Obviously, as with other more traditional police work, it is the presence of line or operational officers rather than supervisors and administrators that determines the success of the enforcement efforts. The responses indicated most of the police personnel working in both a full-time or part-time capacity on environmental crime are "street level" or operational police—sergeants, troopers, and detectives—not personnel in administrative positions.

Arizona reported 15 troopers on a full time basis devoted to the investigation of environmental crimes with 5 administrative officers and one civilian. California reported 9 troopers and 2 administrators. Illinois reported having 40 troopers in the field, 11 supervisors, 14 detectives, and 3 civilians. Maryland indicated they had 3 troopers and 1 administrative officer, while New Jersey reported having no troopers but 9 administrators and 36 detectives. Texas reported having 98 troopers investigating environmental crimes and 34 supervisors. Finally, Kentucky reported its one full time officer as holding an administrative position. However, through follow-up interviews we determined this position is part supervisor (of the 16 part time personnel, one assigned to each police post throughout the state), and part active field investigator. The inconsistency and ambiguity of these numbers suggest that the line between field officer and administrator may be blurred when it comes to determining assignments of police personnel assigned to investigate environmental crimes.

The reported numbers on personnel devoted to the investigation of environmental crimes on a part time basis also widely varied among the state police organizations. Arizona reported 15 troopers and 4 administrative officers. Arkansas indicated that they had 3 detectives working on environmental crimes on a part-time basis. Indiana reported

30 troopers and 2 supervisors, while Kentucky reported 8 detectives and 8 troopers. Mississippi indicated they had 4 detectives working on a part time basis.

Attorneys General: For the attorneys general most of the full time personnel devoted to environmental crime were in-house attorneys: Arizona (4), Delaware (5), Illinois (3), Maryland (3), Minnesota (2), Missouri (2), Nebraska (1), New Jersey (7), New Mexico (1), New York (5), Pennsylvania (5), South Dakota (2), Tennessee (1), Texas (1), Utah (1), Vermont (1), and Wisconsin (1). Pennsylvania also reported utilizing two attorneys from the state EPA to aid their work in the prosecution of environmental crimes. Two states indicated they had paralegels working full time on environmental crimes: Arizona (1) and Illinois (2). Whereas, the state police agencies did not report any secretaries/receptionists working full time on environmental issues, the attorneys general in Arizona, Illinois, and Maryland stated they had two personnel in this category working exclusively on environmental crimes. Nebraska reported one secretary/receptionist, while Pennsylvania reported seven.

There appears to be a demarcation between those attorneys general having personnel devoted to environmental crimes on a full-time basis and those having personnel working on environmental crimes in a part-time capacity only. Delaware, Missouri, South Dakota, Tennessee, Utah, and Vermont are the only states that reported both the full-time and part-time personnel. For the most part, the states appearing on the full-time list are states known for having severe environmental problems or noted for a serious commitment to environmental policy. The states on the part-time list are not in the national consciousness as having severe environmental problems or a commitment to environmental policy. Except for investigators, the numbers for personnel devoted to environmental crimes on a part-time basis, on the average, are higher than those committed on a full-time basis.

This makes sense for two reasons. First, those states not fully committed to the prosecution of environmental crimes understandably would not commit personnel on a full-time basis to this issue. Second, it could also be that their personnel were stretched by limited resources to the point that the resources were just not available to devote any personnel on a full time basis. The number of attorneys dedicated to the prosecution of environmental crimes on a part-time basis ranged from a high of six (New Hampshire) to a low of one (Maine, North Dakota,

Tennessee, and Utah). Colorado, Hawaii, Louisiana, Missouri, and South Dakota reported having two attorneys working on a part time basis; South Carolina, Vermont, and Wisconsin three; Kentucky four; and Delaware five.

Four states (Colorado, Hawaii, New Hampshire, and North Dakota) reported they had one paralegal working on environmental crimes on a part-time basis. With regard to part-time secretaries/receptionists, six states (Colorado, Missouri, North Dakota, South Dakota, Tennessee, and Vermont) indicated they had one position, while Wisconsin reported two and New Hampshire three.

In-House Legal Advisors/Investigators

The state police organizations were asked to indicate their *primary* source of legal advice regarding environmental crimes. Similarly, the attorneys general were asked to indicate who was their primary source of investigators. In this era of limited resources, state police organizations with in-house environmental attorneys suggest the police organization is actively and substantively involved in the criminal enforcement of environmental law. Similarly, the presence of in-house environmental investigators for attorneys general offices should indicate a high level of support for this type of program. Even in-house generalists who can competently advise on or investigate environmental matters should be a rarity and another indicator of the agency's commitment.

Another test of state commitment to the investigation and prosecution of environmental crimes would be if the primary source for legal advice resided with an attorney from another state agency rather than a federal attorney. In other words, if a state police organization had specialist attorneys in environmental crimes anywhere in the state's organization, their presence would suggest a level of commitment to this area of the law. If they did not, however, it could mean the state merely lacks the resources to properly carry out a program even though firmly committed to its philosophy (Lester, 1994). Further research is needed to determine whether the dearth of in-house attorneys or attorneys from other state agencies is an indicator of symbolic or substantive support by the state. For example, states could be using federal attorneys to achieve the criminal enforcement they are committed to but are creatively letting someone else "foot the bill." But the odds are any state committed to criminal enforcement would have at least one attorney skilled in the criminal aspects of environmental statutes, no matter where that attorney is located in the state institutional structure advising the state police on these matters.

Only the Maryland state police reported having an in-house environmental attorney. Keep in mind Maryland was one of those states with an environmental task force involving several state agencies. Five states indicated that generic in house attorneys provided their legal advice. Two of those states, Vermont and Wisconsin, are generally viewed as progressive on environmental concerns. But this perception does not mean you can assume this means their in-house generic attorneys are more informed on environmental issues than the non-progressive states who also reported getting their legal advice from in-house attorneys: Idaho, Mississippi, and Texas.

Most of the state police organizations answering this question rely on outside sources for their legal advice concerning environmental issues. Generally, their source is the state attorney general (Alaska, Arkansas, Illinois, Kentucky, New Jersey, North Dakota, South Dakota, and Washington). Other state police organizations reported getting their advice from local or state prosecutors (California, Nebraska, and Oregon). Indiana reported its legal advice came from the state Department of Environmental Affairs. The differences among the out-of-agency sources of legal advice for the state police organizations are more than likely due to the variation among the states in institutional arrangements and responsibilities.

The attorneys general of eight states (Arizona, Minnesota, New Hampshire, New Jersey, New Mexico, Pennsylvania, Tennessee, and Utah) reported having in-house environmental investigators. Four states (Colorado, Kentucky, Maine, and Texas) reported their investigators came from in-house regular investigators. Reliance on investigators from other sources would not necessarily indicate there was a lack of true commitment to the investigation of environmental crimes but may just indicate the state is doing the best it can with its limited resources (Lester, 1994). South Carolina's investigators came from local police agencies. Delaware, Nebraska, New York, South Dakota, and Wisconsin reported their investigators came from the state EPA, while the state Department of Health provided investigators to the attorney general office's in Hawaii and North Dakota. Finally, a reliance on the state police for investigators may be indicative of a more coordinated state program. Four states (Illinois, Louisiana, Maryland, and North Carolina) reported their investigators were supplied by the state police.

Task Forces

Both the state police organizations and the state attorneys general were asked whether there was a task force dedicated to investigating environmental crimes. If one existed, they were also asked to report when the task force was formed and who initiated the task force. A task force may be an indicator of the seriousness of any specific state toward environmental crimes. Task forces bring together a variety of personnel from different agencies and jurisdictions to coordinate operations and overcome interagency inertia or resistance. Investigating crime drains personnel and resources away from other uses during a time of budgetary constraints. Of course, a task force could be formed as a symbolic political gesture. Thus, the mere reporting of the existence of a task force is not sufficient in and of itself to make the case that a particular state is seriously, actively, and routinely pursuing environmental violations as crimes.

Kentucky, Maryland, Minnesota, New Jersey, and Texas reported having an environmental crime task force. Kentucky's task force started operations in September 1988. Maryland stated its task force was initiated by the state attorney general's office and was began in November of 1982. New Jersey's environmental task force began in January 1991 in the state attorney general's office. Texas gave no beginning date and did not indicate who initiated the program.

In previous studies, 29 states have reported environmental crimes units (Matulewich, 1991). What accounts for the discrepancy in the self-reported numbers and the formal statistics of the FBI? There is no definitive answer to this question, but this type of discrepancy highlights both the positive and negative aspects of this kind of data collection. First, the reliability of the responses is totally dependent on the knowledge and attentiveness of the individual answering the questionnaire. None of the responses can be taken at face value without further inquiry. But the same is true for governmental statistics. The environmental crime units reported in previous studies may ultimately be paper constructs, not viable, active units. Since this survey was designed to garner actual law enforcement activity rather than paper programs, then the self-reported environmental crimes units may be based on activity rather than a paper existence. Granted, some of the missing states may have environmental crimes units but did not respond to the survey, but the number not responding is insufficient to explain away the discrepancy.

Facilities and Equipment

Facilities: Each state police agency was asked questions concerning the facilities, office space, and equipment the agency's environmental personnel had at their disposal. If the police agencies have separate offices, an "800" number available for citizens to report environmental violations, special equipment and vehicles to carry out their investigations in this age of limited resources, this could be an indicator of not only the agency's support for investigating environmental crimes but also the state's commitment to this program. However, we have to keep in mind a dearth of these "extras" does not necessarily indicate a lack of commitment. In an age of budget constraints, a police agency or state may be very concerned and committed but lack the resources to fully operationalize the program (Lester, 1994). Only Vermont indicated an 800 toll free number was available for the reporting of environmental incidents. Six states (Arizona, California, Idaho, Illinois, Kentucky, and Maryland) reported having specialized vehicles beyond the standard issue police car. Six states (Arizona, California, Idaho, Illinois, Kentucky, and Texas) reported having special equipment for the investigation of environmental crimes. The types of special equipment reported included air sampling equipment, protective gear such as boots and gloves, spill kits, fire turnouts, radiation equipment, video cameras and other photographic equipment, and reference publications. The mix of the special equipment represents items to aid the investigation of environmental incidents, acknowledging the fact that standard police issue is insufficient to handle these investigations or provide safety for the investigators.

The police agencies were also asked where their laboratory work was performed and to provide, in percentages, the amount of laboratory work done by environmental in-house crime labs, in-house generic labs, other state owned labs, federal labs and which ones, private labs or others. Specialized environmental in-house labs or even generic in-house crime labs with the ability to do environmental work would be an indicator of agency commitment to this program. Again, if the police agencies turn to outside labs, it may not mean they do not support the program; it just may be due to the lack of resources. Or the police agencies may use outside resources because of the low level of activity. Environmental testing can be very expensive and a laboratory equipped for environmental testing is very costly. Thus, the activity level in the state may not justify the expenditure by the state policy organization even though the state and the police agency may be fully committed to the program.

Kentucky, Maryland, Mississippi, New Jersey, Oregon, South Dakota, and Washington reported all of their lab work was performed by other state agencies. Kentucky, New Jersey, and Oregon specified this outside lab work was performed by the equivalent of a state Environmental Protection Agency. Maryland indicated that its lab work was performed by the Department of Health and Mental Hygiene. Arizona reported that 90 percent of their laboratory work was performed in-house with the remaining 10 percent by an unspecified state agency. Arkansas indicated 75 percent of the work was performed in-house with the remaining 25 percent conducted by an unspecified source. California stated that 45 percent of their work was performed by the Department of Toxic Substances, 35 percent by private sources, and the remaining 20 percent by an unspecified source. Illinois reported 90 percent of their laboratory work was conducted by the state EPA with the remaining 10 percent being contracted out to private laboratories. Finally, Nebraska indicated that 90 percent of their testing was performed by an in house laboratory and with the remaining 10 percent being tested at federal laboratories, specific source unnamed.

From these data, it is obvious that state police information regarding the source of laboratory work is not consistent from state to state. But certain conclusions can be gleaned from the data. Most state police organizations responding to this question have the majority of their laboratory work performed by outside sources. Thus, the interesting question posed by this data is whether or not those states reporting most of their laboratory work was conducted in-house really have in-house laboratories capable of doing this work properly. We pose this question because the states that indicated in-house laboratory work were, for the most part, states not generally considered in the forefront of environmental policy: Arizona, Mississippi, and Washington. However, it could be due to the fact that lacking political and outside institutional support but facing public demand, these agencies have responded in the best way they can. Only further research will determine what is the reality for these states.

Equipment: The questions regarding equipment for the attorneys general were not so extensive. There were no questions concerning special equipment just questions concerning office space and toll free telephone numbers for reporting. Separate office facilities for the prosecution of environmental crimes may be indicative of commitment or work load. Illinois, Maryland, New Hampshire, and Pennsylvania reported separate or additional facilities for the prosecution of environmental crimes. Only New York reported having a toll free number for reporting violations.

Training

The state police and attorneys general were asked if special training was provided for their personnel and if so, how many hours per year, by training source, were provided on the following specific topics: general, nuclear/radioactive, biological, chemical, legal, safety, and other. The agencies were also asked if they provided specialized training in the environmental investigations.

State Police: Among the state police organizations reporting their personnel receive specialized training, there is a wide variety in the number of hours of training received each year. Total environmental training hours, as reported by the state police agencies ranges from a low of 4 (Wisconsin) to a high of 60 (California). The other states reporting total hours of special training were Arizona (40), Illinois (25+), Maryland (24), and Kentucky (16). There was no continuity from state to state as to the types of specialized training the personnel receive in the environmental categories listed in the survey. Arizona reported its personnel received 80 training hours in the nuclear category. For Arkansas, it was 40 hours in chemical environmental hazards. California had the following breakdown among the environmental hazards: nuclear (6), chemical (10), legal (12), and safety (12). Illinois reported nuclear

(8), chemical (8), legal (8), safety (8) and other (8). For Kentucky it was chemical (4) and safety (4). In Texas the state police personnel received specialized training for nuclear (5), biological (5) chemical (5), legal (5), safety (5) and other (5). Finally, Wisconsin reported nuclear (1), biological (1), and chemical (1).

This disparity in training hours and categories among the reporting state police organizations is probably due to the varying environmental conditions among the states and the police agencies matching specialized environmental training to state need or demand. Naturally, legal and safety training should be a concern for any state police agency although the numbers do not bear out this contention.

The sources of training also vary. For most states, the training was in house (Illinois, Kentucky, Maryland, Oregon, Texas, and Wisconsin) or from the state EPA (Idaho, Illinois, Kentucky, and Maryland). California reported its training was obtained from the state Department of Toxic Substances, the Federal Bureau of Investigation and a regional hazardous waste organization. Maryland also reported training to be by a regional hazardous waste organization. Texas reported training for their personnel came from the U.S. Department of Transportation. Finally, Maryland and Oregon stated they received training at the Federal Law Enforcement Training Center at Glynco, Georgia. From the differences in training hours and the variety of sources for that training, it should be obvious there is no standard in this field as to the number of hours per year needed or the best source for that training. This state of affairs is highly suggestive that the investigation of environmental crimes is a very new challenge for police organizations.

Finally, the state police organizations were asked if they provided specialized training to others and, if so to whom. California, Illinois, Kentucky, Maryland, New Jersey, and Texas reported they provided in house training. Kentucky and Maryland also reported providing investigative training to their state EPA agencies. Illinois provided specialized training to other governmental units, while Texas supplied environmental training to city police. Again, there appears to be no standard concerning training in any type or form by police or for police.

Attorneys General: As with the state police organizations, the number of training hours and the source of those training hours vary widely. For attorneys, the main source of training appears to be regional hazardous waste organizations (Colorado, Hawaii, Illinois, Minnesota,

New Hampshire, New York, North Dakota, Tennessee, Utah, Vermont, and Wisconsin), with a variation of 5 hours (New York) to 150 hours (Wisconsin). But attorneys also receive specialized training from the state bar associations (Minnesota, New Mexico, and South Dakota), the state EPA (North Carolina and Wisconsin), other state (Colorado) and federal (Minnesota and Texas) agencies, in-house programs (Minnesota, New Jersey, New York, North Carolina, South Dakota, and Wisconsin), Glynco, Georgia, the federal police training agency (Colorado, Texas and Utah), Continuing Legal Education programs (Colorado and New Mexico) and programs offered by the National Associations of Attorneys General (New Hampshire, New Mexico, and Vermont). Again, as with the state police, it appears there is no organized training procedure for these types of crimes.

While the state police organizations' responses regarding training were scattered among the variety of environmental categories with no apparent pattern, the state attorney's general training was mostly confined to general training rather than specific environmental categories. The states reporting that the training hours for their environmental attorneys were solely confined to general training hours were: Colorado (50), Delaware (10), Minnesota (40), Missouri (15), New Jersey (40), New York (15), and Vermont (10). For nuclear/ radioactive issues Hawaii provided 8 hours of training for their attorneys, the only reporting state to do so. Hawaii was also the only state providing specialized training in the biological category (8). For chemical issues specialized training was provided in Hawaii (8), Illinois (10), New Mexico (20), Tennessee (5) and Utah (15). Colorado was the only state that indicated their attorneys received specialized training in safety (8), North Dakota for hazardous waste (12), and Vermont on Grand Jury litigation (12).

More of the attorneys general indicated they provide training to others regarding environmental crime. In house or internal training was provided by Arizona, Colorado, Kentucky, Maryland, Minnesota, New Jersey, New York, North Dakota, Pennsylvania, South Dakota, Utah, Vermont and Wisconsin. Arizona, Colorado, Illinois, Louisiana, Maine, Maryland, Minnesota, Missouri, Nebraska, New Jersey, New York, North Carolina, North Dakota, Texas, Utah, Vermont, and Wisconsin all reported providing specialized training to other state agencies. These other state agencies included law enforcement officers around the state (Illinois), judiciary, bar association and local agencies (Maryland), regulators (Minnesota), local firefighters and police (New York), classes for the certification of enforcement officers (South Dakota), district attorneys (Texas), and state police (Vermont). Private interests receiving training included business groups, Chambers of Commerce, and regional hazardous waste organizations by Minnesota.

Levels of Activity

The states were asked to report the number of incidents, arrests, and convictions for various environmental crimes and to indicate whether the arrests and convictions were misdemeanors or felonies.

State Police: The responses, although sporadic and somewhat inconsistent, do provide tentative evidence that at least some of the states are slowly moving toward utilizing the criminal provisions of environmental violations. However, several points should be clarified. There is a wide divergence among the states in the numbers reported, with those states popularly considered as more progressive on environmental matters such as California, New Jersey, and Oregon, reporting the higher numbers. But states with "bad reputations" in the enforcement of environmental policy, such as Arkansas, Kentucky, and Mississippi, reported some activity, even though the reported numbers are relatively low. This survey cannot determine the reasons these less progressive environmental states reported any activity. But the answer probably lies somewhere between the institutional arrangements in the state and policy goals, as developed by the legislature and public and interest group activity.

Other questions in this survey provide clues, but further research regarding the number and type of incidents is needed to make a stronger claim that the numbers reported here are indeed evidence the states are moving toward criminal prosecution for those violations. For example, are the reported incidents sensational, highly publicized incidents that cannot be ignored by the state? If so, they may possibly represent only symbolic action rather than a routine, substantive policy and activity level.

The second point to be emphasized is the fact that, again, most of the incidents, arrests, and convictions were confined to those crimes that are more typically thought of as the traditional crimes—illegal transport of some type of hazardous waste—and, more recently, the illegal disposal of waste, both hazardous and nonhazardous, and explosives. However, one nontraditional policing category does have a relatively high number of incidents reported: water pollution. A possible explanation for this may be due to the nature of water pollution and its relationship with the public. Generally, the public gets upset at what they can see but not what they can't see. Thus, often public disgust with environmental degradation is aesthetic in nature. However, water pollution is a qualified exception to that "rule." First, water pollution can be seen—trash, dirty or discolored water, etc. But, trashed rivers do not propel public fear, only revulsion. It is pollutants not seen, e.g., benzene, dioxin, etc., and the perception these invisible toxins contaminate drinking water supplies that fuel the fear and public demand concerning water pollution.

And there are highly publicized incidents, nationally as well as locally, which reinforce that fear. For example, during the summer of 1993 Milwaukee, Wisconsin's public water supply became contaminated with bacteria that sickened most of the city's populace and lead to some loss of life. Jokes abounded such as "drink beer not water" in the beer capital of the nation. There are other, albeit controversial, documented cases of contaminated public and private water supplies, considered the "cause," at least by the affected population, of cancer clusters and a host of other rare illnesses (Brown & Mikkelsen, 1990). As one state police agency indicated, their agency first became involved with water pollution cases due to public demand. People just got tired of their wells being poisoned. However, as with much of the data and discussion in this preliminary report, additional research is needed to verify this contention.

The third and final point to be entertained concerning the reported activity is the wide variance between the number of incidents reported and the number of reported arrests and convictions. Obviously, there can be incidents and the culprits go undetected; thus, there will be no ensuing arrests or possibility of conviction. But our hunch is that it goes much deeper than the obvious for a variety of reasons. First, there is a dearth of specialized training in the investigation of environmental crimes for state police agencies (or any traditional police department for that matter). As the responses under the training questions suggest, there is *no* standardized training in this field; thus, training is a haphazard, hobbled-together affair. Plus, few state police agencies avail themselves of what little and/or limited training that is available, such as that provided by the regional hazardous waste organizations. Training costs time and money both of which is in very short supply among police agencies.

But beyond training there is another problem concerning the investigation of environmental crimes. Criminal investigations of environmental violations, for the most part, are not begun until very "late in the game." Generally, when an incident occurs, the normal investigative procedures used follow those standards governed by civil standards or administrative law and evidence, *not* the standards for criminal investigations. During that initial investigation criminal neglect or malicious intent may be uncovered. But in many cases by the time the evidence concluding that criminal sanctions are in order, the evidence obtained through this process is inadmissible in criminal proceedings. The typical regulator and/or environmental investigator is not necessarily schooled in, nor is he or she concerned with, the rules of criminal evidence. Thus, we should expect, under these conditions, a high ratio of incidents to arrests or convictions. Furthermore, environmental enforcers may be using the threat of criminal sanctions to cajole violators to comply with environmental laws and regulations (DiMento, 1993). Therefore, the investigation may not move into the arrest and conviction stage.

This state of affairs is probably due to the nascent state effort in this aspect of enforcement. More training is needed for all investigators in this area, both civil and criminal. But, again, only more research can truly determine the impact of a dearth of criminal investigative training for environmental violations.

Attorneys General: The attorneys general were also asked to report the number of incidents, arrests, and convictions their office has been involved with or is aware of. As with the state police activity, reported levels of activity varied by environmental category, but most of the activity centered around hazardous materials and water pollution. There were more misdemeanors than felonies as was true for the police organizations. Illinois seems to have the most active attorney general; however, the Illinois State Police did not report any incidents, arrests, and felonies, resulting in only a partial picture of true state activity being painted.

Trends

Agencies were asked to report their activity involving the investigation of criminal environmental violations since 1988 and what they anticipated activity would be over the next two years and to explain their answers.

State Police: No state indicated activity had decreased at any level of measurement, slightly or significantly. Nebraska, New Mexico, New York, North Dakota, South Dakota, Texas, Washington, and Wisconsin reported activity since 1988 had remained the same but gave no reasons. Likewise, those states reporting the activity level had increased slightly (Arizona, Illinois, and Vermont) offered no explanation. Alaska reported its activity level had increased slightly due to the *Exxon Valdez*, while Arkansas indicated its activity had increased slightly due to more requests for help. Indiana indicated the illegal dumping of hazardous waste by out-of-state dumpers lead to a slight increase in activity. Finally, Mississippi indicated its activity had increased slightly but did not give a reason.

All the states reporting a significant increase in activity in the investigation of environmental crimes offered a reason for the significant increase. Both California and Kentucky reported the increased activity was due to increased awareness of the problem. Maryland indicated increased activity was due to sediment violations, while New Jersey stated it was due to marine activity. For the most part, the activity level over the past two years was issue specific. Only California and Kentucky reported their increased activity levels were due to an increased awareness in a generic sense.

The responses are different for the question of what the police agencies anticipate their activity level to be during the next two years. Indiana expected the activity level to decrease significantly, and Alaska anticipated a slight decrease in activity in this area. Neither state gave a reason for its position, but the anticipated decline is probably related to the reasons they gave for the previous question. Indiana officials probably expected some political resolution to the problem of out-of-state garbage, and, for Alaska, the investigation and prosecution of the *Exxon Valdez* were nearing completion.

Arizona, Nebraska, New Mexico, New York, South Dakota, Texas, and Wisconsin all anticipated their activity level would remain the same but gave no reasons for their expectations. California portended their activity level would remain the same due to a lack of resources, and Vermont indicated their activity would remain unchanged because they needed more proficient investigators, which they did not anticipate as forthcoming.

Mississippi was the only state that anticipated a slight increase in activity without giving a reason. Arkansas anticipated a slight increase in the investigation of environmental crimes due to public demand. However, Illinois indicated there would *only* be a slight increase because of the need for more proficient investigators. The other states in this category (Maryland, New Jersey, and North Dakota) also gave rationales indicating that their activity level would be higher if they had more support. Both Maryland and North Dakota reported they needed more resources. New Jersey reported they would not receive replacement personnel for retirements and resignations. Thus, in the responses to this category we see some police agencies do see this as a problem but just do not have the resources to combat it properly.

Two states indicated they believed activity in the investigation of environmental crimes would increase significantly during the next two years. Kentucky stated the activity level would be due to continuing and increasing public pressure. Oregon reported activity would rise significantly due to an increasing number of incidents.

Attorneys General: The trends, as portrayed by the attorneys general, are very different from those painted by the state police agencies. Most of the attorneys general indicated during the last two years their activity level had increased slightly or significantly. Only New Hampshire reported their activity had slightly decreased due to less criminal activity concerning the environment. There is no way to tell from the data whether the decrease was due to past activity that deterred criminal activity or a decreased attentiveness to the issue. Nebraska, New York, and Vermont stated their activity level remained the same over the last two years. Nebraska did not give a reason for this state of affairs, but both New York and Vermont indicated budget cutbacks were the reason their activity level remained the same.

Arizona, Colorado, Hawaii, Kentucky, Maryland, North Carolina, North Dakota, Pennsylvania, South Dakota, and Tennessee stated their activity level in the last two years had increased slightly. Kentucky, North Dakota, and Pennsylvania gave no indication why they responded in this manner. Both Maryland and North Carolina indicated their increased activity was due to additional and stronger criminal provisions in state environmental statutes. The remainder of the states indicating their activity level during the past two years had increased slightly gave a variety of reasons. Arizona reported it was due to better enforcement, while Colorado indicated it was a new program and there had been a recent discovery of the problem. Hawaii stated the reason was due to training and awareness, while South Dakota indicated the increased activity was due to more reporting and effort. Finally, Tennessee reported the increased activity level was due to better coordination with district attorneys who have the ultimate authority for this program.

Delaware, Illinois, Louisiana, Maine, Minnesota, Missouri, New Jersey, New Mexico, Texas, Utah, and Wisconsin indicated their activity had increased significantly in the last two years. Both Delaware and Maine indicated one person in a key position was responsible for their increased levels of activity. Delaware indicated the increase was due to the commitment by the attorney general. On the other hand, for the attorney general's office in Maine, their increased activity level was due to one person at the state natural resources department who was highly committed to an environmental crimes program. Illinois, New Mexico, and Utah indicated their activity level increased due to the recent discovery of a problem. Louisiana reported activity increased because of effort and interest by the agency. Both Minnesota and Missouri indicated their activity level increased due to a state environmental crimes task force.

Again, the attorneys general paint a different picture of what they anticipate the activity level concerning environmental crimes will be during the next two years. None of the attorneys general anticipated the activity level would decrease. Arizona, Maryland, New Hampshire, New York, and Vermont all indicated the level of activity would remain the same. Vermont did not give a reason for its claim, but the rest of the states indicated their activity would remain the same due to a dearth of resources or budget cutbacks.

Hawaii, Kentucky, Maine, Nebraska, New Mexico, North Carolina, North Dakota, Pennsylvania, and South Dakota all stated they anticipated their activity level would increase slightly over the next two years. North Carolina and New Mexico indicated the increased activity would be due to additional and stronger criminal provisions in the environmental statutes. Kentucky said it was due to the attorney general's commitment to this program. North Dakota indicated their increased activity would be due to the illegal transport of waste from other jurisdictions. Both Hawaii and South Dakota suggested the increased activity level would be due to new administrative regulations and a new effort and focus on this issue area. Finally, Maine stated their activity would increase slightly due to the lack of resources suggesting it would increase more if there were more resources available.

The state attorneys general indicating they anticipated a significant increase in activity tended to give similar responses to the question. Colorado, Tennessee and Utah stated it was due to a new effort and focus by the agency. Closely related to that reason, Illinois and New Jersey said it was due to training and awareness. Again, Minnesota and Missouri claimed that task forces work. Finally, Delaware indicated the increased activity would be due to public demand.

Assessing Environmental Threats and Impediments to Prosecution and Investigation

Finally, each state police organization and attorneys general office was asked the following: (1) Which violation poses the greatest threat to the environment? (2) What is the greatest obstacle in the pursuit of criminal environmental violations? (3) Which violation is the most difficult/easiest to enforce?

Threats

State Police: California reported the greatest threat to its environment was the illegal disposal of hazardous waste. The rationale for this statement was hazardous waste had far-reaching effects and cleaning up the problem was very expensive. Illinois, Maryland, and Oregon also reported the illegal disposal of hazardous waste as the greatest threat to their environment. Both Illinois and Oregon said this activity contaminates well water, while Maryland reported it was a problem because the waste was dumped in the sewer systems. Kentucky indicated water pollution in general was their greatest threat. And Mississippi stated hazardous waste and explosives were their biggest problems. Oil vessel spills were the greatest threat to the environment in New Jersey. Both South Dakota and Wisconsin reported the illegal transport of chemicals as being their biggest headache—South Dakota because it represented the largest volume and Wisconsin for the far-reaching effects and expense involved. Even though the responses differ, there is a commonality among all the responses: polluted water supplies. Thus, it appears for police involvement the environmental criminal activity they are most concerned with is a direct threat to human health and life. This type of threat, then, fits nicely with the traditional reasons society utilizes police and the responsibilities police agencies historically are assigned.

Attorneys General: Again, as with the state police agencies, the greatest threat facing the states, as reported by most of the attorneys general, was related to hazardous waste and water pollution. Only Maine gave a response to this question that was not along this line. Maine indicated their greatest threat was ozone pollution that drifted into the state from out-of state sources. Arizona claimed its greatest threat was water pollution because of the limited water supply. Water pollution was Maryland's greatest threat due to the increasing use of sewers to dispose of waste. New Mexico reported hazardous waste as the greatest problem, North Dakota claimed it was the illegal disposal of hazardous waste, and Vermont indicated it was water pollution. Interestingly, all three states gave the same reason—these activities are a threat to groundwater supplies. New York indicated solid waste and water pollution were their biggest headache due to midnight dumpers. Delaware, Hawaii, South Dakota, and Tennessee all gave similar reasons, geographical location or military installations for their greatest threat but listed different hazards. Delaware indicated its greatest threats were air pollution, the disposal of hazardous waste, and water pollution. Hawaii, South Dakota, and Tennessee reported their greatest threat was the illegal disposal of hazardous solid waste. Both Missouri and New Jersey said their greatest threat was hazardous waste and water pollution. They indicated this had become their greatest threat due to the increased costs of legal disposal. Because of the human health and environmental risk, Minnesota said the greatest problem was knowing endangerment and the illegal disposal of hazardous waste. For the same reason, Pennsylvania claimed any disposal of hazardous waste was a threat. And Illinois and Utah said the illegal disposal of hazardous solid waste was their biggest problem because it was the greatest activity.

Colorado said any disposal of hazardous waste was their gravest problem due the history of mining in the state. Several states identified threats but offered no reasons for those being their greatest threats. Indiana and North Carolina listed any disposal of hazardous waste, and Kentucky listed hazardous waste and water pollution. For Louisiana there was a laundry list of problems: air pollution, disposal of hazardous waste and water pollution. Finally, Texas said they didn't know what the biggest obstacle facing the attorney general's office was because of the lack of experience.

Obstacles

State Police: The police agencies were also asked what the biggest obstacle facing their department was in the investigation and enforcement of criminal environmental violations. Although the responses to this question varied widely, most were related to a dearth of resources.

Arizona, Arkansas, California, Kentucky, Mississippi, Nebraska, New Jersey, New Mexico, Texas, and Wisconsin reported that their biggest problem was a lack of funding. The lack of personnel was the biggest obstacle confronting Arkansas, California, Illinois, Kentucky, Maryland, Mississippi, Nebraska, New Jersey, New Mexico, Texas, and Wisconsin. And it was a dearth of specialized equipment that hindered Maryland and Nebraska. Some responses to this question were not resource related. Illinois, New Mexico, and Wisconsin stated that one of the biggest obstacles they faced in the investigation of environmental crimes is they did not have clear cut authority. For California and Oregon one of their biggest problems was due to the fact policy makers did not view environmental violations as a crime. Mississippi reported that being a rural state was a liability. Finally, Indiana indicated its biggest obstacle was out-of-state garbage haulers, an issue specific response.

Attorneys General: For the attorneys general, the biggest obstacles to agency success were similar to those reported by the state police agencies. Maryland and South Dakota reported they needed more and properly trained investigators. The states responding they needed more personnel in all aspects of investigating and prosecuting were Colorado,

Missouri, New Jersey, and Vermont. Arizona, Louisiana, Minnesota, New York, North Carolina, Texas, Utah and Wisconsin responded they need more resources for everything. Budget cuts were the problem in Maine. Non-resource responses by the attorneys general included inadequate laws (Delaware and New Mexico) and the lack of statutory authority (Indiana and Pennsylvania). North Dakota indicated its biggest obstacle was due to the fact violators resided outside their jurisdiction. This state was having a big problem with the illegal disposal of waste from outside sources. The implementation of new administrative regulations was the biggest obstacle for Hawaii. Illinois stated the biggest obstacle was the court system: judges don't view environmental violations as real crimes. The Tennessee attorney general responded that inertia of the status quo was their biggest problem in combating environmental crime.

Investigation and Prosecution Efforts

State Police: For the crimes reported as the hardest to enforce, there were a variety of answers and some commonalities, too. Kentucky responded air pollution violations were the hardest to enforce due to a dearth of equipment. South Dakota found its most difficult task to be illegal loads, because of the mobility of the perpetrators. For this same reason Wisconsin claimed its biggest headache to be the illegal transport of chemicals. California gave the same reason for naming the illegal transport of hazardous waste. Illinois and Maryland reported their toughest investigations to be the illegal disposal of hazardous waste since the conduct of this activity occurs in hard to access industrial areas. New Jersey, also, indicated that water pollution was their biggest enforcement problem because the activity occurs in industrial areas. Finally, Mississippi said the hardest enforcement was the illegal disposal of hazardous waste, because it is a rural state where much activity can occur without detection.

The state police organizations responding to the question of which violations were the easiest to enforce also gave a variety of responses. California said it was stationary pollution, because it is the most visible. For the same reason, sediment pollution was the easiest for Maryland. Illinois, contrary to those states in the previous question, claimed the transport of hazardous waste was the easiest to enforce due to the fact this activity is extensively regulated and there is a documentary trail to follow. Kentucky found water pollution the easiest to enforce because of the access to equipment. Finally, probably the most fitting response, Wisconsin said none is easy.

Attorneys General: The attorneys general varied in their response to this question. Four states, Delaware, Indiana, Minnesota and New Jersey, indicated that the hardest prosecutorial problem they faced was air pollution. Indiana gave no reason for their response while Minnesota indicated air pollution was the hardest to prosecute because proof, detection and location of the source were difficult. Delaware indicated that it was not only air pollution but also water pollution and the disposal of hazardous waste that were the hardest to prosecute. The attorney general from Delaware said these crimes were difficult due to the complicated regulatory scheme and dearth of investigators. For the reason proof, detection, and the location of the source was so difficult New Jersey indicated solid waste as well as air pollution as the hardest enforcement issues. Arizona and New Mexico said their hardest prosecutions were water pollution. For Arizona this state of affairs was due to the fact that the proof, detection and location of source are difficult. New Mexico indicated their difficulties are caused by inadequate state oversight and enforcement. Three states, Kentucky, Missouri, and South Dakota, indicated the hardest cases to prosecute concerned the illegal disposal of nonhazardous waste. Kentucky laid the blame on the lack of public education. Missouri said their problems stemmed from the fact defendants did not have enough assets to correct the situation and the criminal laws for this violation were weak. The ever-popular difficulty of proof, detection, and location of source was given by South Dakota in response. Closely related to the illegal disposal of nonhazardous waste was North Dakota's response that the hardest cases to prosecute are the illegal transport and disposal of waste from sources outside of the state. The attorney general from North Dakota gave no reason for this response.

The remainder of the attorneys general gave a variety of answers to this question. Maryland indicated their hardest enforcement was the illegal storage of hazardous waste due to the vagueness of the laws and regulations. Pennsylvania said it was used oil for the same reason. In Illinois, the biggest prosecution problem was the overcharging by contractors in the state leaking underground storage tank program. The attorney general's office in Illinois indicated that the problem had developed due to inadequate state oversight and enforcement. For Maine the problem was false reporting because the violators conceal the falsification of records. And North Carolina said that single-event unpermitted discharges were their hardest to prosecute without giving a reason why. Finally, there was a group of states not responding with a specific environmental category. Hawaii and Louisiana stated they had confronted no substantial obstacle so far. Vermont said all of their environmental prosecutions were difficult due to the complexity and vagueness of the regulatory rules. Tennessee indicated all of the cases were difficult because of judicial, prosecutorial, regulatory, and industry resistance to addressing the problem. Finally, both Colorado and Texas said they could not properly answer the question due to their lack of experience in criminal environmental law.

Again, the attorneys' general responses were more varied than those of the state police agencies regarding which environmental offenses were the easiest to pursue. However, keep in mind more of the attorneys general fully responded to the survey. The attorney general responses to this question, for the most part, focused on aspects of court or trial activity. Delaware and New Jersey stated water pollution violations were the easiest to enforce. Delaware said water pollution was the easiest to enforce because these violations were source specific. Due to the broad definition of criminal negligence and culpability contained in the water pollution laws the New Jersey attorney general indicated it was easier to prosecute water pollution violations than other environmental laws. Missouri indicated the illegal disposal of hazardous waste was its easiest case for a different reason—the criminal provisions in hazardous waste statutes were stronger than in most environmental laws. Both Kentucky and Maine said the illegal disposal of hazardous waste represented their easiest cases for the same reason—citizens and/or employees see the violations, get upset, and report them.

Arizona, Illinois, Indiana, and Pennsylvania all said solid waste landfill violations were the easiest to prosecute. Arizona indicated the reason was that the management of landfills was paper intensive, leaving a well-documented evidentiary trail. For Illinois, these violations were easy because citizens and/or employee witnessed violations and reported them. Pennsylvania simply stated these were the easiest to prove, while Indiana gave no reason for this response.

Conclusion

This relatively new police enforcement issue is also a relatively new research program for academics. From this precursory examination of the activity level of state police organizations and attorneys general, we have seen, in at least some states, a movement toward utilizing the criminal provisions of environmental statutes for enforcement and compliance. Comparisons or correlations of state activity in environmental crimes and other aspects of state environmental policy will provide clues to understanding and determining the conditions under which states undertake a program of utilizing the criminal statutes as an enforcement technique for environmental violations.

Our thesis is that the states turning to criminal enforcement will do so for two basic reasons. First, they will be states with severe environmental problems, especially water pollution, but which lack adequate environmental institutions to properly monitor and enforce their environmental statutes and regulations. The inability may be due to a dearth of resources or commitment (Lester, 1994). These conditions will interface with public demand to find solutions to problems that fuel public fear.

This research identified many issues requiring further inquiry. This study was, in part, an effort to ascertain what is known about environmental criminal enforcement in the states and what additional research is necessary to fully understand this newly developing phenomena. For example, there exists a real need to determine the difficulties prosecutors encounter when shifting from civil to criminal enforcement. Also, we need to more thoroughly understand what types of environmental violations are more apt to be prosecuted criminally rather than civilly and why. Furthermore, we need to ascertain the deterrent factor of the utilization of environmental crimes and perhaps, most importantly, the relationship between public demand and activity concerning the investigation and prosecution of environmental crimes. After all, environmental policy represents one of those policy topics almost totally driven by public demand and participation in our democratic system. If the specific environmental agencies aren't responding, then the public may be turning to the non-traditional environmental agencies to resolve their demands.

Finally, through further research, we need to determine a precise and proper definition of what constitutes an environmental crime. This may very well be the most critical task when it comes to assessing the investigatory and prosecution efforts by the states. Police agencies throughout the country are gearing up to take off on this new dimension of law enforcement. The International Association of Chiefs of Police has a committee on environmental crime in policing. Others such as the National Institute of Justice are conducting research into local police agencies and their activity concerning environmental crimes. But without an operational definition of environmental crime, police activity regarding the environment could be as futile and frustrating as the efforts currently in place in the "War on Drugs." The persistence of a drug problem in this country has been, in part, due to the failure to develop a precise definition of a "drug related" crime and to define the problem. Without such definitions it has been almost impossible to agree on how to achieve a solution to the problem. For environmental crimes, resolving this definitional phase beforehand is critical lest enforcement activity on environmental crimes produce few positive results and waste valuable and limited law enforcement resources.

NOTES

1.   The focus of this research lies on criminal enforcement efforts at the state, rather than local, level. This does not mean efforts by substate governmental units (cities, counties, etc.) are unimportant; however, true "statewide" commitment to criminal enforcement is evidenced through organized state effort by state organizations, not random or haphazard local governmental interest.

2.   Of the 99 surveys administered, 49 to state police agencies (Hawaii has no state police agency) and 50 to state attorneys general, there were 79 responses, 41 from state police agencies and 38 from attorneys general. In 32 states both the state police and attorney general completed the survey. Of the remaining 18 states, 14 had at least one of the two agencies respond (9 by state police and 5 by attorneys general). Neither survey was completed by only four states.

3.   The International Association of Chiefs of Police (IACP) has classified state police organizations into two categories—highway patrol and state police. A "Highway Patrol" agency is defined as "a state law enforcement agency with a uniformed field patrol. Police services restricted to or concentrated on traffic, vehicle, and highway related activities" (e.g., Alabama, Arizona, California, Colorado, Florida, Georgia, Iowa, Kansas, Minnesota, Mississippi, Missouri, Montana, Nebraska, Nevada, North Carolina, Ohio, Oklahoma, South Carolina, South Dakota, Tennessee, Texas, Utah, Washington, Wisconsin, Wyoming). While a "State Police" agency is defined as: "a uniform field force. Responsible for general police services" (Alaska, Arkansas, Connecticut, Delaware, Idaho, Illinois, Indiana, Kentucky, Louisiana, Maine, Maryland, Massachusetts, Michigan, New Hampshire, New Jersey, New Mexico, New York, Oregon, Pennsylvania, Rhode Island, Vermont, Virginia, West Virginia). Therefore, it has to be acknowledged the responses from the state police organizations may vary because of these different jurisdictional lines.

REFERENCES

Abrams, Robert (1991). "Safeguarding the Workplace: Environmental Hazards May Be Criminal." *Trial* (June): 20-23.

Bowman, Ann O'M. (1984). "Intergovernmental and Intersectoral Tensions in Environmental Policy Implementation: The Case of Hazardous Waste." *Policy Studies Review* 4 (2): 230-244.

_____ (1985). "Hazardous Waste Management: An Emerging Policy Area Within an Emerging Federalism." *Publius: The Journal of Federalism* 15: 131-144.

Brown, Phil, and Edwin J. Mikkelsen (1990). *No Safe Place: Toxic Waste, Leukemia, and Community Action.* Berkeley, CA: University of California Press.

Comment (1985). "Putting Polluters in Jail: The Imposition of Criminal Sanctions on Corporate Defendants Under Environmental Statutes." *Land and Water Law Review* XX: 93-108.

Crotty, Patricia McGee (1987). "The New Federalism Game: Primacy Implementation of Environmental Policy." *Publius: The Journal of Federalism* 17: 53-67.

_____ (1988). "Assessing the Role of Federal Administrative Regions: An Exploratory Analysis." *Public Administration Review* (March/April): 642-648.

DiMento, Joseph F. (1986). *Environmental Law and American Business: Dilemmas of Compliance.* New York: Plenum Press.

_____ (1993). "Criminal Enforcement of Environmental Law." *ANNALS, AAPSS* 525 (January): 134-136.

_____ (1990). "Polluters Beware." *The Economist* 315 (April 7): 38.

Habicht, F. Henry, II (1984). "Justice Cracks Down on Environmental Crimes." *EPA Journal* (March): 16-17.

Hammett, Theodore M., and Joel Epstein (1993). "Local Prosecution of Environmental Crime." *Issues and Practices*. Washington, DC: The National Institute of Justice.

"Justice Environmental Crimes Unit Wins Record Number of Indictments" (1985). *Inside EPA* (September 6): 5-6.

Kelly, Brian (1978). "Allied Chemical Kept that Kepone Flowing." *Business and Society Review* 21 (Spring):17-22.

Kentucky Land, Air and Water (1991). "Crimes Workgroup Opens 64 Cases." (Fall): 16.

Leon, Richard J. (1990). "Environmental Criminal Enforcement: A Mushrooming Cloud." *St. John's Law Review* 63: 679-690.

Lester, James P. (1994). "A New Federalism? Environmental Policy in the States." In Norman J. Vig and Michael Kraft (eds.), *Environmental Policy in the 1990s* (2nd. ed.) (pp. 51-68). Washington DC: CQ Press.

Matulewich, Vincent A. (1991). "Environmental Crime Prosecution: A Law Enforcement Partnership." *FBI Law Enforcement Bulletin* 60: 20-25.

McMurry, Robert I., and Stephen D. Ramsey (1987). "Environmental Crime: The Use of Criminal Sanctions in Enforcing Environmental Laws." *Land Use and Environment* 18: 427-463.

Moorman, James W. (1978). "Criminal Enforcement of the Pollution Control Laws." Report before the American Bar Association (pp. 25-28).

National Penalty Report: Overview of EPA Federal Penalty Practices, FY 1990 (1991). Compliance Policy and Planning Branch, Office of Enforcement (April): 23.

Reich, Michael R. (1991). *Toxic Politics: Responding to Chemical Disasters*. Ithaca, NY: Cornell University Press.

Reitze, Arnold W., Jr., and Glenn L. Reitze (1976). "Overview." *Environment* 18 (2): 2-5.

Ringquist, Evan J. (1993). *Environmental Protection at the State Level: Politics and Progress in Controlling Pollution*. Armonk, NY: M. E. Sharpe.

Russell, Clifford S. (1991). "Monitoring and Enforcement." In Paul R. Portney (ed.), *Public Policies for Environmental Protection* (pp. 243-274). Washington DC: Resources for the Future.

Stanfield, Rochelle L. (1984). "Ruckelshaous Casts EPA as 'Gorilla' in States' Enforcement Closet." *National Journal* (May 26): 1034-1038.

Starr, Judson W. (1986). "Countering Environmental Crimes." *Environmental Affairs* 13: 379-395.

Stone, Christopher D. (1976). "A Slap on the Wrist for the Kepone Mob." *Business and Society Review* 22 (Summer): 4-11.

Tejada, Susan (1984). "A Day in the Life of a Criminal Investigator." *EPA Journal* 11 (1): 25-26.

Tennille, Jr., Norton F. (1978). "Criminal Prosecution of Individuals: A New Trend in Federal Environmental Enforcement?" Report before the American Bar Association (pp. 20-22).

CHAPTER ELEVEN

Environmental Crime and Organized Crime: What Will the Future Hold?

William D. Hyatt
Tracy L. Trexler

This chapter addresses the possible, probable, and potential for the involvement of organized criminal groups in the future destruction or degradation of the environment. The scope is not intended to encompass all environmental crime or all of the groups who will engage in it but rather to focus on those organizations whose foundation and purpose is criminal activity and who seem likely to attack the environment in a variety of ways, often because it is a relatively easy and unprotected target. As the term is used in this chapter, organized crime is neither restricted to the traditional view of the Mafia families nor is it so broad as to include legitimate companies who, in the course of trying to improve their profitability resort to criminal destruction of or damage to the environment (although such companies will often employ organized criminal groups formed for the specific purpose of exploiting and avoiding environmental regulations). The groups who commit the criminal acts will be the focus here.

Describing what shape environmental crime is going to take next year is an ambitious undertaking, and predicting what is going to take place as we enter the next century seems foolhardy. Nevertheless, unless we attempt to prepare now for what is likely be in store for us in the next century, we will likely find ourselves victims of events rather than shapers of our own destiny. The purpose of this chapter is to call attention to trends that are emerging in our society which suggest likely future scenarios. Most of the predictions here are not couched in terms of what might possibly be but are based on events which are beginning to occur now and which in all likelihood will accelerate in the future. In the words of Naisbitt and Aburdene (1990): "the most reliable way to anticipate the future is to understand the present."

The following discussion will be in terms of three groups of criminal activity: (1) depletion of scarce environmental resources, (2) destruction or degradation of the environment, and (3) damaging, or the threat of damaging, the environment for political purposes.

Globalization of Environmental Crime

For the past few years organized crime has been portrayed in the media as a decaying institution with a very limited life span. This chapter will challenge that assumption and suggest that organized crime in all parts of the world, particularly in the environmental crime arena, is poised for a "great leap forward" which may well rival the progress it achieved in the United States in the 1920s and 1930s. In the early part of this century, organized crime in America truly became organized and simultaneously moved from being controlled by the politicians to controlling them, primarily as a result of the enactment of prohibition (Abadinsky, 1990).

In *The Third Wave*, Alvin Toffler (1980) describes how events moved us from a hunter-gatherer society to an agrarian society, then through the Industrial Revolution to an urban industrial society and with the development of the technology of recent years to a new age (the "information age"), free of many of the restraints that shackled society during the industrial age. This technology appears to be the vehicle which will move the groups that we cumulatively refer to as "organized crime" from the present criminal age to an age of information utilization which will free them from many of the constraints imposed upon them by current laws, law enforcement, politicians, and geography. This new age will allow them to become true international organizations in the sense of having no border restrictions. And it is the form they will take in this period that will present the greatest challenge to law enforcement.

Over the last decade, although all criminal activities on an organized scale have become internationalized, to some extent, environmental criminal activity must be singled out for special consideration as global in nature because environmental crimes in any country are very likely to affect all countries. This is perhaps the one crime that cannot be compartmentalized or ignored in that the effects of environmental crime touch millions; often in ways unforeseen at the time of the commission of the crime.

Effect of Ethnicity on Environmental Crime

Newspapers have repeatedly chronicled the demise of the Mafia in the United States. They have at the same time documented the unprecedented proliferation of ethnic gangs operating here and in many of the territories formerly the exclusive province of the Italian/Sicilian Mafia. These emerging ethnic gangs include factions from Russia, Israel, China, Japan, Thailand, Vietnam, Mexico, Colombia, and Jamaica, just to name a few. As with the Mafia, which kept its ethnic ties to its homeland and made profitable use of those ties, the emerging groups are likely to do the same. This strong tie to a friendly "home base" makes enforcement and investigation of criminal violations difficult. The ability of investigators to "pierce" these gangs is hampered since many of the members will move back and forth between their native country (both physically and technologically) with an ease and rapidity previously reserved for legitimate international trade. As each of these new organizations emerges, they will bring their own cultural backgrounds and experiences to their criminal endeavors, severely straining the capability of governmental units assigned to the fight against organized crime since an understanding of each of these ethnic backgrounds will be needed to successfully investigate them.

In the days when the Mafia was virtually the only target, investigation was relatively easy. Federal and state law enforcement communities maintained surveillance on and records of the most "notorious" members in particular geographic areas and/or "trades." Under these circumstances investigation of criminal activities was comparatively easy, particularly since most of the organizations were geographically shackled because of their need for political assistance as well as the necessity for geographical proximity to their victims.

When working on the Miami Organized Crime Strike Force, the primary author found that two of the targets, in addition to the Mafia, were the Colombians and the Jamaicans. These targets presented considerably more of a challenge because they had no real roots in the United States, and although the target group stayed the same, the active players continually changed. An investigation was often thwarted when a suspect simply retreated to his home country for a period of time. As travel and communication between countries becomes increasingly easier, these targets will become more and more difficult to focus on and correspondingly more difficult to prosecute unless new levels of international cooperation are developed.

Many of these new groups will have little regard for the environmental damage they effect in the United States or in any industrialized country, not only because of the conditions that they are likely to have in the country in which they were reared but also because of the opinion in much of the world that the First World countries have been destroying the environment, particularly in Third World countries, for decades.

World Democratization Will Lead to New Targets

Law enforcement in the United States has never had the "advantage" of fighting crime through unrestrained techniques and tactics. Here, all criminal processes by the government must be conducted in an atmosphere governed by numerous personal rights and liberties guaranteed to suspects and defendants. While the U.S. law enforcement community operates under the principles of "innocent until proven guilty" and "due process," totalitarian countries were able to effectively suppress most of what we call organized crime largely because they were not bound by the legal protections afforded suspects and defendants in a democratic society. As a result, most of the Iron Curtain countries have never developed what we would consider an effective criminal investigation technique. With the demise of strong central governments in these countries and the likelihood their policing agencies will not enjoy the unrestrained freedom of the past, the Eastern

European countries seem destined for considerable difficulty in coping with the organized crime gangs of the future. These difficulties are especially likely given that many of these gangs are imported part and parcel from the countries offering trade and economic assistance. A prime example of such "importation" of gangs and gang-related criminal activity is the *Yakazu* who will, in all likelihood, become a major factor in criminal activity as Japan becomes more of a trade partner with these countries. Indeed, the recent events in the former Soviet Union, with the attempts to market weapons-grade nuclear material, underscore the difficulties these countries will have in the future, particularly since environmental degradation has been the norm in those countries in the past.

The likely difference in technological capabilities between the newly emerging countries and the gangs will, in most instances, tilt heavily in favor of the gangs. This advantage, together with the experience of these gangs in evading prosecutions in democracies will likely cause severe problems for both the countries involved and for the corporations and countries who will suffer the consequences of their actions. By analogy, imagine the problems currently being experienced in the New York construction trade with organized crime, then transfer those problems to a jurisdiction whose law enforcement officers had, until very recently, worked only as writers of parking tickets, and consider the difficulty that jurisdiction would have.[1]

These problems will be exacerbated by the technological advances which will eliminate much of the need for on-site activity by the gang members. It will be not only possible but technologically logical for gangs in Tokyo, New York, and even Hagerstown, Maryland, to commit crimes a continent away in the safety and comfort of their living room via telephones and television screens (Moore, 1994).

Third World Production: Opportunity for Environmental Crime

It is widely predicted that in the next century most of the industrialized world will emerge as service and information societies while the current Third World societies will become the industrial production centers of tomorrow (Toffler, 1980). As with the Iron

Curtain countries previously discussed, these countries will be ill prepared to cope with the sophisticated criminal activities of today's organized criminal organizations, particularly given the current lack of sophistication in both laws and law enforcement in those countries. These countries currently have been protected, at least to some extent, by their poverty and lack of industrial base. In other words their protection, to now, is that they have little if anything that is worth the effort to steal.

In the future, as their industrial base grows, these countries will have worthwhile assets to be plundered, even though in many instances the assets may be owned or controlled by corporations located in the so-called sophisticated countries. These corporations, although accustomed to dealing with organized crime in their home environments, will find the going considerably more difficult in Third World countries where the laws are not geared to combat such threats and the law enforcement agencies are better suited to the enforcement of simple crimes. It is also likely that some businesses will move to these areas specifically to avoid the economic effect of environmental laws as was argued during the debate of the recently enacted North American Free Trade Agreement (NAFTA) legislation. Thus, whether by bad intention or simply the inability to cope with the emerging groups, protection of the environment is likely to be much more difficult in the future, either by the law enforcement agencies of these newly industrialized countries or by the corporations doing business there.

The United States Will Be an Exporter of Environmental Criminal "Know-How"

There has been much recent talk about the changing of the American economy, particularly the predictions that we will phase out much of our industrial base to the Third World and will become primarily a service and information economy. It seems likely that this will occur as we find that the future is more and more in the area of selling of information and know-how. It also seems reasonable to assume that criminal groups in the United States will find themselves in much the same position, namely, that it will become more profitable for them to supply know-how and technological expertise in sophisticated environmental crimes rather than to commit the actual crimes themselves. Just as we have gone from a substantial importer of marijuana in the late 1960s and early 1970s to a net exporter in the 1980s and 1990s, it seems likely that we will go from an importer of criminal technology in the 1900s (from Italy and Sicily) to a net exporter of such technology to countries where not only will democracy and industry be evolving but so will organized criminal activities.

With regard to sophisticated white collar and environmental fraud, our criminal organizations are unsurpassed, and the market for their expertise will be in heavy demand, particularly in the newly opened parts of eastern Europe, South America, Asia, and Africa. Likewise in money laundering and reinvestment, it is likely our organizations will be ready, willing, and able to provide expertise for a price.

U. S. Organized Crime: Aggressively Targeting Environmental Crime

Most of the predictive research data seem to suggest street and violent crimes will be substantially reduced in the future for a variety of reasons. It seems likely that we will instead see well-run criminal organizations moving away from the current physically-oriented crimes in the future. Not only will future crimes be safer for the criminal than the more "open" operations of yesteryear, but they are likely to be infinitely more rewarding financially. Because of the technology available today, a criminal with a computer will be able to earn more in a few hours than a burglar could earn with twenty years of diligent effort.

Just as many drug dealers in California and elsewhere are able to avoid prosecution with "designer drugs" which, because of their currency, have not yet been made illegal, criminal organizations of the future will look for opportunities in the environmental area where criminal laws and enforcement techniques have not yet caught up with the potential for abuse. This seems particularly likely to be true in countries where no administrative sophistication has yet been developed and law enforcement is still geared to deal in reactive fashion with traditional criminal activities.

While many small concerns cannot afford adequate insurance protection in today's competitive environment, much of American business will find itself merely "one of many" in the world economy rather than world leaders. Many of these businesses will find that they can neither afford measures necessary to protect the environment nor the financial burden that will accompany compliance with environmental regulations, particularly in the United States.[2]

In such a scenario, one solution for many small businesses might be to succumb to an "offer they can't refuse" in terms of having their environmental compliance problems solved by people they strongly suspect are not going to solve them in any responsible way. Because most governments are currently seeking to protect the environment through regulation rather than criminal enforcement, it will seem relatively safe and attractive to the weak willed or the financially stressed to deal with their waste disposal and related problems in such a manner.

As we are all aware, the cost of disposing of refuse is becoming increasingly expensive for industries and governmental units. The proper disposal of toxic waste is rapidly becoming prohibitive from a business perspective and will only become more so in the future. Organized crime groups have already begun to assist in the "disposal" of these toxic substances for legitimate businesses who turn to them because their "charges for disposal" are much less expensive (Block & Scarpitti, 1985). It is likely that these gangs in the future will organize themselves through a series of shell corporations with at least one shell corporation being in a country where incorporation records are secret, such as the Cayman Islands, so that ultimate ownership of the corporations cannot be traced. These corporations will then contract to dispose of toxic wastes for considerably less than the price being charged for legitimate disposal. The charges can, of course, be reduced because the criminal organization has no intention of disposing of the waste in any proper or responsible fashion. In fact, disposal will likely take the form of either mislabeled waste which will be deposited in landfills or other disposal sites, or simply "midnight dumping" at any convenient and isolated site.

With the globalization of the criminal activities it seems likely that criminal organizations will also seek out compliant leaders in Third World countries who will allow their countries to become a toxic waste disposal site for the proper monetary consideration. This presents a problem for the world for, although many of these dumping incidents will ultimately affect the entire world, they will likely be legal under the manipulated laws of the "receiving" country, and national sovereignty has traditionally been respected.

The benefit to the criminal organization will be that the crime, unlike the crimes of assault or robbery, will not be discovered immediately and possibly for some considerable period of time, which allows ample time for the covering of criminal tracks. The benefit to the corporations is twofold. Most obvious is the enormous saving in disposal cost, but of equal importance is the availability of a "fall guy" if and when the criminality of the disposal is discovered. If the corporation were discovered to have illegally dumped the waste, the damage to their image, not to mention the criminal prosecution of their officials, would make the illegal disposal unattractive. But in this instance they can take their place as victims along with the public, wringing their hands at how they were taken in by these con men and criminals and finessing the question of why they did not realize something had to be amiss since the cost of this "bargain" was so much less than the normal cost of legitimate disposal.

Toxic Waste Recycling

There was recently a rather terrifying incident of a road having to be closed because it caught fire and took several days to extinguish the blaze. The roadbed was actually built on, and to some extent composed of, highly flammable waste (Miller, 1986). If we do not develop techniques for preventing reoccurrences of such events in the future, such incidents may become the norm rather than a startling and unique occurrence. The rationale is the same as was described in the previous section. Because of relatively small enforcement staffs, disposal of toxic chemicals and materials by passing them off as nontoxic becomes a relatively safe and certainly economical way to dispose of material. A company which is in the road construction business and controlled indirectly by a criminal organization purchases fill material for the road bed from a company who offers an attractive price for delivery of the material. The company offering the fill has collected toxic waste from a chemical or paper company for the purpose of seeing it properly disposed of, but their records either do not indicate the final disposition of the material or they falsify the records of its disposition. No real check is currently made of such companies' records to determine whether the hazardous material has been disposed of responsibly, and, because of the prohibitive cost of such a check on all but the most dangerous or radioactive chemicals, it is unlikely to be made in the future.

Thus, the dangerous material becomes part of the roadbed and eventually seeps into the ground water and begins to seriously erode the environmental quality of its surroundings. The damage will be noticed years, possibly even decades, later. At this point, fixing criminal or even civil liability will be difficult if not impossible. From both the corporation's and the criminal's point of view, this is a win-win situation, except in the extremely rare case where one of the "bad guys" happens to live in the affected neighborhood.

Third World Belief That It Is Their Turn To Make Money with Pollution

The President of Argentina recently commented that the First World has had its turn at polluting the environment, and now that it has grown rich from disregard of the health of the environment, it has no business interfering: "It is our turn" (to pollute the environment in order to become industrialized and thus wealthy). This attitude, which will, at best, be difficult to reverse, will be exacerbated if Third World countries can see that we have not solved our own environmental destruction problems and are lamely crying that it is not our fault that criminals are violating our laws. This excuse is not likely to hold much sway with Third World countries trying to improve their economies. In other words, we must get our environmental house in order before we ask others to do the same.

Depletion Of Endangered Species and Materials

The business of organized crime has always been, in one form or another, the supplying of desired but illegal goods to a willing market of consumers, particularly in America, Japan, and Western Europe. While we currently have laws against the importation of endangered species of both animals and materials into the United States, anyone who is interested either in animals or wood knows that both are being imported and sold in the United States despite the ban. One of the authors of this chapter has considerable interest in wood working and is therefore continually looking in magazines to see what exotic woods are available; rosewood is frequently found. Rosewood imports were banned by the Convention on International Trade in Endangered Species in 1992, but, if anything, there are now more offerings of this beautiful but extremely scarce wood than before the passage of this agreement. Although some of these offerings may be, for a variety of reasons, exempt from the ban on importation, it is quite unlikely that all of these advertisements are for legal import. The collection of rosewood, which is usually only a single slow-growing tree in perhaps a 50 acre forest tract, represents substantial damage to the environment because not only is this rare tree removed but the removal of the tree from the forest often does substantial damage to neighboring trees which are in the way of its removal not to mention the animals whose habitat is destroyed.

Currently, much of the trade in both banned animals and materials is relatively unorganized, primarily because the profit available has not been a sufficient incentive, and there is some risk involved in the smuggling. The exception to this involves the trade in ivory and rhinoceros horns; this "business" thrives in a very organized criminal environment. However, organized criminal groups, with their smuggling networks and corrupt officials long in place, will be the vehicle of the future in expanding the importation market as the demand for these items grows and their scarcity increases. While we have had some limited success in preventing the harvesting and importation of these items up to now, that success is unlikely to continue as the value of the items grows and more organized and sophisticated criminal organizations enter the arena.

Environmental crime involving the depletion of natural resources, including wildlife and endangered lands, is an issue that we must face. With the growing market for the exotic animals, most of which are endangered and protected under the Endangered Species Act, animals ranging from ostriches, kangaroos, llamas, camels, and zebras to water buffalo, primates, rare birds, and reptiles are being sold on the auction block for thousands of dollars in most of the First World countries. Citizens of these countries of origin are willing participants in the destruction of their country's environment because of the money to be made in the trafficking in these animals and materials. The sellers of these animals and materials are raping their own land and the bounty mother nature has provided them. Some of these animals are responsible for playing specified ecological roles, and when the animal or material becomes extinct, their ecological contribution is eliminated to the detriment of all of us. Another criminal act which contributes to the overall reduction of our natural resources is the depletion of our nation's wetlands. A U. S. Department of the Interior study in 1991 estimated that there are roughly 103.3 million acres of wetlands remaining. The annual reduction is estimated at 200,000 to 300,000 acres. Although there are regulations governing the conversion or filling of wetlands, these regulations are currently being circumvented through incestuous relationships between criminal elements and public officials.

Once again, this holding the environment hostage will only increase in the future. Environmental crimes that scar and destroy the land for years to come are crimes that need to be prevented or at least reacted to as quickly as possible. Since law enforcement agencies assume a reactive role in the course of an accident involving hazardous materials, they need to be trained to act accordingly when environmental crimes occur. Yet most law agencies involved in protecting the environment have only minimal criminal enforcement staffs, and these are trained in reactive rather than in proactive modes.

A pressing issue for police organizations in the future will be how to train officers how to deal with environmental criminality. According to U. S. Department of Transportation estimates, there are at least 500,000 shipments of hazardous material daily in the United States.[3] These are shipped by all means of transportation--air, water, railways and highways. The response time and the manner in which the responding officers deal with the illegal disposal of waste is vital for environmental and population protection. If an improper disposal involving hazardous material occurs near a source of water, then a large number of people may be affected. If the reaction time by law enforcement officials is slow and steps are not immediately taken to prevent future incidents, then irreversible environmental damage may be inflicted. To maintain our environment, it is the duty of law enforcement agencies to assume a proactive position. Proactive measures by law enforcement agencies such as "sting" operations and special environmental crimes units will be critical in the future; once the hazardous material has soiled the environment, the effects will plague us for generations. If it is that easy to poison our environment unintentionally, as was the case in the *Exxon Valdez* incident, imagine how easy it will be for those who wish to intentionally harm the environment to pursue their agenda of destruction and/or terror.

Environmental Terrorism

Although the United States reports a substantial number of domestic terrorist incidents each year, these do not normally fall in the category of environmental crime. (While a cross burning in one's front yard or the firebombing of an abortion clinic is undoubtedly terrifying to those at whom it is directed, it is not the type of terrorism to which the people of Northern Ireland or Lebanon have become accustomed.) One has only to listen to any news broadcast to realize that America and its inhabitants are not currently the most popular country or people in the world, particularly with the inhabitants of many Third World countries. This unpopularity, which now results in terrorist acts against Americans living or traveling abroad, will likely be brought home to America during the next decade.

While these countries and people do not possess the means to confront us directly, they do have, thanks to the technology explosion, the ability to do us considerable harm by way of terrorist acts committed in our country. They also believe they have the right and sometimes the duty to commit acts against us which will punish us for what they see as our meddling in affairs in their region, however well intentioned our actions are.

It is axiomatic that a truly free open and democratic country cannot effectively protect itself from terrorist activities. In order to be truly free, our citizens must have open access to virtually all areas of the country, to much of the structure of government and free travel throughout the country without the necessity of obtaining or displaying identity papers on the command of authority. While such freedom from restrictions makes us comfortable in our lifestyles, they make us extremely vulnerable to attack by determined terrorists. Increasingly countries are discovering that while they cannot challenge the leading industrial countries militarily, they can make life uncomfortable and difficult for them through the use of terrorist tactics, particularly in countries such as ours which are large and have a mobile and diverse population.

While we have lived with the threat of terrorism for some time throughout the world, the United States has been exceptionally fortunate to have not been the target of any major terrorist activities. FBI statistics indicate that there are some 1500 terrorist incidents in the United States each year, almost exclusively of a minor domestic nature, other than the World Trade Center bombing. Furthermore, the United States has experienced no international environmental terrorist incidents of consequence. While it would be wonderful if this remained the case, that seems extremely unlikely.

Currently, one of the greatest environmental concerns of the law enforcement community is the vulnerability to environmental terrorism. Given the shift in the balance of power in the world in the last five years, it seems likely that the United States territory will increasingly become the target of terrorists and that it is quite possible that the attacks will take the form of environmental terrorism perhaps in some of the following forms:

Water Supplies: Since the goal of any terrorist attack is to create the maximum fear in the general target population at the minimum risk to themselves, environmental crime fills the bill perfectly. Not only are the targets of environmental crime lightly guarded or completely unguarded, but the attack can be made and the resulting damage not be apparent for hours, days or even weeks, leaving the terrorists adequate time to flee the scene. Imagine if you will, a terrorist attack on a large city water supply. The terrorists would likely be faced with no more than a having to navigate an eight-foot-high chain link fence and possibly avoid a security guard who might make occasional rounds. The terrorists contaminate the water with a chemical or bacteria that will not be affected by the chemicals in the water and leave the scene. During the next few days there is widespread illness and a number of deaths that at first cannot be traced to a specific source. Then the terrorists contact a newspaper announcing responsibility and making demands which, if not met, will result in the poisoning of other water supplies. Further, the terrorists announce that in the future their attacks will be directed primarily at small and medium size cities and towns who will not have the financial resources to protect their water supplies, particularly since the water can be contaminated at a variety of sources and does not require that someone climb into the reservoir area to complete the act. The panic in this country would be almost complete and the terrorists would be virtually impossible to stop. Unlike the World Trade Center bombing, which took a certain amount of sophisticated equipment and supplies, poisoning a small water reservoir might take no more than obtaining a gallon of rat poison from a hardware store in another state, making the attack both simple and relatively safe.

Electricity Supplies: There are currently about 500 Extremely High Voltage transformers (EHV) in the United States, which can be found by maps available to anyone, including terrorists. These are the basis of the nation's electric distribution grid and are located for the most part in isolated areas which are at the present time entirely undefended. While the destruction of these may seem to some a blessing rather than a blow to the environment, the effect on our nation would be catastrophic. While these would require the acquisition of explosive materials on the part of the terrorists, and the results would be quickly known, the effect on the public would be substantial and, because of the location of the grids, would make the act a relatively safe one.

Infrastructure: Liquid Metal Embrittlement (LME) is a new technology which will soon be available in a form not unlike a magic marker. LME is a substance that when applied to various metals will, over a period of time, cause the equivalent of metal fatigue and thus can be used to destroy bridges, buildings, airplanes, storage facilities and other items of public use or infrastructure.

Arson: The western United States has always lived with the threat of forest fires, many caused by humans, whether through arson or negligence. It is quite possible to see a time when terrorists could literally hold our forest hostage to their demand. Because of their size and isolation, it would be literally impossible to protect our forests from arson attacks. As a parallel to the attack on our water supplies, attacks could also be made on our lakes and streams, destroying the life in them and making them unusable for long periods of time.

Conclusion

To borrow a line from Ebenezer Scrooge: "are these the visions of things that might be or things that must be?" The scenarios and outcomes outlined above are only pessimistic possibilities and can perhaps be prevented by proper action and cooperation on the part of governments, businesses, and individuals. It does seem quite possible, given the current direction of the world in general and the United States in particular, that absent substantial changes in attitudes, that the world will find, paraphrasing Mark Twain, the report of the demise of organized crime is greatly exaggerated, particularly with regard to environmental crime.

NOTES

1. Although environmental criminal statutes have existed in the United States since 1899, until the 1980s virtually no enforcement was available. In the early 1980s only Louisiana, Maryland, Michigan, New Jersey, New York, and Pennsylvania even had units. Since that time twenty-three states have developed environmental crimes enforcement units. The Pollution Prosecution Act of 1990 has mandated that the federal government must have 200 investigators by October 1, 1990, in addition to the some 35 agents of the Federal Bureau of Investigation now working environmental crime. While this is obviously an enormous improvement, it is still a very small group to investigate the huge potential for these crimes throughout the States. For an examination of the scope of the problem see: Matulewich, V. (1991). "Environmental Crimes Prosecution." *FBI Law Enforcement Bulletin* (April): 20-23.

2. Prior to the Resource Conservation and Recovery Act of 1976 (RCRA), the cost to a business of disposing of a fifty-five gallon drum of hazardous waste was $3.00-$5.00. That cost in 1991 had risen to $300.00 to $500.00 with the cost of some hazardous wastes being in excess of $1500.00 per drum. For a full analysis of the cost problems for businesses, see: Block, A. & F. Scarpitti (1985). *Poisoning for Profit: The Mafia and Toxic Waste in America.* New York: William Morrow.

3. The United States has gone from generating about 500,000 metric tons of hazardous waste in the years shortly after World War II to some 300,000,000 metric tons in 1986. See: United States Environmental Protection Agency Office of Solid Waste (1986). *RCRA Orientation Manual.* Washington, DC: Author.

REFERENCES

Abadinsky, H. (1990). *Organized Crime* (3rd ed.). Chicago, IL: Nelson Hall.

Block, A., and F. Scarpitti (1985). *Poisoning For Profit: The Mafia and Toxic Waste in America*. New York: William Morrow.

Matulewich, V. (1991). "Environmental Crimes Prosecution." *FBI Law Enforcement Bulletin* (April): 20-23.

Miller, P. (1986). "Organized Crime's Involvement in the Waste Hauling Industry." A Report from Chairman Maurice D. Hinchey to the New York State Assembly Environmental Conservation Committee (July 24).

Moore, R. (1994). "The Activities and Personnel of Twenty-First Century Organized Crime." *Criminal Organizations* (Summer): 3-11.

Naisbitt, J., and P. Aburdene (1990). *Megatrends 2000*. New York: William Morrow.

Toffler, A. (1980). *The Third Wave*. New York: Bantam Books.

United States Environmental Protection Agency Office of Solid Waste (1986). *RCRA Orientation Manual*. Washington, DC: Author.

Contributors

Freda Adler is Distinguished Professor of Criminal Justice at Rutgers University. She has served as President of the American Society of Criminology; Regional General Secretary General (North America), International Society for Social Defense; and Permanent Representative to the United Nations, *Centro Nazionale di Prevenzione e Difesa Sociale*. Author of over 70 scientific articles and monographs, she has published several books on drugs, gender issues relating to crime, criminology, criminal theory, and criminal justice. She has served as a consultant to the National Commission on Marijuana and Drug Abuse, the United Nations Crime Prevention and Criminal Justice Branch, and the Office of Juvenile Justice and Delinquency Prevention. She also serves as a faculty member of the National Judicial College, consulting editor to the Journal of Research in Crime and Delinquency and the Journal of Criminal Justice, and member of the Editorial board of Criminology. She received her B.A., M.A., and Ph.D. (Sociology) from the University of Pennsylvania.

Valerie J. Cass is a doctoral student in Criminology, Law, and Society in the School of Social Ecology at the University of California, Irvine. Her research interests include multinational corporate regulation and environmental crime. She received her B.A. from the University of California, Irvine and M.A. from the University of Colorado.

Sally M. Edwards is an assistant professor of Political Science at the University of Louisville. Her research interests include environmental crime and justice, clean air, coal policy and congressional elections. She received her B.S. from the University of Louisville, her M.S. from The Florida State University, and her Ph.D. (Political Science) from Indiana University.

Terry D. Edwards is an assistant professor of Justice Administration at the University of Louisville. His research interests include environmental crime, criminal law, constitutional law, and legal issues relating to police. He currently serves on the Environmental Crime Committee for both the International Association of Chiefs of Police and American Bar Association. He previously worked as a state trooper and military attorney. He serves as the Second Vice-President of the Southern Criminal Justice Association, and for three years was Secretary/Treasurer of the organization. He received his J.D. from the University of Louisville.

Michael Esler is an assistant professor of Political Science at Southern Illinois University at Carbondale. His research interests include public law and judicial process, environmental politics, and American political thought.

Charles B. Fields is Professor and Chair of the Department of Criminal Justice at the California State University-San Bernardino. He has a B.A. (1980) and M.A. (1981) in Political Science from Appalachian State University and a Ph.D. (1984) in Criminal Justice from Sam Houston State University. His research interests include drug policy and comparative justice systems. He has edited *Innovative Trends and Specialized Strategies in Community-Based Corrections* (Garland, 1994) and (with Richter H. Moore, Jr.) *Comparative Criminal Justice: Traditional* and *Non-Traditional Systems of Law and Control* (Waveland, 1996).

Carol Hays is a doctoral student at Southern Illinois University at Carbondale. Her current research involves the relationship between environmental quality and economic development in the states.

Scott Hays is an assistant professor of Political Science at Southern Illinois University at Carbondale. His research interests include environmental policy at the state level. He has published in the *Journal of Politics* among others.

William D. Hyatt is a professor of Criminal Justice at Western Carolina University. His research interests include organized crime, white collar crime, and criminal law. He previously worked with the U.S. Department of Justice for 17 years where he served in the Organized Crime and Racketeering Section, Criminal Tax Section, and as Chief of the Organized Crime Strike Force. He received his J.D. from the University of Cincinnati and his LL.M. from Georgetown University.

Gerhard O.W. Mueller is Distinguished Professor of Criminal Justice at Rutgers University. He has a J.D. from the University of Chicago, an LL.M. from Columbia and a Dr.Jur. (h.c.) from the University of Uppsala (Sweden). From 1974-82 he was Chief of the United Nations Crime Prevention and Criminal Justice Branch and has been on the faculties of law at the University of Washington, West Virginia University, New York University and the national Judicial College. A renowned expert on several facets of crime and justice worldwide, he has authored or edited some 50 books and 250 scholarly articles.

Donald J. Rebovich has been the Director of Research for the American Research Institute (APRI) since 1990. He is responsible for the direction of a number of national research programs dedicated to the study of the prosecution of environmental crime, organized crime, domestic violence, and drug-related offenses. He has authored numerous works including *Dangerous Ground: The World of Hazardous Waste Crime* (Transaction Publishers, 1992). Prior to coming to APRI he served for 10 years with the Office of the New Jersey Attorney General and was responsible for the research and evaluation of environmental and drug enforcement initiatives. He received his B.S. (Criminal Justice) from Trenton State College and his M.A. and Ph.D. (Criminal Justice) from Rutgers University.

Debra Ross is a doctoral student in Criminal Justice at Rutgers University. She is currently completing her dissertation on a test of the deterrence doctrine among environmental criminals. She has instructed a number of courses including courses on white Collar crime. She previously served as a research assistant on a NIJ project on drug market analysis and was involved in the preparation of two publications while a research assistant at Northeastern University. She received her B.A. (Sociology/Criminology) from Eckerd College and M.S. (Criminal justice) from Northeastern University.

Mark Seis is a doctoral student in the criminology program at Indiana University of Pennsylvania and currently is an instructor at Wheeling Jesuit College in Wheeling, West Virginia. He is completing his dissertation, an ecological critique of the Clean Air Act. In addition to the study of environmental law and crime, his interests include theoretical criminology, epistemological issues regarding the study of crime, and ethical issues concerning current trends in criminal justice system operations.

Thomas C. Shevory is an associate professor of Politics at Ithaca College. He has published two books on Chief Justice John Marshall's law and politics and a variety of articles on law and public policy related to health and environmental issues. He is currently working on a book which analyzes property and privacy in terms of human reproduction and environmental policy.

Tracy L. Trexler is an officer with the Mecklenburg Metropolitan Police Department. Her research interests include police issues and criminal law. She received her B.S. from Western Carolina University.

Nanci Koser Wilson is an associate professor of Criminology at Indiana University of Pennsylvania, where she is also a member of the Women's Studies faculty. Her research has focused on issues of gender and crime, and more recently on environmental crimes. Recent publications include articles in Women and Justice and Female Criminality. She received her B.A. and M.A. from the University of Kansas and her Ph.D. (Sociology) from the University of Tennessee.

Index

Abbey, Edward 164, 183-186, 196
Abolitionists 192
Abwasserabgabengesetz 10
accretion 21
acid rain 166
Acquired Immunity Deficiency Syndrome (AIDS) 169, 197
Africa 198, 251
air pollution 35, 138, 207, 209, 237
Air Quality Act of 1967 5
Alaska 21, 212, 214, 216, 220, 230
Alco Pacific 103, 111
Aleutian Islands 166
Alexander, George 188
Allied Chemical 17
Altamirano, Rene 114
Amazon
    Basin 18
    rubber tappers 199
American Bar Association
    Section on Natural Resources, Energy, and Environmental Law (SONREEL) 215-216
American Prosecutors Research Institute 80, 88, 95-96
American Revolution 127, 175, 189

animal clan 130
Argentina 254
Arizona 164-165, 212-218, 220, 222-224, 226, 230-232, 234-235, 237-238
Arkansas 208, 212, 214, 216-217, 220, 223-224, 227, 230-231, 235
Asia 251
Association of Oregon Loggers 176
Baja peninsula 101
Bald Mountain 186
Basel Agreement 114, 115n
Bhopal (See India)
"Billboard Bandits" 164
biocentrism 168, 176, 197-198, 200
biodiversity 168
bioregions 121-122, 127-128, 130-131, 134, 139
bird clan 130
Black Mesa Defense 164
Black Panthers 189
"Bolt Weevils" 164
Bookchin, Murray 199
boreholes 41
Brazil 18
Bridger-Teton National Forest 165
Britain (See United Kingdom)